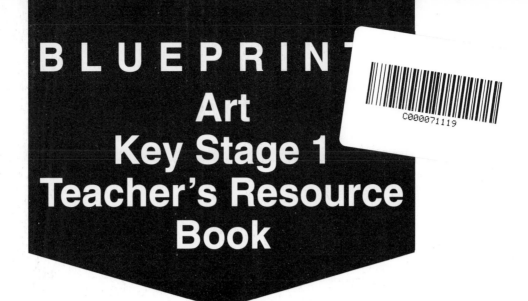

BLUEPRINT
Art
Key Stage 1
Teacher's Resource
Book

Ron Adams

Stanley Thornes (Publishers) Ltd

Do you receive BLUEPRINTS NEWS?

Blueprints is an expanding series of practical teacher's ideas books and photocopiable resources for use in primary schools. Books are available for separate infant and junior age ranges for every core and foundation subject, as well as for an ever widening range of other primary teaching needs. These include **Blueprints Primary English** books and **Blueprints Resource Banks**. **Blueprints** are carefully structured around the demands of the National Curriculum in England and Wales, but are used successfully by schools and teachers in Scotland, Northern Ireland and elsewhere.

Blueprints provide:
- *Total curriculum coverage*
- *Hundreds of practical ideas*
- *Books specifically for the age range you teach*
- *Flexible resources for the whole school or for individual teachers*
- *Excellent photocopiable sheets – ideal for assessment and children's work profiles*
- *Supreme value.*

Books may be bought by credit card over the telephone and information obtained on **(01242) 577944**. Alternatively, photocopy and return this **FREEPOST** form to receive **Blueprints News**, our regular update on all new and existing titles. You may also like to add the name of a friend who would be interested in being on the mailing list.

> Please add my name to the **BLUEPRINTS NEWS** mailing list.
>
> Mr/Mrs/Miss/Ms _____
>
> Home address _____
>
> _____ Postcode _____
>
> School address _____
>
> _____ Postcode _____
>
> Please also send **BLUEPRINTS NEWS** to:
>
> Mr/Mrs/Miss/Ms _____
>
> Address _____
>
> _____ Postcode _____
>
> To: Marketing Services Dept., Stanley Thornes Ltd, FREEPOST (GR 782), Cheltenham, GL50 1BR

First published in 1993 by:
Stanley Thornes (Publishers) Ltd
Ellenborough House
Wellington Street
Cheltenham GL50 1YW
England

97 98 99 00 / 10 9 8 7 6

A catalogue record for this book is available from the British Library.

0–7487–1623–8

Typeset by Tech-Set, Gateshead, Tyne & Wear
Printed and bound in Great Britain by Redwood Books, Trowbridge, Wiltshire

CONTENTS

INTRODUCTION

What is *Blueprints: Art*?

Blueprints: Art is a practical teacher's resource that provides structured materials for developing art in line with the requirements of the National Curriculum. It is, however, organised in such a way that it can be used just as profitably by teachers and schools not following National Curriculum courses. It is intended to be used flexibly, either as an ideas bank for individual teachers or as a workable core resource for a whole school scheme of work in art.

Blueprints: Art consists of material for Key Stages 1 and 2. For each stage there is a Teacher's Resource Book and a book of Pupils' Copymasters. This Teacher's Resource Book provides hundreds of practical ideas and activities for 5- to 7-year-olds and can be used on its own, as a freestanding resource, without the accompanying Copymaster book. The book of Pupils' Copymasters provides 103 photocopiable worksheets linked to the many activities in this book. The worksheets reinforce and extend activities already done and provide opportunities to develop art skills in a structured way.

Blueprints: Art will provide you with coverage of all the requirements of National Curriculum Art. It is written around the requirements of the Programmes of Study and provides complete coverage of the Statements of Attainment at Key Stage 1. You will find a full explanation of National Curriculum Art and how it is covered in the following chapter. The key feature of *Blueprints: Art* is that it is a skill based, progressive resource not a collection of isolated one-off activities, and this is reflected in its structure, as well as the contents.

The general features of *Blueprints: Art* are in line with both the requirements of the National Curriculum and the realities of the primary school classroom, as follows:

- It provides a balanced programme of art, craft and design which allows children to meet the full range of art activities, in both two and three dimensions and in a variety of scales.
- It provides activities which integrate the two art Attainment Targets, as recommended in the Non-Statutory Guidance on art.
- It stresses the newly emphasised role of art history in children's artistic development.
- It allows you to work flexibly from either topics or skills or directly from the National Curriculum programmes of study if you so choose.
- It assumes a realistic amount of time in class and takes account of the need to fit art into an over-crowded primary curriculum.

This book consists of two parts. The first part uses nine common infant topics to provide a bank of structured, skill based art activities. The second part provides a section of basic skills and knowledge, in line with the requirements for AT1 and AT2. You will find the skills and knowledge also referred to quite widely during the topics, and the sections are closely cross-referenced. The content of the topics is in fact structured around these areas of study to provide the balanced programme of art, craft and design activities that the National Curriculum demands. The areas of study are:

 Art history

 Ceramics

 Design

 Drawing

 Modelling

 Painting

 Print-making

 Textiles.

Art history relates to AT2: Knowledge and understanding, the other areas to AT1: Investigating and making. The logos for these areas are used widely throughout the book.

Art through topics

Constraints on time and the nature of the infant day mean that topics will provide the most frequent opportunities for art. With this in mind nine topics have been chosen as a context for developing art skills. These are:

- My family and myself
- Homes
- Clothing
- Water
- Circuses and fairs
- Transport
- Living things
- Colour
- Materials.

You will find that cross-curricular links are made but each topic is focussed quite specifically on art, and the activities are related throughout to art in the National Curriculum. You can see the coverage in outline on the chart on page xi. The topic webs are structured in such a way that all the main areas for study mentioned earlier are specifically covered in each topic and highlighted through the use of logos mentioned earlier. The topics include a huge range of activities that provide coverage of all these specified areas of National Curriculum art. You will also find that a topics index has been included on page xiii to enable you to use many of the ideas in the nine topics to resource a wide range of other topics.

Although they may be used in any order you like, the order of the topics is loosely developmental. Earlier topics make fewer demands on knowledge and understanding (AT2). They focus more on investigating and making activities (AT1). These activities also tend to be simple rather than ones which link together a number of processes and skills. They are therefore more suitable for younger classes. Later topics lay more stress on knowledge and understanding and on activities that combine more complex processes and planning. You can see the developing coverage of the topics in the chart on page xi.

Skills and knowledge in art

The second substantial section of the book is structured around the specific requirements of the two ATs. Art history provides activities that relate to AT2, the other seven skill areas relate to AT1. One of the fundamental aims of the National Curriculum is to develop the notion that art involves the progressive development of particular skills, that there is a vocabulary of visual literacy and skills which needs to be taught and developed systematically. Whilst the National Curriculum sees that 'there is more to learning in art than acquiring technical skills', it does also emphasise a systematic development of these skills through practical activities as set out in AT1.

The idea of developing art skills systematically will be an unfamiliar one to many teachers. There is a common tendency to regard art with children as being primarily about inspiration and imagination, and that these qualities must not be interfered with by the structured teaching of skills. The progressive development of skills is, however, one of the key features of the National Curriculum. In this respect art is not unlike music: music teachers know how essential it is to use a variety of exercises to build up skills. Similarly, language teachers know that leading children towards verbal literacy includes a number of well established methods and approaches. Common to all literacy skills is the foundation of the alphabet, followed by exercises to build listening, reading and writing skills: children are not expected to come across the alphabet by accident. The same applies to the field of visual literacy. Artistic skills can and must be taught. Teaching skills, individually, in groups or as class activities should enhance children's adventurous and daring spirits, while a balance of activities will give scope for individuality, flair and a sense of craftsmanship.

The skills section aims to provide a developmental alphabet of knowledge and skills in each area through a course of progressive activities. You will find that the development of these areas of study is threaded through the topics, but this section provides you with a coherent development for the eight areas mentioned previously:

 Art history

 Ceramics

Design

 Drawing

 Modelling

 Painting

 Print-making

 Textiles.

The skills are very firmly linked to practical activities. Art history relates to AT2 (Knowledge and understanding). The remaining skill areas comprise AT1 (Investigating and making). These are based on an analysis and breakdown of the activities set out in the examples in the programmes of study. Of the practical activities, drawing is dominant because it is a basic skill which underpins art. The National Curriculum recommends that ratio of work in AT1 to AT2 should be approximately 2:1.

The skills activities can be used either as a reference source or to build a course that relies on class teaching rather than topic work. There are no hard and fast rules about the levels of the activities. Some are at the cross-over between Key Stage 1 and Key Stage 2 and are included to ensure progression. It is important that you do not set the exercises in isolation. Ensure that you provide a relevant and well resourced context for all work. You may also find the skills section invaluable for enhancing your own skills.

Assessment in art

There is no statutory end of Key Stage assessment in art, but the non-statutory guidance does make suggestions about teacher based assessment which are interesting, if rather complicated. It is important that you do find a simple and straightforward way to develop a critical awareness of your pupils' performance in art so that you are able to help them develop further and provide a progressive programme. It will also be necessary to provide parents and future schools with information.

With this in mind *Blueprints: Art* provides a simple record keeping sheet at Key Stage 1 (Copymaster 103) which is straightforward, comprehensive and easy to use and also provides a checklist of criteria to use when assessing children's work. Alongside this it will be helpful to keep a portfolio of annotated and dated samples of your children's work. The skill based copymasters can comprise a useful part of this portfolio. When taking photographs take care to include a rule alongside the work and to use a tripod and light it properly. Fuzzy photographs of vague objects in the distance are worse than useless as records and as exemplars in the visual arts.

How to use this book

Blueprints: Art can be used flexibly to meet your needs. It allows you to work from either Topics or Skills or directly from the National Curriculum. You do not need to have the Copymasters to use this Teacher's Resource Book, but the Copymasters are dependent on it.

If you have only this *Teacher's Resource Book:*

If you want to work from topics integrated into the rest of your curriculum planning, you can use any of the nine core topics to do so. You will find that the cross-curricular links are clearly stated and that the map of art activities is outlined in the web at the front of the topic. If you are planning to integrate art into topics other than the nine specifically covered, go to the Topic Index on page xiii which will allow you to access ideas across the book.

If you want to treat art as a separate subject and start from skills, go to the relevant skill section and start from there. You will find each provides a bank of skill based activities which can provide a module of progressive learning. You can also use the skills index on page xiv to help you do this. Remember that it is important to provide interesting contexts in which to develop skills. Although art history (AT2) doesn't provide many specific activities, it may be seen as a vital first step. The way it is arranged relates the knowledge specifically to practical areas.

If you want to start by looking at the National Curriculum programmes of study, go to the charts on pages xi–xii where you will find an outline of how the activities provide coverage. Again it is important that any subject-based approach to art is securely grounded in contexts which have real meaning for infants. In general we recommend that you work mainly from a topic approach at Key Stage 1, that you integrate art into your overall curriculum planning and use the record sheet to record pupil progress. You will probably want to dip into the skills section at certain points to focus learning as you work within a topic, as well as to provide yourself with a basic alphabet of necessary art skills.

I recommend that you allow an hour a week for specific art activities whether they are related to a topic or not. You will find that making a practical link between AT2 and practical activities is both logical and enriching.

If you have the pupils' *Copymasters* as well:
At first sight it may appear odd to provide copymasters for a subject such as art. The copymasters in *Blueprints: Art* are all designed to do specific and purposeful tasks, either by providing opportunities for developing quite specific focussed skills, or by providing a bank of visual resources that can be used to stimulate activity in a wide range of situations. The sheets can also form part of a child's art portfolio. Many sheets are locked quite specifically into particular activities in this book and you will find them referred to in the text where notes on their use are provided. You will find the appropriate sheets

referred to in this book with this symbol:

Acknowledgements
Many thanks to Veronica Parker, Headmistress and her staff at St Stephen's Primary School, Bath; Fiona Godfrey, MA, of Birmingham University.

For reference purposes, the programme of study and Attainment Targets are set out below for Key Stage 1. Alongside these are printed the accompanying examples, which are non-statutory. You will also find a chart showing in outline how the sections of the book meet the requirements of Key Stage 1. The general requirements for programmes of study are also included.

For general purposes it is worth mentioning here some of the key features of Art in the National Curriculum, as follows:

- There are no levels of attainment for National Curriculum Art, and no statutory requirement for formal assessment.

- There is a need to provide a balanced programme of art, craft *and* design activities. You will find that *Blueprints: Art* meets this need.
- Children should work in two and three dimensions and have opportunities to meet a wide range of art styles. For the first time children are required to see examples of art from around the world and from across the whole history of art. This is an important new dimension to primary art, which forms the core of AT2: Knowledge and understanding.
- Art skills are now an essential part of primary art, as embodied in AT1: Investigating and making.
- The two ATs need to be continuously integrated in the work provided and the emphasis should be laid most heavily on AT1: Investigating and making.

Programme of study

Art should be interpreted as 'art, craft and design' throughout.

Pupils' understanding and enjoyment of art, craft and design should be developed through activities that bring together requirements from both **Investigating and Making** and **Knowledge and Understanding**, wherever possible.

1. Pupils should be given opportunities to experience different approaches to art, craft and design, including those that involve working individually, in groups and as a whole class.

2. In order to develop visual perception, pupils should be taught the creative, imaginative and practical skills needed to:

   a express ideas and feelings;

   b record observations;

   c design and make images and artefacts.

3. In order to develop visual literacy, pupils should be taught about the different ways in which ideas, feelings and meanings are communicated in visual form.

4. Throughout their work, pupils should be taught about visual and, where appropriate, tactile elements, including:

   a pattern and texture in natural and made forms;

   b colour matching and how colour is mixed from primary colours;

   c how images are made using line and tone;

   d the use of shape, form and space in images and artefacts.

5. Pupils should be introduced to the work of artists, craftspeople and designers, *eg drawing, painting, printmaking, photography, sculpture, ceramics, textiles, graphic design, architecture*, in order to develop their appreciation of the richness of our diverse cultural heritage. The selection should include work in a variety of genres and styles from:

   a the locality;

   b the past and present;

   c a variety of cultures, Western and non-Western.

6. Pupils should be taught to use materials, tools and techniques for practical work safely and in accordance with health and safety requirements.

Investigating and making

7. Pupils should be given opportunities to:

a record responses, including observations of the natural and made environment;

b gather resources and materials, using them to stimulate and develop ideas;

c explore and use two- and three-dimensional media, working on a variety of scales;

d review and modify their work as it progresses;

8. Pupils should be taught to:

a record what has been experienced, observed and imagined;

b recognise images and artefacts as sources of ideas for their work;

c select and sort images and artefacts, and use this source material as a basis for their work;

d experiment with tools and techniques for drawing, painting, printmaking, collage and sculpture, exploring a range of materials, including textiles;

e experiment with visual elements, *eg pattern, texture, colour, line tone,shape, form, space*, to make images and artefacts, using the range of media in 8d;

f review what they have done and describe what they might change or develop in future work.

Knowledge and understanding

9. Pupils should be taught to:

e develop understanding of the work of artists, craftspeople and designers, applying knowledge to their own work;

f respond to and evaluate art, craft and design, including their own and others' work.

a identify in the school and the locality the work of artists, craftspeople and designers;

b recognise visual elements, *eg pattern, texture, colour, line, tone, shape, form, space*, in images and artefacts;

c recognise differences and similarities in art, craft and design from different times and places;

d respond to the ideas, methods or approaches used in different styles and traditions;

e describe works of art, craft and design in simple terms, and explain what they think and feel about these.

PROGRAMME OF STUDY COVERAGE OF THE TOPICS ▶

A black circle indicates considerable coverage. A white dot indicates more limited coverage.

AT	Pupils should be taught to:	My family	Homes	Clothing	Water	Circus/ fairs	Transport	Living things	Colour	Materials
1a. Record responses etc	a. Record what has been experienced, observed and imagined	●	○	●	●	○	●	●	●	●
1b. Gather resources etc.	b. Recognise images etc.	○	○	●	○	○	○	●	○	●
	c. Select and sort images etc.	○	●	●	○	○	○	●	○	●
1c. Explore and use 2 and 3 D etc.	d. Experiment with tools and techniques etc	●	●	●	●	●	●	●	●	●
	e. Experiment with visual elements, e.g. pattern etc.	●	●	●	●	●	●	●	●	●
1d Review and modify etc.	f. Review what they have done etc.	○	○		○	○	●	●	●	●
2e. Develop understanding of the work of artists etc	a. Identify in the school work of artists etc		○	○	○		○	○	●	
	b. Recognise visual elements, e.g. pattern etc.	○	●	○	○	○	●	○	●	
	c. Recognise differences and similarities	○	●	○	○	○	●	○	●	
2f. Respond and evaluate etc.	d. Respond to ideas in styles etc.	○	●		○	○	○	●	●	
	e. Describe works of art, etc.	○	●	○	○	○	●	●	●	

PROGRAMME OF STUDY COVERAGE OF THE SKILLS ▶

A black circle indicates considerable coverage. A white dot indicates more limited coverage.

		Art History	Ceramics	Design	Drawing	Modelling	Painting	Print-making	Textiles
AT	Pupils should be taught to:								
1a. Record responses etc	a. Record what has been experienced, observed and imagined	●	○		●	○	●		
1b. Gather resources etc.	b. Recognise images etc.	●	○	○	○	○	○	●	
	c. Select and sort images etc.	●	○	○	○	○	○	●	
1c. Explore and use 2 and 3 D etc.	d. Experiment with tools and techniques etc	●	●	●	●	●	●	●	●
	e. Experiment with visual elements, e.g. pattern etc.	●	●	●	●	●	●	●	●
1d Review and modify etc.	f. Review what they have done etc.	●		●	●	○	○	●	○
2e. Develop understanding of the work of artists etc	a. Identify in the school work of artists etc	●		○	○		○	○	○
	b. Recognise visual elements, e.g. pattern etc.	●	○	○	○	○	●	●	○
	c. Recognise differences and similarities	●			○		○	○	
2f. Respond and evaluate etc.	d. Respond to ideas in styles etc.	●			○		○	○	
	e. Describe works of art, etc.	●		●	○	○	○	●	○

TOPICS AND SKILLS INDEX

Blueprints: Art is structured around nine topics but ideas within it can be used to resource a far wider range of other topics. The index below shows you, by activity number, how ideas within the book can be used to resource a wider range of other overlapping topics. You will also find an index of all the skills that the book contains, for easy reference.

TOPICS INDEX

SKILLS INDEX

BIBLIOGRAPHY

General background titles for teachers

Berger, J., *Ways of Seeing*, Penguin, ISBN 0 14 013515 4. (Very theoretical.)

Carlson, *Guide to Landscape Painting*, Dover, ISBN 0 4862 2927 0

Carr, W., and Leonard, M., *Looking at Paintings*, British Museum Press, ISBN 0 7141 1725 0 (Very good.)

Children's Books of the Year, Children's Book Foundation, from Book House, 45 East Hill, London, SW18 2QZ. Tel. 081 870 9055

Kellog, R., *Analysing Children's Art*, Mayfield publishing, ISBN 0 87484196 8

Leach, B., *Potter's Book*, Faber, ISBN 0 571 10973 4

Picture this Century – an introduction to 20th century art, Hodder & Stoughton, ISBN 0 340 54867 3. (Very good.)

Read, H., *The Meaning of Art*, Faber, ISBN 0 571 09658 1. (Very theoretical.)

The Craftsman's Directory, Angle Press from The Rural Crafts Association, Brook Road, Wormley, Godalming, Surrey, GU8 5UA

Art books linked to National Curriculum requirements and as a visual stimulus

Barnicoat, *Posters, A Concise History*, Thames and Hudson, ISBN 0 500 20118 8

Burn, *Greek and Roman Art*, British Museum Press, ISBN 0 7141 1297 6

Carpenter, *Hiroshige*, Kodansha International, ISBN 4 77001658 1

Duchen and Cook, *Understanding Modern Art*, Usborne, 1991, ISBN 0 7460 0475 3

James, T. G. H., *Egyptian Painting*, British Museum Press, ISBN 0 7141 2038 3

Lister, *Paintings of Samuel Palmer*, Cambridge University Press, ISBN 0 521 31855 6

McHugh, C., *Animals*, Wayland, 1992. This title is part of the *Discovering Art* series

Master of Art Series, Thames & Hudson. Titles include: *Van Gogh, Cezanne, Constable, Klee, Leger, Monet, Picasso,* and *Turner*

Micklethwaite, L., *An Alphabet in Art*, Collins, 1992. ISBN 0 00 664184 9

Prats and Okuyama, *Art Playbook Series*, Abrams. Titles include: *Magritte – the Double Secret*, ISBN 0 8109 3601 1, *Picasso the Minotaur, Delauney the Eiffel Tower, Kandinsky Sky Blue*

Richardson, W. and R., *The World of Art Series*, MacMillan, 1989. Titles include: *Animals, Cities, Water, Families, The Natural World, Entertainers*

Vallance, *Art of William Morris*, Dover, ISBN 0 4862 5647 2

Wilkin, *Braque* from the *Abbeville Modern Masters* series, Abbeville, ISBN 0 89659947 7

Woolf, *Picture This*, Hodder & Stoughton, ISBN 0 340 55991 8

Wrede, S., *Modern Poster*, Museum of Modern Art, ISBN 0 87070 571 7

SUPPLIERS AND USEFUL ADDRESSES

Card and paper products
Celloglas Mirri Products (Mirriboard), Unit 12C, Exeter Way, Theale Commercial Estate, Theale, Reading, Berkshire, RG7 4AW. Tel: 0734 303656

Daler–Rowney Ltd, Southern Industrial Area, PO Box 10, Bracknell, Berkshire, RG12 4ST. Tel: 0344 424621

Frisk Ltd, 4 Franthorne Way, Randlesdown Road, London, SE6 3BT. Tel: 081 698 3481

Oram and Robinson Ltd, Cadmore Lane, Cheshunt, Waltham Cross, Hertfordshire, EN8 9SG. Tel: 0992 27376

Paperchase Products Ltd, 213 Tottenham Court Road, London, W1. Tel: 071 580 8496

Slater Harrison & Co Ltd, Lowerhouse Mills, West Bollington, Macclesfield, SK10 5HW. Tel 0625 73155

Wiggins Teape Ltd, (Paper Point) 63 Poland Street, London, W1. Tel: 071 439 4414

Clay
Clayglaze Ltd, Kings Yard Pottery, Talbot Road, Rickmansworth, Herts. Tel: 0923 87107

Wengers Ltd, Etruria, Stoke-on-Trent, ST4 7BQ. Tel: 0782 25560

General art supplies
Berol Ltd, Oldmeadow Road, King's Lynn, Norfolk, PE30 4JR. Tel: 0553 61221C

Caran D'Ache, Jakar Int. Ltd, Hillside House, 2–6 Friern Park, London, N12 9BX. Tel: 081 445 6377

Faber–Castell (UK) Ltd, Crompton Road, Stevenage, Herts., SG1 2EF. Tel: 0438 316511

Reeves Ltd, Whitefriars Avenue, Whealdstone, Harrow, Middlesex, HA3 5RH. Tel: 081 427 4343

Staedtler 9UK0 Ltd, Pontyclun, Mid-Glamorgan, Wales, CF7 8YJ. Tel: 0443 237421

Winsor & Newton, Whitefriars Avenue, Whealdstone, Harrow, Middlesex, HA3 5RH. Tel: 081 427 4343

Textile Techniques, 47 Storths Rd, Birkby, Huddersfield, HD2 2XW

General educational suppliers
E J Arnold & Son Ltd, Parkside Lane, Dewbury Road, Leeds LS15 5TD

James Galt & Co. Ltd, Brookfield Road, Cheadle, Cheshire SK8 2PN

Hestair Hope Ltd, St. Philip's Drive, Royton, Oldham, OL2 6AG

Nottingham Educational Supplies, 17 Ludlow Hill Road, West Bridgford, Nottingham NG2 6HD

Materials for print-making
Daler-Rowney, Westminster Road, Wareham, Dorset BH20 4SW. Tel: 09295 6621

Hunter Penrose Ltd, 7 Spa Road, London, SE16. Tel: 071 407 5051

T. N. Lawrence & Son Ltd, Bleeding Hart Yard, Greville Street, Hatton Garden, London, EC1N 8SL. Tel: 071 242 3534

Process Supplies Ltd, 19 Mount Pleasant, London, WC1. Tel: 071 837 2179

Sericol Ltd, 26 Parsons Green Lane, London, SW6. Tel: 071 736 3388

Photography
Kodak Ltd, PO Box 66, Station Road, Hemel Hempstead, Herts, HP1 1JU. Tel: 0442 61122

Specialist pencil and felt tip suppliers
C. W. Edding (UK) Ltd, Merlin Centre, Acrewood, St. Albans, Herts, AJ4 0JY. Tel: 0727 34471

Royal Sovereign Ltd, 6/7 St George's Industrial Estate, White Hart Lane, London, N22 5QL. Tel: 081 888 7029

Textiles
Whaleys (Bradford) Ltd, Harris Court, Great Horton, Bradford, W Yorkshire, BD7 4EQ. Tel: 0274 576718

Suppliers of multi-cultural arts and crafts resources
Jackson Contra-Banned, Unit 2, Gatehouse Enterprise Centre, Albert Street, Lockwood, Huddersfield HD1 3QD. Tel: 0484 530855

Useful addresses
Children's Book Foundation, Jean Egbunike, Book House, 45 East Hill, London SW18 2QZ. Tel: 081 870 9055

Crafts Council, 12 Waterloo Place, London, SW1Y 4AU

Regional Arts Association (CORAA), Litton Lodge, 13a Clifton Road, Winchester, Hampshire, SO22 5BP. Tel: 0962 51063

NSEAD (National Society for Education in Art and Design), 7a High Street, Corsham, Wiltshire, SN13 0ES. Tel: 0249 714825

Schools Library Association, Executive Secretary, Valerie Fea, ALA, Liden Library, Barrington Close, Liden, Swindon, Wiltshire, SN3 6HF. Tel: 0793 617838

Group For Education in Museums, Care of Regional Convenor, Museum of London, London Wall, London EC2Y 5HN

MY FAMILY AND MYSELF

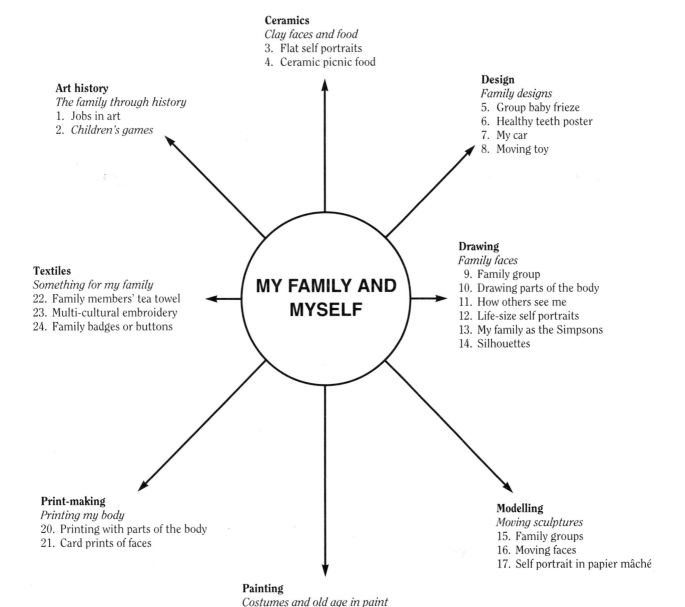

Ceramics
Clay faces and food
3. Flat self portraits
4. Ceramic picnic food

Design
Family designs
5. Group baby frieze
6. Healthy teeth poster
7. My car
8. Moving toy

Art history
The family through history
1. Jobs in art
2. *Children's games*

Drawing
Family faces
9. Family group
10. Drawing parts of the body
11. How others see me
12. Life-size self portraits
13. My family as the Simpsons
14. Silhouettes

MY FAMILY AND MYSELF

Textiles
Something for my family
22. Family members' tea towel
23. Multi-cultural embroidery
24. Family badges or buttons

Print-making
Printing my body
20. Printing with parts of the body
21. Card prints of faces

Modelling
Moving sculptures
15. Family groups
16. Moving faces
17. Self portrait in papier mâché

Painting
Costumes and old age in paint
18. The wedding or christening
19. 'When I'm 64'

CROSS-CURRICULAR LINKS ▶

Design and technology Designing and making, mechanisms

Drama and dance Family related, role-play

Environmental studies Our garden (local environment), recall and trace where pupils were born, make a map of their journeys

History Families long ago, famous families, babies past and present, equipment, customs, jobs, in factories, offices, outdoor, on the land. Make a chart of a family tree (famous families)

Language Reportive writing about family and self, using words in correct context

Mathematics Measuring body parts, comparisons and differences, simple graphs and charts showing hair, eye, skin colours. Illustrated surveys of family pets, presented as bar charts

Music 'Me and my Teddy Bear', Jungle Book songs

RE Being aware of oneself and the need to care for others as well, emotions and feelings

Science Variety of life, parts of the body, this is me, five senses, simple cooking, health and hygiene, growth

ABOUT THIS TOPIC ▶

General points

You will need to be sensitive as you introduce the topic, as not all families are the same and many children will not be in conventional family units. Try to make a positive feature of our differences and similarities. We all need a safe, attractive, warm home, with enough food provided by loving parents. Art is an ideal medium for work on the senses. There are also many celebrations that are directly linked to family life in various cultural settings that can stimulate exciting possibilities for art activities. There is also the need to be sensitive to the psychology of young children. Here artwork can be very helpful in understanding their emotional state.

Displays and resources

Collect photographs of the children and family weddings and christenings; souvenirs of their very early days such as baby clothes and shoes and examples of pictures of family groups. Try to include examples of artefacts that illustrate changes in family life. These could include domestic items, coins and tokens, games, toys, children's costumes from the Victorian age, family bibles, baby gas masks. The Health Education Council has produced sets of material to support 'My body' projects. You may find that models and sets of posters can be borrowed through your library or museum service. Adam Rouilly produces excellent models that include ears, eyes, noses, fingernails, feet, hands, hearts, full scale and small scale skeletons and a series of models of foetal development.

STARTING POINTS ▶

- You may be able to borrow works of art and ceramics from your library or museum service to make a display. Models of various parts of the body and of babies in the early stages of development can also be borrowed from some LEAs. All such resources, together with relevant books, can form an important part of your display.

- Children may explore how they discover things by using the five senses and may make observational drawings of themselves. They can identify and understand the functions of individual body parts. (What can be done without hands? Try, for example, sticking lolly sticks to fingers.) A visit of a baby or toddler to class will generate a lot of interest and

discussion. (Look at size and stages of development).

- Discussion of important family events such as weddings and christenings, how faces are shaped differently (use **Copymaster 2** for this) and how different people look, will all focus attention clearly as a starting point. Such discussions can easily lead to individual and group work such as a photo-montage of 'different people'. Use **Copymaster 2** to identify the different types of face shapes to be found in your class. Make drawings of various class members on the sheets which can be used as part of a class display.

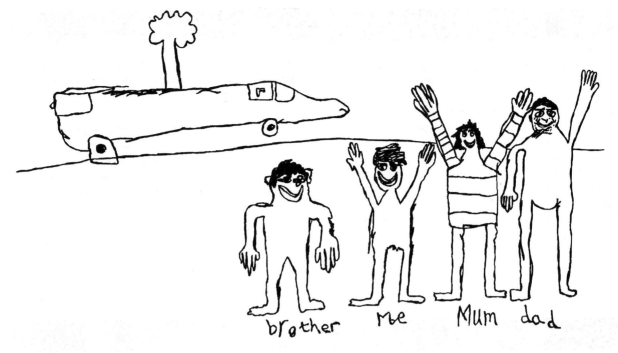

My family and I on a trip

MY FAMILY AND MYSELF ACTIVITIES C1–C10

 ## The family through history

Before you start

Introducing work on 'My family and myself' can be enriched immensely by providing good quality prints and reproductions. For very young children it is sufficient to provide a rich and stimulating environment simply by making images available which show that there are many ways of seeing the family and ourselves. As the children grow they will engage in more complex analysis of why they like or dislike pieces of work.

You can find a good range of books at your local library or you may be able to ask staff at your local school library service for help. The following suggested artists and sources cover aspects of 'My family and myself': the bold and colourful images of Andy Warhol (Elizabeth Taylor, Marilyn Monroe and the 16 Jackies); Leonardo da Vinci's Madonna and child paintings and drawings; the drawings of the holy family by Raphael: *La Belle Jardinière, La Granduca Madonna, Madonna of the Chair*, various portraits are also worth including; the Rembrandt series of self portraits from the age of 20 until the year of his death are a must. The family life of Rembrandt is also particularly interesting and is punctuated by portraits of his mother, wives and son Titus. Also noteworthy are his drawings of the holy family; Caravaggio, *The Rest on the Flight into Egypt*; Grunewald produced some wonderful portraits of old women and the superb Christmas, *Angel Concert* and

Nativity; Goya, *The Family of Charles IV*; Van Gogh (series of well known self portraits and portraits plus couple of paintings of children); Velasquez, *Royal Family* and *The Adoration of the Magi*; Kathy Kollwitz, A few mother and child drawings; Frans Hals, *A Family group in a Landscape*; Pieter De Hoogh, *Courtyard of a house in Delft*; Charles Leslie, The Grosvenor family plus other family scenes, some of poverty; The Simpsons cartoon characters use **Copymaster 1**.

Activity 1: Jobs in art

Ask the children to make pictures of themselves and their mother and father at work. Obviously it is

The postman

necessary to be sensitive to the probability that some of your children's parents are unemployed. Discuss the idea of housework as a job. Is all the family involved? What little jobs do the children do? Cleaning shoes? Clearing the table? Talk about the usual outside work that Mum or Dad does and whether or not special clothes or tools are used. Add costumes and artefacts to your display and include such images of people at work as Van Gogh's *Postman*.

You need
Reproductions of people at work, pencils, crayons, felt tip pens, paper, paints, brushes, clay or Plasticine®, costumes, protective clothing, tools of trades.

Activity 2: *Children's games*
Show a reproduction of Breugel's picture and discuss it. What is going on in the picture? Was it painted recently? Can you see any games that you play today? Are some people nearer to you than others? What makes them seem closer? The picture is really just paint on a flat surface but your pupils may feel that they could walk into it. Ask them. Why is this? Can they see how the picture is divided up into dark and light areas? Is it as good as a photograph? Can you see different colours? After a thorough discussion get the children to make drawings of their friends playing games such as leapfrog, tag or marbles. Ask them to show some details of arms, legs and heads. Should the shapes of the bodies give us a clue about the games being played?

You need
The materials mentioned above, illustrations of children's games, reproductions of the painting by Pieter Breugel.

 ## Clay faces and food ▷

Before you start
Make sure that tables are covered with newspaper and the children are wearing protective clothes.

You need
Clay, rolling pins (without handles), wooden boards to roll out clay on, coloured slip and glazes, tools for making textured surfaces, pastry cutters and illustrations of food, **Copymasters 3** and **4** on Food shapes.

Activity 3: Flat self portraits
Get the children to follow up the drawings they have done on the shape of their own faces by producing a self portrait with clay. First, get the children to roll out a small lump of clay until it is about 1 cm thick and about 15 cm square. Ask them to cut the clay so that the outline of their own face is produced. With the spare pieces of clay, they can roll out thin 'sausages' which can then be applied to the flat base to produce eyes, ears and other features including eyebrows and hair. Use nailbrushes and other textured surfaces to press into the damp clay to represent freckles or hair effects.

Children can pinch and form the faces to give an impression of three dimensions. Apply different coloured slips to the damp clay. Dry thoroughly and fire the faces in the kiln. When the children are fixing eyes and ears, it is important that the clay is sufficiently damp and has been scored a little to ensure a good join.

Clay face

Activity 4: Ceramic picnic food
Discuss going on a picnic and make a list of the kinds of food that the children like to eat in the open air. The types of food will depend on the variety of cultures that are represented in your class. Making sandwiches involves rolling out clay, cutting out small triangular shapes to represent bread and circular shapes for cucumber and tomatoes. When the clay is still damp but not wet, make up the sandwiches, using a brush dipped in slip to ensure a good fix. After biscuit firing, use coloured glazes to paint the different elements of the sandwiches. Jam tarts can be made by pushing the clay that has been already rolled out and cut by a pastry cutter into a small textured cake tin to get the right shape and surface markings. Glaze the centre of the jam tart with bright red or orange. Pork pies are good fun to make and can be modelled by rolling a lump of clay into a thick sausage about 3 cm across and cutting it to form a squat pie shape that can be finished easily. Cakes, doughnuts, biscuits, samosas, kebabs, pizzas and all kinds of fruit and vegetables will provide a range of progressively interesting challenges. You can introduce the idea of accurately copying shapes by using **Copymasters 3** and **4**. These contain simple silhouette shapes of different kinds of food. Photocopy these onto card. Cut out the templates (you may have to help with this) and let your children use them to produce shapes on their clay. The clay shapes can be cut out and the modelling of the food finished by hand. Instead of glazes, coloured slips (made with oxides and body stains) can be used before biscuit firing.

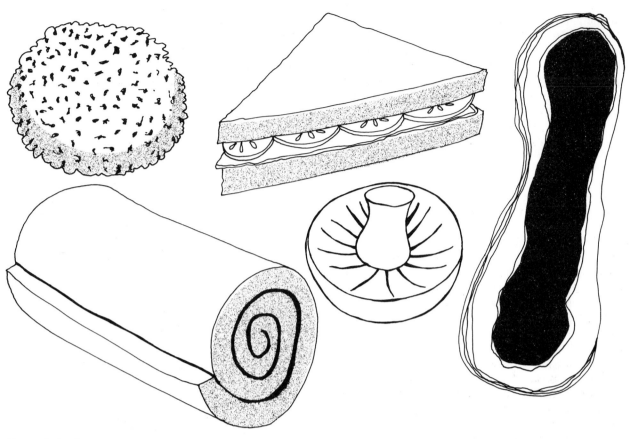

Ceramic food

 ## Family designs ▷

Activity 5: Group baby frieze
The idea is to produce a decorative, attractive frieze that will include the alphabet, or numbers up to ten, in a friendly and nicely coloured composition. An easy way to organise this is to work in pairs on specific numbers or letters that are then joined together to form a large wall display. If a parent is able to bring a baby into class, then discussing with the children what will make a baby happy, is a good way to start this work. It is important to stress that the frieze needs to be friendly and coloured accordingly. Look at nursery books and posters of popular characters.

You need
A roll of lining paper or a number of sheets of white paper stuck together, paint, brushes, pencils, and a supply of nursery books, posters and numbers.

Activity 6: Healthy teeth poster
After discussing the need to look after ourselves, get the children to look at their teeth with the mirrors. Consider what happens when sugar is left on teeth. After doing some observational drawings of their teeth, set the task of producing a poster to encourage dental hygiene.

You need
Books on health and care of teeth, paper, paint, brushes and mirrors.

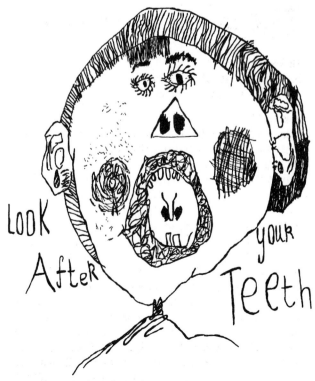

Poster on teeth

5

Activity 7: My car

Talk about the kinds of cars the children's families have got or ask the children to bring in their favourite toy cars. Look at the colours and what sorts of shapes the various elements of the cars are like. Get the children to use squares, rectangles, circles and strips to make up a picture of their car.

You need
Sticky paper, white paper, scissors, books on cars and shapes.

Activity 8: Moving toy

Look at the kind of toys that can be pulled and see how the movement is created. What kind of toy will you make? An animal? A monster? Which part of the toy will move? It is important to be very careful when very young children are handling materials and tools such as those listed below. In small supervised groups, however, children can start to learn how to cut wood with a simple saw and fix things together. Children need to work in pairs or in groups of three or four. When they have completed their toy, they will need to paint it and generally finish it. Simple movement mechanisms are given on **Copymaster 5**, these involve rubber bands and cotton wheels and are easy to follow.

You need
Copymaster 5, junk materials, boxes, lollipop sticks, plastic containers, dowelling and balsa wood, card or plywood wheels, wire, string, plastic tubes, glue, junior hacksaw, a collection of children's pull along toys, magazines with toys.

 Family faces ▷

You need
Pencils, charcoal, paper, a roll of lining paper, black paper for silhouettes, felt tip pens, crayons, rulers, tape measures, A4 Mirriboards, illustrations depicting family life, a projector and **Copymasters 2, 6–8, 79**.

Activity 9: Family group

Talk about how tall various family members are and any strong characteristics that they have. Ask the children to draw their family. The drawings of very young children are likely to be very simple with just size changes and colouring differences with approximations of the height of various family members and the colour of hair, eyes and ears shown. Crayons are very immediate in producing satisfactory results. If you want more detailed drawings then felt tips are better.

Activity 10: Drawing parts of the body

Get the children to work in pairs. Using large pieces of paper and crayon, put the paper on the floor and trace the outline of each child in turn. Once the outlines are complete the children can measure their own head sizes and complete their full size portraits. The main features can be named and the height and width of the outlines marked in.

Activity 11: How others see me

Show some portraits painted by Picasso. Discuss what the individual parts of the face look like. Look at and discuss **Copymasters 2, 6, 7** and **8**. Pay particular attention to noses, ears and eyes and differences in colour, hair and skin. Ask questions such as: 'How big are your ears?' 'What shape are your eyes?' Get your children to work in pairs to produce pictures of individual features until all the components of the face are ready, use rulers to measure accurately. Now the individual drawings of features can be assembled to make a collage of back, side and front views. Make up an identikit picture from the selected bits and pieces of the partner.

Activity 12: Life-size self portraits

Give each child a Mirriboard or a mirror, a piece of A3 paper and a choice of drawing materials. Ask the children to make their self portrait about as big as a piece of A4 paper. Get them to follow this simple rule: 'Think, Look and then start Drawing'. Extend this activity by using **Copymasters 7** and **79** on proportions. These sheets shows the various proportions of a standard face and different views.

Activity 13: My family as the Simpsons

Collect examples of cartoon families such as the Simpsons. Get the children to make up their own cartoon drawing of their families. Use **Copymasters 7, 8** and **79** to discuss the relative sizes of adults, children and the elements of the face. Help your children to get the sizes of the cartoon characters about right.

Activity 14: Silhouettes

Show examples of Victorian silhouette portraits and talk about the shape of heads as viewed from the side. What is a profile? Working in pairs and assisted by helpers use a projector to cast clearly defined outlines of the children's profiles. Use chalk to draw the outline carefully as projected onto black paper. When complete cut out the heads and mount onto white backing paper for class display.

 Moving sculptures ▷

You need
Copymasters 2, 6 and **7**, card, Plasticine®, sticky and coloured paper, wool, glue, PVA and paste, straws, butterfly clips, paper clips, scissors, clay, papier mâché and boards on which to work with papier mâché.

Activity 15: Family groups

Ask the children to make a small sculpture of a favourite family activity such as going to the swimming pool, going out in the car, watching television or taking the dog for a walk. Try to offer Plasticine® that still has individual colours so that they are able to colour different sections of their sculptures as they wish.

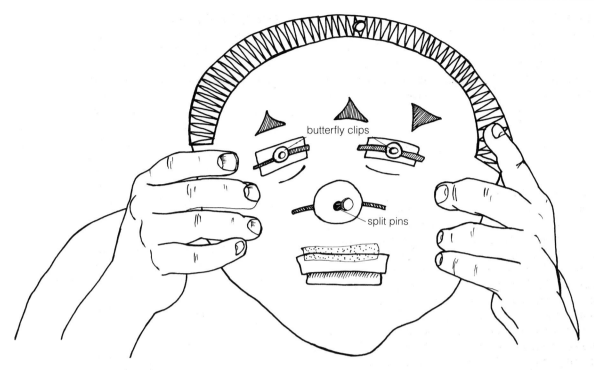

Face with moving parts

Activity 16: Moving faces

Discuss our faces and the parts that move (eyes, eyelids, tongues and mouths) and consider in which direction the parts move. First, get the children to do drawings of their own faces using the **Copymasters 2, 6** and **7** to help get the outlines and proportions right. Then cut out a basic face shape from one colour card. Make all the various parts in different colours. Some pieces will then be glued totally while others only partially to allow movement (to lift and shut).

See the illustration showing how to fix eyelids and use butterfly clips. The butterfly clips can be used for the eyes. They can also be used to move the eyes around and by making a slit they can be moved from side to side. Make cuts in the face for the tongue to slide through. Invite the children to suggest ways of making the moving parts stay in place.

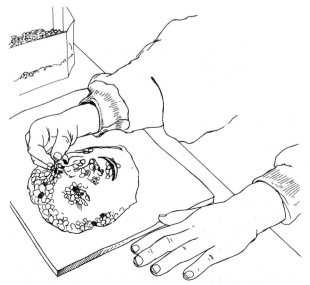

Building up shapes on baseboard

Activity 17: Self portrait in papier mâché

Make up enough papier mâché according to the recipe in the Modelling skills section of this book (see page 110). For 30 children making up small bas relief sculptures you will probably need slightly more than a gallon of mâché. Get the children to cut out the shape of their faces from a sheet of thin card, place this on the board and build up the sculpture from this outline. Use tools to form openings and add textures. When dry the sculptures can be painted and displayed.

Costumes and old age in paint

You need

Photographs of Mum and Dad's wedding, your (or relative's) christening, family photographs of grandparents throughout their lives, paints, paper and brushes. Reproductions of famous paintings and posters showing marriage, wedding dresses, top hats and saris. You may need to have gold paint available.

Activity 18: The wedding or christening

Your children may have richly differing experiences of marriage because of the cultural diversity of our country. Discuss what happens at weddings in Christian, Islamic, Hindu and non-religious ceremonies. Set the children the task of painting a family group including the bride and groom or a group during the christening or naming ceremony. Pay particular attention to the colour of skin, eyes, hair, and costumes. If you have a variety of cultures to use as a resource you will be able to mount a comparative display of paintings.

7

Activity 19: 'When I'm 64'

This activity is self explanatory and is introduced by showing images of how people change throughout their lives. It is a way of introducing a drawing activity on ageing. Look at the photographs of the children's grandparents as young, middle aged and old people and play the Beetles' song 'When I'm 64'. Ask the children to paint pictures of what they think they will look like when they are 12, 21 and 64. Use **Copymaster 9** for this.

You need
A series of reproductions of self portraits by Rembrandt and Van Gogh that show startling changes over a period of time. The Beetles' 'When I'm 64' from the Sergeant Pepper album, mirrors, paints, paper, family photographs, **Copymaster 9**.

Printing my body

You need
Paper (newsprint), fingerpaints, printing ink, sheets of perspex (40 × 30 cms approx.), hard rollers.

Activity 20: Printing with parts of the body

Printing with parts of the body is as well established in schools as it is fun. Normally with young children, finger paints are rolled out onto a sheet of perspex or Formica topped table, the hand or foot pressed into it and then the paint covered hand pressed onto a piece of paper. Such printed images can then be cut up and used as part of a mobile or class collage. Often the prints are very blobby and indistinct because too much paint is picked up then deposited. If you wish to make clearer images that can be examined with a magnifying glass try an alternative approach. First roll out some finger paint smoothly onto the Perspex, place the child's hand or

foot on the paint, then transfer the hand or foot, while still wet with paint and press the wet hand firmly onto another piece of clean perspex. Place a piece of paper immediately onto this 'off-set' image and rub, then peel off the paper. Such an approach can give a more detailed and exciting result.

Activity 21: Card prints of faces

Cut out the shape of faces from a piece of card, also cut out the shapes of eyes, noses, mouths and ears. Ink up individual shapes and press print these onto clean pieces of paper, start with the face and add all the elements until the printed multi-coloured self portrait is complete.

Elements of a face print

Something for my family

You need
Unprinted tea towels, old sheets, open canvas for embroidery, embroidery silks and needles, potatoes, textile crayons (make sure they suit the fabrics being used), dyes and an iron for fixing dyes.

Activity 22: A family members' tea towel

This is a simple and direct activity. Ask the children to do pencil sketches of all family members, including the pets. Now with fabric dye crayons copy the drawings onto clean tea towels, making sure that the space is well used up and not half empty. When complete, follow the manufacturers instructions to fix the dyes permanently to the fabric.

Activity 23: Multi-cultural embroidery

Using **Copymaster 10**, do simple cross stitch examples of how family scenes and faces are shown in different cultures. Refer to the Textiles skill section of this book (page 125) for more information about simple embroidery.

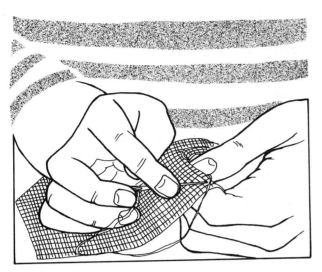

Family embroidery

Activity 24: Family badges or buttons
Roll out clay and cut round shapes about 3 or 4 cms across, allow to dry. When dry, paint little pictures of the family members one per button, when finished and quite dry fix a safety pin to the reverse as shown below.

You need
Make a collection of different types of buttons and badges, clay, water-based paints, safety pins.

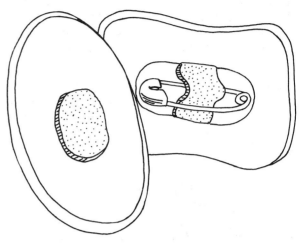

Badge fixings

HOMES

Ceramics
Cups and animals
30. Design and make tiles
31. Cups and saucers for a dolls' house
32. The home I would like
33. Noah's ark

Art history
Homes through the ages
25. Interiors
26. Exteriors
27. Murals and graffiti
28. Domestic pottery
29. Treehouse

Design
Ideal homes
34. Redesign home corner or bedroom
35. Patterned floors for the different rooms
36. *The Three Little Pigs* puppets

HOMES

Textiles
Designs on fabrics
50. Batik curtains
51. A sampler

Drawing
Drawing my home
37. My home from memory
38. The nosey window cleaner
39. The town

Print-making
Home decorating
47. Printing the wigwam covering
48. Wallpaper
49. Rubbings

Modelling
Model homes
40. Make a class wigwam
41. Make a model of a house or a castle
42. Design and make a bird table
43. Papier mâché garden in relief
44. Repoussé of my home or castle

Painting
House painting
45. Street scene
46. Shapes of homes

10

CROSS-CURRICULAR LINKS ▶

Design and technology Designing and making homes for pets (a nest) or toys, make a plan and redesign the home corner, modern domestic appliances, strong shapes for building, problem solving in building strong structures, structures to support specific weights. Safety in the home, the use of colour for safety coding, safe places, say no to strangers

Drama and dance Activities in the home corner, miming, role-play, acting out stories and rhymes

Environmental studies Animal and human homes, endangered species

History Homes at different times, the development of building materials, domestic items and appliances, lighting, caves, castles, cots, house-boats, small and grand, caravans, change of use i.e. Church to house

Language Descriptive, reportive and imaginative writing, extensions to vocabulary, stories and poems about homes and domestic activities, word search of 'homes' words

Mathematics Plane and solid shapes, tessellations, finding shapes, comparing sizes and shapes

Music Pentatonic Song, 'Lord of the Silver Birch' (chorus to be sung as a round)

RE House of God (sanctuary), homelessness (the wilderness), refugees

Science Building with solid shapes, making a pond or wormery

ABOUT THIS TOPIC ▶

General points

What is a home? It should be a warm and emotionally safe place. Unfortunately for many children this is not the case. Children may be subject to abuse, living in poverty, suffering the trauma of repossession or in the centre of a divorce case, all of which will make the home something of a nightmare place. This topic will have to be approached in a sensitive and careful way.

Drawings of houses that your youngest children do are unlikely to be very sophisticated. Remember that your pupils are moving from scribbles to a more clearly defined schema (a schematic way of using simple visual elements for different subjects). Try not to let your personal taste become the final measure of achievement; stereotype drawings are dull and without value. Also remember that the drawings may contain significant signals about the psychological state of your children. Obviously disturbed or oppressively dark images may merit your sensitive concern.

The history of art is littered with a rich array of images of homes through the ages. A varied collection of images and models will allow you to introduce the topic in an historical and visual way that will engage the interest of the children without accentuating their own housing problems.

Displays and resources

Your local museum and library services may be able to provide artefacts such as models of cottages, houses and castles as residences, Roman hypocausts, domestic appliances such as vacuum cleaners, spinning wheels, domestic pottery and kitchen utensils, games and toys, wallhangings from other cultures, carpet beaters, mob caps, scrubbing boards, pestles and mortars and the like. The John Judkyn Memorial Museum (John Judkyn Memorial Museum, Freshford Manor, Freshford, Nr. Bath, Avon) has a superb range of North American resources including Indian artefacts that are available for hire to schools. You will need books, posters and reproductions of works of art such as Van Gogh's series of well known interiors and houses, Pieter De Hoogh 'Courtyard of a house in Delft', Vermeer's paintings of interiors that include *The lacemaker* and *The view of Delft*.

STARTING POINTS ▶

You may introduce the topic through reading and role-playing stories and rhymes such as *Hansel and Gretel, Old woman who lived in a shoe, 'I'll take you to Mrs. Coles'*. You may look at interiors from art history and consider how different rooms and notions of comfort and furnishings have changed. You could take an historical approach, examining the styles and periods of homes or look at the different kinds of homes that exist. For example, permanent and mobile homes, homes on water, in the air, space, animal and human homes. Include a study of domestic items through the ages.

Homes through the ages

Before you start

It is important that children are encouraged to enjoy simply looking at lovely things. It is not always necessary to seek a practical result. You can introduce the variety of homes through looking at paintings, wood engravings, visits to stately homes, and finding interesting houses in the local environment. You may find examples of how the use of buildings has changed; castles modified into grand residences, windmills, old schools and churches turned into eccentric homes. Here the art history activities may simply be appreciation. Nevertheless they can form a positive context for more practical work.

You need

A substantial range of books and reproductions showing as varied a range of homes that you wish to encompass. Try to focus on the real area of interest. Paintings and drawings or prints by the following artists will be useful: Vermeer, Thomas Bewick (1753–1828), Giotto, Lowry, Breugel, Bratby, Canaletto, Saenredam, Sir Muirhead Bone (1876–1953), Claude, Adriaen Brouwer (1605–38), Sickert, Cezanne (1839–1906), Chardin (1699–1779), Constable (1776–1837), Cotman (1782–1842). Illustrations of canal barges, caravans, African huts, North American Indian wigwams, cave dwellings. **Copymaster 11** for stained glass, **Copymasters 12–14** for house styles.

Activity 25: Interiors

Collect and sort a range of images of interiors including illustrations from magazines, kitchen and bathroom brochures, paintings and drawings by Vermeer. Discuss the changes in style and the need for comfortable surroundings. Use magazine pictures to make a photo-collage of different types of interiors. Visit your local church, talk about the 'House of God'. On your visit use **Copymaster 11** to make drawings of stained glass windows. Make drawings of effigies, the exterior and interior of churches, draw attention to the darkness (and sources of light) and the quiet of the interior.

Activity 26: Exteriors

Look at the different styles of houses in your display, whether they are models, posters or illustrations in books. Ask why certain houses are more or less attractive than others. Include facilities (such as running water, warmth and the physical appearance and decoration of the houses). Talk about how old the children's homes are and whether or not they are flats, semi-detached, terraced or detached houses. What kinds of materials are used? Collect examples of tiles, bricks, wood. Give your pupils copies of **Copymasters 12, 13** and **14** which contain illustrations of different

styles of homes. Organise a walking tour around the school. Get your children to do drawings of homes similar to those shown on the copymasters. On the tour your children can also take photographs of houses, make drawings of details and street furniture and using lining paper and crayons take rubbings of interesting features. Later in school they can add to their drawings on the copymasters.

Activity 27: Murals and graffiti

Show illustrations of cave paintings, murals by Giotto (1267–1337), Michaelangelo, Piero della Francesca (1410–1492), Rivera (1886–1957) and contemporary wall paintings on the outsides of buildings and trains. Choose a topic for a class mural, such as our homes or the street. Ask each child to make their own painting of a house, shop or other building. Your children may find it useful to do architectural work on gridded paper. Use **Copymaster 17** or **18** to produce 1 cm or 2 cms squared paper. Also, on this paper, you could work out an overall plan and allocate a small section to be completed by the children working in pairs. For this approach you will need to give each section a number to be noted on the plan. When complete, assemble according to the plan and fix to the wall.

Activity 28: Domestic pottery

Collect a range of domestic pottery. Try to include in your display pots from the children's homes and examples of domestic pottery made by local craftsmen. Include willow pattern plates. Read the story to your children. Give each child a copy of **Copymaster 15** which contains a number of simple profiles of cups, jugs and pots. Get them to match the profiles with the words. Let them colour the outlines so that they match items from the display. Ask your children which style of pottery they like best. Make lists of likes and dislikes. Make sure your discussion involves an appreciation of the shapes, feel and utility of the pieces. Contact the Craft Council for information about supplies of good domestic pottery. Use **Copymaster 16**, ask the children to answer the questions about the *Willow pattern* story.

Activity 29: Treehouse

Ask your children to make a drawing of their garden or their ideal garden. They should include a carefully planned treehouse or garden playhouse. Before setting the task discuss the kinds of features that would be important, such as stairs (or alternative way of getting in), furniture and perhaps a way of communicating with the house.

Cups and animals

Activity 30: Design and make tiles

Make up square or rectangular frames from 2 cm square wood (balsa wood can be used). It is best to restrict the size to a maximum of about 10 cms by 10 cms. This simple mould needs to be fairly strong so gluing and pinning are recommended. Place the frame on a board and lightly oil with vegetable oil, or talc, the inside of the frame. Each child will need a piece of clay around the size of a tennis ball. This is placed inside the frame and thumped until it has spread out to fill the frame to an even depth of about 1 cm. The surface can be built up or cut into to produce a patterned design or a picture of the child's home or even a heraldic image for mounting on the wall of a castle (for wall mounting remember to pierce the clay with mounting holes before it dries). A variation on this approach is to build a relief picture to fit inside the frame and then press the clay over this to produce an imprinted tile. Tiles that have a relief design or pattern can, when dry, be used as a base for simple repoussé (see page 111 of the Modelling skill section) work. The tiles can be coloured by using slip or glazes after biscuit firing and fired. For further information about making tiles see the Ceramic skill section of this book (page 90) and Activity 44.

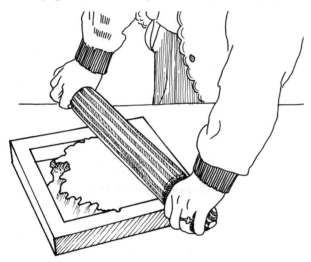

Making a tile

You need
Wood for the frames, clay, glazes or slips, tools, scrap materials for the relief picture from which the tile may be imprinted, glue, pins.

Activity 31: Cups and saucers for a dolls' house
If the children are making a model house or you have a doll's house on display you can set them the task of making cups and saucers that are about the right size (to scale).

You need
Clay, Newclay® or Plasticine®, examples of toys, tea sets, pictures of cups and saucers, a model house with dolls.

Activity 32: The home I would like
This can be an extension of the technique for making tiles, or the houses can be made freehand. First make up some regular slabs, as the tiles above. Remove them from frames when semi-dry and make up a basic box shape. Take care to join the corners well by using slip on the edges to be fixed and pressing them firmly into place. The roof can be made the same way. Holes can be

cut for windows and doors. Textures can be pressed into the damp clay. For very young children the task can be much more open-ended without the need for making slabs and the results more sculptural. Either way the finished pieces of work in natural clay can be coloured with glazes or slips while Newclay® can be painted.

You need
Clay or Newclay® boards, tools, frames (moulds), glazes, slips, paints and brushes and kiln (optional). Objects and materials to press into clay for textures.

Activity 33: Noah's ark
Noah's ark is a favourite unusual home and is a tremendous way of ensuring fun with clay. It is best for the children to work in pairs making a whole range of small animals. As the ark may be too difficult a task for very young children you may need to help them. The ark can be tackled by first making a slab base, then using coils to build up the walls following the outline of the base. Smooth the coils to form the walls of the ark. Cut out doors, windows and then, using slabs, form the roof. Do not make the ark too big (about 20 cms by 20 cms) and remember to use strong shapes and supports to hold the structure together. For more information about coil work please refer to the Ceramic skill section of this book (pages 89–90).

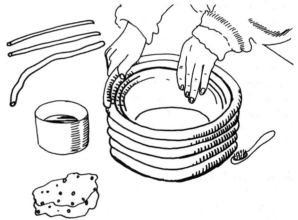

Forming coiled walls

Ideal homes

Before you start
Ask your children what they think makes an ideal home. Invite them to bring in their soft toys as part of their home brought to school. The Teddies and Cindies will probably need somewhere to live in school.

Activity 34: Redesign home corner or bedroom
If you have a home corner, you can set children the task of redesigning it to improve it, or they can redesign their own bedroom. To improve the way things are arranged it is first necessary to see how they are at present. Ask the children to do a memory drawing of their bedroom or a sketch of the home corner (with as many features as possible). Now give each child copies of **Copymaster 17** or **18** printed onto thin card. These grids are to be used for planning the layout of the

children's bedrooms or the home corner and for making up models. Ask the children to draw their beds, chairs, toys, windows, doors and walls onto the squares. You may be able to introduce a simple form of scale. For example: if the chair is two squares by two squares and the table is four squares by four squares, how big is the door? Later as children progress to Key Stage 2 the grids can be used for modelling in three dimensions.

You need
Paper, squared paper and cards, pencils, felt tip pens, rulers, **Copymasters 17** and **18**.

Activity 35: Patterned floors for the different rooms
If you have done some of the ceramic activities earlier in this topic you may already have got the children to make their own individual tiles. You can now discuss the idea of tessellation and show examples of simple and more complicated patterns. If you have examples of bricks in your display, you can then physically show the structural value of tessellating with building materials. **Copymasters 19–24** contain tessellated patterns based upon traditional Islamic Quranic designs. Give the children copies of one or more and ask them to make their own coloured patterned floors, using two, three, four or more colours. Ask them to think about the colours that they would use for the room. What colours would suit a bathroom? Which a kitchen?

You need
Copymasters 19–24, illustrations, examples of building materials, tiles, parquet floor strips and bricks, felt tip pens, paints brushes.

Activity 36: *The Three Little Pigs* puppets
Read the story of *The Three Little Pigs*. Discuss what kinds of materials are good for building the pigs' homes and how they could be used as part of a puppet production of the story. Using a variety of materials the children can then make strong and weak homes. They need to be the right size to fit into your puppet theatre.

These homes, together with all the characters, can be used to give a presentation of the story in front of the whole class.

Sometimes children need to get on with making something before exploring and analysing problems further. With very young children break the problems down into manageable parts, 'try this first and see how you get on'. If the children are very young the puppets will need to be very simple such as a lollipop stick puppet: 'I got a piece of toilet roll. I flattened it and I stuck a lollipop stick inside. I cut a long piece of card for the arms'.

Lolly puppet

In the Materials topic (pages 73–5) you will find a detailed account of how to make a puppet theatre. The puppets for *The Three Little Pigs* can be used in the puppet theatre.

You need
A wide range of resources to enable children to take control and make decisions for themselves. The children will then have to employ and develop skills of modifying the material to suit their purpose. Provide old toilet roll tubes, cardboard cartons, lolly sticks, straw, paints, glue, fabric scraps.

 ## Drawing my home ▷

You need
Pencils, paper, felt tip pens, Biros®, crayons or pastels. **Copymasters 17** and **18** grids to assist in accuracy and **Copymasters 25–7**.

Activity 37: My home from memory
The National Curriculum puts emphasis on drawing from memory, imagination and observation. Setting the

task of drawing their homes from memory can be a good point of departure for other activities. Discuss what kinds of homes the children have: a flat, house, caravan? Does it have a garden? Is there a park nearby? Emphasise the various elements that need to be considered, the garden, kitchens, greenhouses, and garages. Use **Copymaster 26** and ask the children to draw the front and back of their house, each floor and some details of furniture and windows and the garden. Ask them to make a special effort to remember what they look like. These drawings will enable follow-up tasks to be set. (It is a good idea to ask your children to bring in photographs afterwards to compare with the drawings.) As a follow up activity ask your children to make a model of their home. All the models together would make a fine display.

Activity 38: The nosey window cleaner
Discuss the kind of people who come to work in the home. Window cleaners, child minders, plumbers and electricians. What must their home look like to strangers? Ask the children what it would be like to be a window cleaner visiting their home. What would the view through each window be like? Would every room be tidy? What would their bedrooms look like through the frame of a window? Use **Copymaster 27** as a template for drawings of the important rooms of the home as viewed by a window cleaner.

Activity 39: The town
Show some of Klee's paintings of towns and houses. Give each child a copy of **Copymaster 25**. Ask them to select colours and to design their own town from the tessellated shapes on the sheet. Will all shapes be coloured? Is it night or day?

Model homes

Activity 40: Make a class wigwam
The activity of making a class wigwam involves designing and making the structure and printing the fabric. The printing is dealt with separately under Activity 47.

Introduce a discussion about how other people in other times and cultures have provided homes for themselves. Make sure that your display has examples of homes of various cultures, including North American Indians. The Indian teepee or wigwam is a sound and very mobile home. Set the task of designing and making a teepee and associated Indian domestic items for use in the home corner. First of all decide how many children will be involved in the making of the teepee itself and how many in making the other domestic items. If the teepee has six sides then three children can work on each section. The remaining children can work on the ceramics and other artefacts. Get the wigwam makers to make a small model of the tent. They can then think about how to design and decorate their own section. This is an excellent problem-solving activity.

Cut old sheets into six equal isosceles triangular sections as shown in the diagram. The front opening will be made by cutting up half through one triangle as shown. Now print the fabric as explained in Activity 47 and fix the colours. Once the printing is complete and the fabric is dry it is time to make up the covering. The canes will have to be long enough (two metres) to protrude through the open apex of the wigwam. Cut the fabric sections, with sufficient over for a hem and pieces with which to attach to the framework of canes. You will probably have to help with the sewing together of the sections. When the cover is complete, fix it to the canes and erect it in the home corner decorating it with the artefacts made by the other children.

You need
Old cotton sheets, paper, ceramics (as above), canes, printing materials (see below), sewing equipment (you may need to use a machine).

Activity 41: Make a model of a house or a castle
Copymasters 28 and **29 a** and **b** can be used as guides to making either a house or a castle. Scrap corrugated card or thin card can be used. Thin card is easier to cut, score and fix. The basic elements of the castle, cones, cylinders and walls are given on **Copymaster 28**. Once these have been assembled and fixed it is possible to cut doorways and plan stairs so that the castle can have a dungeon. The net for the house can be photocopied onto sheets of thin card and made up in a similar way. For older children these activities can be modified so that original designs can be made on squared paper and converted into nets drawn on squared card. To add realism to these models you can copy the building finishes on **Copymasters 30–37**. These contain scale patterns of various building materials such as stone, tiles and bricks. These can be copied onto card, coloured and used to finish the buildings by being fixed with glue.

An important part of learning to work with sheet material such as card is investigating the many ways in which it can be folded, shaped and formed to give it increased strength and rigidity. The models can be decorated as desired. It is wise to experiment with scraps of card first to see what results there might be. For more information please refer to the Modelling skills section (page 106).

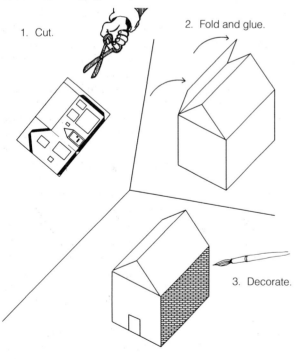

1. Cut.

2. Fold and glue.

3. Decorate.

You need
Thin card, **Copymasters 28–37**, rulers, cutting boards, safety rulers, glue, paints and brushes, paper clips to hold elements in place while glue dries.

Activity 42: Design and make a bird table
Discuss what kinds of homes birds inhabit and talk about whether the children have gardens, window boxes, verandas or nothing at all. What kind of bird table would be best? First draw the various details for the finished design. Include water dishes, hanging nuts, roof, support, doors and windows. Make up the designs as models. A point to watch is stability and balance when birds land. Ensure that the base is big enough.

You need
Wood, card, old toilet roll tubes, boxes, Sellotape®, plastic, glue, paint, netting, saws.

Activity 43: Papier mâché garden in relief
Get the children to make drawings of their gardens. Trees, swings, sandpits and paddling pools should all be shown. Use these drawings of their gardens as a starting point for modelling in papier mâché. Decide what size the miniature gardens will be. 35 cms to 45 cms square is big enough for children working on their own. Make up a wooden frame, from 2 cm square wood. Back it with a thin sheet of card as illustrated and place on a board covered with a piece of polythene. Pack out the frame with a layer of papier mâché. Features can be built up and cut away to provide ponds, hillocks, sheds and trees. Use sand to add textures. Additional features can be modelled from papier mâché or scrap materials. Let the models dry thoroughly and then paint.

An alternative activity to this is to make a desert island home with caves and mountains using papier mâché.

You need
Papier mâché (see Modelling skills section page 110 for recipe), 2 cm square section wood, card, boards, glue, corner pieces, paint, brushes, scrap materials, sand.

Activity 44: Repoussé of my home or castle
If the children have produced tiles with relief images of homes or castles on them then you can introduce repoussé work. Take the finished and hardened tiles, cut a piece of metal foil (aluminium cooking foil) slightly larger than the tile. Place it over the tile which is now being used as a shape former and simply press the foil

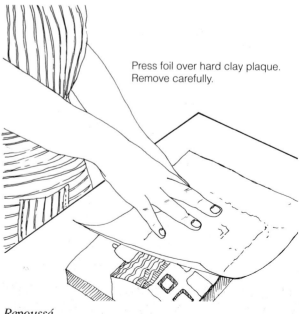

Press foil over hard clay plaque. Remove carefully.

Repoussé

16

into the indentations. When complete carefully remove the foil and mount onto a card support for wall display. (See Modelling skill section, page 111.)

You need
Foils, relief tiles.

 ## House painting ▷

Before you start
There are many painting activities about homes, such as imaginative work based upon stories such as *Hansel and Gretel, The old woman who lived in a shoe*, etc. The two activities given below have been included because they relate to the shapes associated with homes. Gently introduce the idea of abstract shapes.

Activity 45: Street scene
Extend drawing activity 39 and show examples of paintings of houses by different artists including Klee, *Flagged town* and *Seaside town*, Lowry, and *The view of Delft* by Jan Vermeer (1632–1675) and Canaletto (1697–1768). If you are able to show slides of these pictures as a warm up exercise get the children to sketch anything they like while the pictures are being projected. Include details such as rooftops, doors, windows.

After the opening session tell your children that you would like them to concentrate on the shapes that make up their houses. Give them pieces of A3 white paper and black felt tip pens. Ask them to do large drawings of their homes using the black felt tip pens without taking their pens from the paper until the drawings are complete. This technique is shown in the diagram. When complete these drawings can be painted with flat areas of colour for each separate shape that has been drawn. Mount all the works as a mural.

Keeping pen on paper. Designing and making a bird table.

Activity 46: Shapes of homes
Get the children to paint rectangular shapes of different sizes using different colours. Ask them to try to make their shapes as clear and simple as possible. The rectangles should be both big and small, and should be arranged in different ways on the paper: horizontal, vertical and diagonal. Also try working with sticky paper as follows. Give the children strips of sticky paper of various widths. Now ask the children simply to make the shapes that best represent their homes on a white backing sheet. By breaking the shapes down and then constructing with them your children will develop understanding about space and shapes.

 ## Home decorating ▷

Activity 47: Printing the wigwam covering
This is an extension of modelling activity 40. The North American Indians based their symbolism on their experience of their environment, taking birds, animals and other natural forms and rendering them in a simplified or abstract form. Part of the class may well be using clay to model pots and animals with which to decorate the wigwam. Those engaged on printing designs onto the cloth may use potatoes or clay.

To use clay simply take a small ball of firm clay and thump it onto a table top. Your children can either design their own abstract patterns directly into the clay or prepare small designs on tracing paper. If they use tracing paper then the design can easily be transferred to a clay block using a sharp pencil. These 'blocks' are then used for printing. All manner of objects or tools can be used to press into the flattened surface of the clay. Once a pattern has been produced the clay printing block should be tapped again onto the table to ensure that it is flat. Now place pieces of foam sponge into the bottom of an old ice-cream container and pour over quantities of fabric printing ink such as that produced by Berol. Press the clay block against the sponge and print onto the fabric. **Copymaster 38** contains simple Indian symbols for use with this activity.

This is a very easy method and you should take care that the children plan where they will print on the sheet sections before actually starting to print. This is such an easy process that it can get out of hand when used as a method of printing onto paper. When experimenting prior to printing on the fabric give each child a limited quantity of newsprint and encourage them to produce a variety of images on the single sheet of paper, before making up their finished plan for their piece of work on a new piece of paper. Once they are happy, they can print on the wigwam sections. Make sure that the children work in a clean way and wipe the blocks clean after each colour. Favourite clay printing blocks can be allowed to harden and can be reused for a long period of time. When each section of the wigwam cover has been completed, follow the manufacturer's instructions for fixing the dyes permanently.

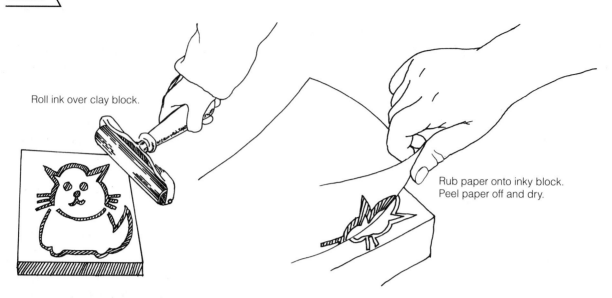

Roll ink over clay block.

Rub paper onto inky block.
Peel paper off and dry.

For further information about developing this method refer to the Print-making skills section on page 120).

You need
Clay, objects for making impressions in the clay, fabric crayons or wet dyes, potatoes, a collection of signs and symbols that are common in early civilisations (see **Copymaster 38**) as part of your display.

Activity 48: Wallpaper
A similar approach to that outlined above can be followed for printing wallpaper, with the exception that ordinary finger paints may be used. Talk about the examples of wallpaper that form part of your display. Which ones would the children like for their homes? Why do they like these? Can they make better designs? Set the task of designing a simple image (silhouette) as a motif for their wallpaper (flowers, animals, robots). Discuss how simple repeated patterns can be made. Look at the Islamic patterns again.

To arrange a repeat pattern take the piece of paper to be printed and fold it so that it is creased into squares which are slightly larger than the image to be printed. Demonstrate how to make a pattern in this way. Get them to plan where each image will be placed. The motifs can be printed from clay blocks or from potato cuts. As an alternative to this your children can make simple stencils. For very young children take small squares of paper 10 cms square, fold and cut small patterns from the centre. Flatten out and cover both sides of the edges with wax crayon to stop the paper becoming saturated with paint. Use a sponge to pad through paint onto the paper. Craft knives should either be used by adults or the children should be supervised very closely.

You need
Either clay, potatoes or paper for stencils. Scissors, wax crayons to cover the edges of the cut paper with brushes, finger paints, palettes.

Activity 49: Rubbings
If you are able to visit some houses around the school the children can take rubbings of a variety of building materials. These rubbings can be used as part of the background to class collages on homes. Cut small sections of the rubbings and mount on **Copymaster 39** as a permanent record of the textures.

You need
Lining paper, chunky wax crayons, **Copymaster 39**.

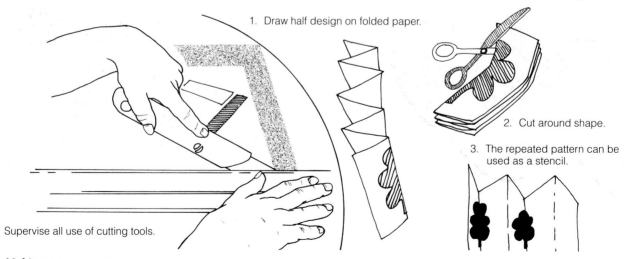

1. Draw half design on folded paper.

2. Cut around shape.

3. The repeated pattern can be used as a stencil.

Supervise all use of cutting tools.

Making a repeat pattern

Designs on fabrics ▷

Activity 50: Batik curtains

The Javanese craft of batik work can be undertaken quite safely with top infants provided you limit the number of pupils involved and you manage the activity properly. Working with groups no bigger than six should allow you to supervise the use of molten wax. First get the children to work out some ideas with paint or crayons on paper. These will not be followed rigidly but will allow for some forward thinking before moving to batik. Rough outlines can be sketched onto the fabric with a soft pencil, then using tjanting (a batik wax pen) carefully apply lines, blobs and splodges of wax to the fabric. When the first stage is complete scrunch up the fabric and dunk it into cold water dye such as Dylon, remove, rinse, dry and then iron out the wax between sheets of absorbent paper. Repeat the process until the design is finished. For the sake of economy, only smallish samples of curtain materials should be made up. For further information about batik see the Textile skills section on page 126.

You need
Cotton fabric, batik equipment, cold water dyes, buckets, iron, protective clothes including rubber gloves, clean newsprint.

Activity 51: A sampler

Making something to take home always appeals to children; it will also reinforce ideas of helping and what a home can mean. The task here is for the children to design and embroider a small sampler or picture. **Copymasters 40** and **41** show large scale drawings of embroidered or woven fabric. These can be used to introduce the idea of sewing through fabric. The children can colour the copymasters in a number of interesting ways. Children can make their own designs up on the special **Copymaster 42** of canvas sized squares. Keep the designs simple, use a few coloured pencils. Help your children to transfer the designs to canvas, using coloured thread. For further information see the Textile skills section on page 125.

You need
Canvas, embroidery needles, cottons or silks, **Copymasters 40–42**, paper.

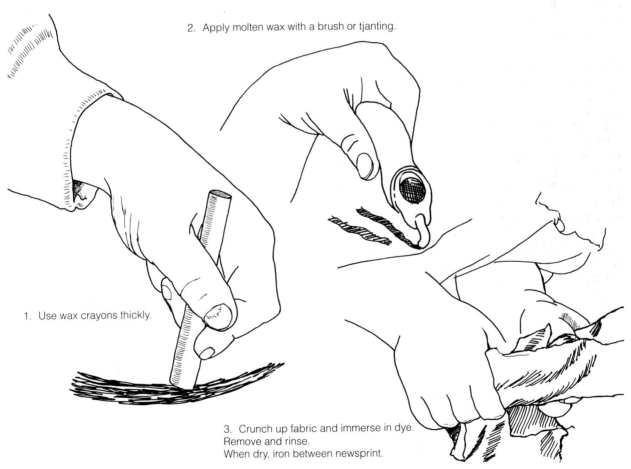

2. Apply molten wax with a brush or tjanting.

1. Use wax crayons thickly.

3. Crunch up fabric and immerse in dye. Remove and rinse. When dry, iron between newsprint.

Batik

CLOTHING

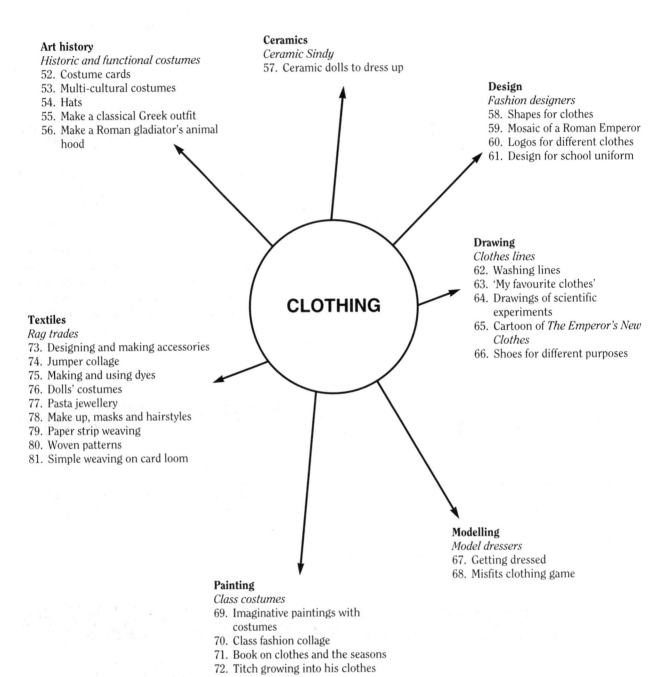

Art history
Historic and functional costumes
52. Costume cards
53. Multi-cultural costumes
54. Hats
55. Make a classical Greek outfit
56. Make a Roman gladiator's animal hood

Ceramics
Ceramic Sindy
57. Ceramic dolls to dress up

Design
Fashion designers
58. Shapes for clothes
59. Mosaic of a Roman Emperor
60. Logos for different clothes
61. Design for school uniform

Drawing
Clothes lines
62. Washing lines
63. 'My favourite clothes'
64. Drawings of scientific experiments
65. Cartoon of *The Emperor's New Clothes*
66. Shoes for different purposes

Textiles
Rag trades
73. Designing and making accessories
74. Jumper collage
75. Making and using dyes
76. Dolls' costumes
77. Pasta jewellery
78. Make up, masks and hairstyles
79. Paper strip weaving
80. Woven patterns
81. Simple weaving on card loom

Modelling
Model dressers
67. Getting dressed
68. Misfits clothing game

Painting
Class costumes
69. Imaginative paintings with costumes
70. Class fashion collage
71. Book on clothes and the seasons
72. Titch growing into his clothes

CROSS-CURRICULAR LINKS

Design and technology Clothes for different purposes, fashion
Drama and dance Role-play in imaginary clothes shops, fashion shows
Environmental studies Multi-cultural clothes links, protective clothes, natural and made fabrics
History History of costumes, changes in style and materials
Language Imaginative, factual and reportive writing, extensions to vocabulary, stories, use word search for clothing words

Mathematics Comparisons of size, matching, pattern making, sequential dressing
Music 'The Altogether' (*Emperor's New Clothes* song)
RE The importance of ceremonial clothing in different religions, pride, envy and jealousy
Science Testing fabrics for differing qualities i.e. insulation, water-proofing, durability, effectiveness of dyes, safety and special clothes like hard hats on building sites

ABOUT THIS TOPIC

General points
Clothes are made from natural and made materials. They are designed with specific purposes of keeping us dry, warm, cool or safe and for specific occasions or activities. While the cross-curricular aspects of clothing are very important, when considering art activities the main emphasis is on looking at the history of clothes, the multitude of purposes for clothing and accessories, dyeing, weaving, pattern making (size) and designing and making.

Displays and resources
Collect different artefacts, shoes, riding hats, flippers,

uniforms, examples of historical costumes from museum and library services. You may be able to get 'dressing up boxes', that include many types of garments from the Victorians to the present day, from your museum and library services. Collect fabrics, hats (if possible), handbags, shoes, gloves, scarves, belts, ties, braces, waistcoats. Dekker toys produce a range of role-playing outfits that are really quite inexpensive, durable and repairable. The space-suits are very good and include helmets with visors. Get the children to bring in toys that include clothing of any kind, especially those that have changeable clothing.

STARTING POINTS

- History of clothing.
- Stories such as *You'll Soon Grow Into Them, Titch* by Pat Hutchins and old chestnuts such as *The Emperor's New Clothes* and *Cinderella*.
- Toys brought in from home.
- Dressing-up and drama activities.
- Visits by policeman, postman, fireman, diver,

surgeon followed by discussions about clothing for particular purposes.
- Collection of illustrations of contemporary and historical costumes, party wear, work wear, sports-wear.
- Visit of costume keeper of a theatre group.

CLOTHING ACTIVITIES

C43– 50

Before you start
Clothing seems to have been developed for a number of different reasons. When introducing this topic consider the different functions of clothing. Protection and display are very important as is a magical element (it was a method of warding off hostile magic). Bangles and necklaces of the teeth of powerful animals may have been worn as the first jewellery with the object of endowing the wearer with great strength, only later on would the beauty of the bangles be considered.

 ## Historic and functional costumes

You need
Illustrations, or examples of protective clothes, costumes, and garments for different purposes. From the history of costume try to have a few illustrations of Cretan and Minoan costumes (these are unlike

'Classical' Greek robes; Egyptian costumes and jewellery (often based on animals and insects); Bronze age jewellery; Greek chitons (in either wool, linen, or silk – your children can use dyed, old pillow cases with openings for head arms and legs, plus a cloak); illustrations on how to wear these can be found on Greek ceramics and sculptures; illustrations of types of sandals; toga and tunica of Southern Italy and the Roman Empire; gladiators' animal hoods and masks (different lengths for men and women); make up, masks and hairstyles; mosaics of Roman Emperors; Saxon and Viking costumes; Norman armour and helmets. A range of costume dolls including some of the following: 12th century builder, fisherman or farmer; 15th century court jester; 16th century Walter Raleigh, a lady spinning, a Tudor night watchman, 17th century cavalier and roundhead, puritan man and woman, seaman, straw and basket vendor; 18th century Captain Cook and Nelson; 19th or 20th century milkseller; plus agricultural garments including a smock and gaiters and multi-cultural costumes including saris.

Activity 52: Costume cards
Use **Copymaster 43** to produce outlines of men, women and children on thin card. Help the children to cut out the basic dolls. They can then design and make their own clip-on clothes for historical or multicultural costume designs by tracing the outlines.

Activity 53: Multi-cultural costumes
Give the children **Copymaster 44** of different multi-cultural costumes. Help them to find out which costumes they are and to colour and identify the costumes and their country of origin correctly.

Activity 54: Hats
Look at pictures of different kinds of hats on **Copymaster 45**. Discuss the idea that a hat somehow gives the wearer prestige, the ultimate being a crown and the antithesis the dunce's cap. Have a tea-party with your own 'Mad hatter'. Make up a collection of hats and use as part of your display. Hats worth looking at include those odd beak shaped hats designed to protect the wearer from the plague, crowns, hard hats on building sites, space helmets, baseball hats, police and firemen's

helmets, bridal head coverings from different religions, boaters, cook's hats, surgeons hats and mob caps. Get your children to find and name the various types of hats on the **Copymaster 45**. Certain colours will be particularly associated with different hats. Get your children to colour them and explain why they have used the chosen colours. The examination of hats may easily be developed into many practical activities such as making a protective helmet for a soft toy or a decorative hat for a special occasion.

Activity 55: Make a classical Greek outfit
Look at illustrations of classical Greek figures on sculptures and ceramics. Using old pillowcases, get the children to mark where the head and armholes should be cut out. Cut out the holes and try the pillowcases on the children for size. Modify openings to suit. Children can use crayon dye sticks to decorate around the openings with lines or patterns. Using old sheets, children can make up cloaks to finish off their outfits and, using **Copymaster 46**, can try to make simple sandals from card. (Check that the dye sticks are suitable for cotton.)

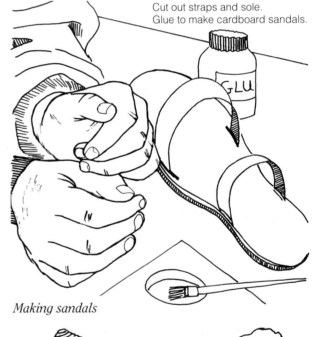

Cut out straps and sole.
Glue to make cardboard sandals.

Making sandals

Hats

Activity 56: Make a Roman gladiator's animal hood

With scraps of white fabric, get the children to design their own leopard skin hood. The fabric needs to be stretched and a rough plan of the flattened heads sketched using crayon. Fill in the patterned areas with crayon dye sticks and fix according to the manu-facturer's instructions.

Ceramic Sindy dolls ▷

Activity 57: Ceramic dolls to dress up

You will need to direct this activity positively and it will be sensible to work with a small group wearing overalls. Prepare your work area with newspapers or canvas on top of polythene sheets.

Get the children to look at their Sindy® and Action Man® dolls and ask them to make up their own small versions (10 cms high) using clay. Roll out solid cylinders of clay for the trunk and the legs and arms. Fix these solidly together using slip or form them as part of the whole body. The legs may need to be joined down to the knees or even feet. You will need to help to ensure that the dolls are stable on their feet. Use a ball of clay for the head and squeeze to shape. Once the clay has dried a little, finishing with tools can be done more easily. It is better if the figures can be fired in a kiln. If you do this, please look at the Ceramics skills section of this book (page 91) for guidance on firing solid shapes. The figures can be glazed after biscuit firing and used as a basis for activity 76.

You need
Examples of Sindy® dolls and Action Man®, clay, boards, modelling tools.

Fashion designers ▷

Activity 58: Shapes for clothes

Copymasters 47 and **48** contain simple outlines of clothing. Use these for this very simple activity. It is suitable for younger infants and involves tracing the shapes of shirts, trousers, skirts and hats onto different coloured card, cutting them out and using the results as part of the display. The names of the various garments can be added to the shapes.

Activity 59: Mosaic of a Roman Emperor

Show examples of Roman mosaics and the costumes the Romans used to wear. As a group activity get the children to make their own design about 60 cm high on paper, then using cut up sticky paper make up the design as a mosaic.

Draw outlines.
Fill in shapes with torn, coloured paper.

Mosaic of emperor

Activity 60: Logos for different clothes

Discuss what kind of clothes are needed on cold days and warm days and make a list. In order to present the findings of a survey of what children wear, ask the children to design a logo or symbol that is easily understood for each item of clothing. Use the best designs to create a bar graph detailing their findings.

CLOTHES SURVEY

	white	red	black	blue	yellow

Activity 61: Design for school uniform

Make a chart to show visually 'The clothes we wore to school today'. Discuss whether or not school uniforms are popular. What colours would be best? Will it suit both boys and girls? How many individual items of clothing will need to be designed? Is there a school badge? Will it be included in the designs? How will the clothes be fastened? Give the children paper, pencils and felt tip pens and ask them to make designs of the uniforms they would like. For very young children ask them just to paint a picture of themselves dressed in their idea of a nice school uniform.

You need
Drawing paper, selections of pencils, felt tip pens, crayons, samples of fabrics, buttons, adhesives, examples of fastenings such as velcro, examples of patterns and illustrations of designs.

Clothes lines

Activity 62: Washing lines
Discuss and make lists of all the kinds of clothes that the children can think of and their characteristics (warm, cool, dry, furry). Get the children to draw pictures of different garments using felt tip pens. Try to show the textures. Cut out the clothes, name them and hang them from a washing line in the home corner.

Activity 63: 'My favourite clothes'
Ask the children to bring in one item of clothing they particularly like. Using a combination of media, pencils, biros, felt tip pens, and charcoal, ask them to do representative drawings of their favourite clothing. Add a description of why the clothes are liked and use it as part of a class display.

Activity 64: Drawings of scientific experiments
If the children are experimenting with clothing, fabrics or dyes, help them to make diagrams of these experiments as part of a record of the activities. A simple device is to include a scale so that the size of various items can be judged.

Activity 65: Cartoon of *The Emperor's New Clothes*
After reading the story, show examples of strip cartoons from comics and talk about the way time is shown by moving from one picture to the next. Give each child a copy of **Copymaster 49**. Ask them to draw four pictures to illustrate four important features of the story in sequence. Use colour to finish the drawings nicely.

Activity 66: Shoes for different purposes
Collect together flippers, ballet shoes, football boots, running shoes, wellingtons, riding boots, trainers, and if you can, a pair of huge clown's shoes. Make a still life of the shoes. Get the children to use different materials to represent the different styles, shapes and textures of the shoes.

Model dressers

You need
Card, pencils, felt tip pens, **Copymaster 43**, paper clips.

Activity 67: Getting dressed
Get the children to do a drawing of themselves on coloured card about 15 cm high without any clothes on. Use some tracing paper to trace the outline of the figure they have drawn and trace this image on to two or three sheets of white card. On those traced outlines draw the various items of clothing that they would normally wear to school. Colour and help them to cut out the individual items of clothing which can then be used as part of a sequencing story of themselves getting dressed.

Sequencing clothes game

Activity 68: Misfits clothing game
Using **Copymaster 43**, trace the outlines of men and women. Trace the outlines onto other pieces of card and design clothing to suit. Colour and cut out. The clothing can then be used either on the men or the women with amusing results. If the children work in a group they can produce a very varied collection of costumes and clothes for a misfits game.

Class costumes

Activity 69: Imaginative paintings with costumes
Show reproductions of famous portraits that include well known people in period costumes, for example, 'Iron and coal' by William Bell Scott, Ford Madox Brown's 'Pretty baa-lambs', and images of Queen Victoria and Albert. Discussions of such set-up pictures can be combined with dressing up activities. Get the children to paint pictures either from imagination or observation of their friends dressed in the clothes of famous characters. This should be a lot of fun as the role-playing can extend to striking poses as models and, of course, the artists (with stuck on whiskers and proper palettes!).

You need
Illustration of famous costume paintings, costumes, paint, paper and brushes, props.

Activity 70: Class fashion collage

Collect and sort illustrations of all kinds of fashion from all over the world. Cut these pictures out carefully and get your children to arrange them for a class fashion collage. The costumes can be sorted into colour groupings (all red, etc), clothing types or clothes for warm or cold days. Drawings and paintings can be produced by the children and combined as a full scale collage mounted onto hessian or coloured paper mounted on the wall.

You need
Illustrations from books and magazines, paint, felt tip pens, sticky paper and paper.

Activity 71: Book on clothes and the seasons

A class book (A2 size) made from sugar paper is a good way to collect various activities together and present them as a story of the topic's activities. Take five or six sheets of A1 sugar paper. Fold them in half and punch two holes through the folded margin as shown in illustration. Reinforce the holes with fabric reinforcing-circles and thread the whole thing together with wool, so that the book could be hung from the wall. The book will have 20 sides that can be used. Cut two circles of contrasting sugar paper each approximately 15 cm in diameter. On one circle children can mount cut out illustrations of winter clothes and on the other a set of summer clothes. If you overlap the circles you can mount clothes that are worn all year round in that common area. A book such as this, can hold examples of work for up to eight children. The kinds of things to include are paper strip weaving, designs for jumpers, photocopies for 'Our favourite clothes' and illustrated graphs of 'The clothes we wore today', experiments

about different fabrics, pictures of Titch growing into his clothes, examples of national costumes, results of surveys of shoe sizes and pictures of the Emperor's new clothes.

Activity 72: Titch growing into his clothes

You'll Soon Grow Into Them, Titch by Pat Hutchins is a great favourite with young children, many of whom will sympathise with the way Titch inherited clothes. After reading the story ask the children to paint pictures illustrating: Pete giving away his clothes; Titch being told that he will soon grow into them; Titch going shopping; Titch finding that they are still a 'bit too big' and, finally, Titch saying that the baby will soon grow into them.

Extending this activity can focus attention on the problems for people without enough money to buy clothes. Referring to the history of clothing you can explain that during the last century many poor people could not afford any new clothes and streets often echoed to the cry of the Old Clothes' Man: 'This man cries old clothes! To buy or to sell; Hats, coats, shoes and hose, What more I can't tell'.

 # Rag trades ▷

Activity 73: Designing and making accessories

Sewing can be introduced by designing and making simple accessories such as bags, bangles, belts and scarves. To make a bangle: measure the wrist and cut two strips of felt, (about 5 cms wide by 8 cms longer than the circumference of the wrist) in contrasting colours. Cut a point on one end of the two strips (see diagram overleaf), lay the strips so that they are offset, showing the colour below. Form into a bangle shape by

Winter   All year   Summer

Class book with summer and winter clothes

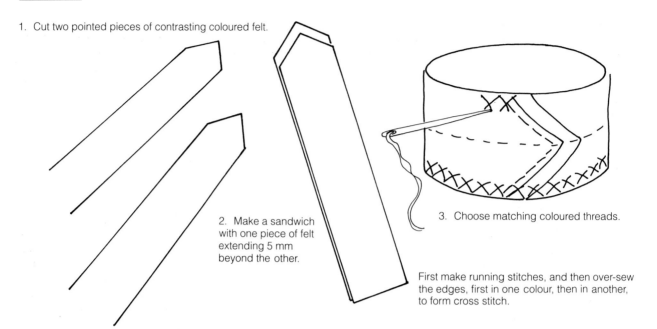

1. Cut two pointed pieces of contrasting coloured felt.

2. Make a sandwich with one piece of felt extending 5 mm beyond the other.

3. Choose matching coloured threads.

First make running stitches, and then over-sew the edges, first in one colour, then in another, to form cross stitch.

Making bangles

laying the pointed ends over the straight end, check for size and tack in place. Choose two colours of embroidery cotton to match the colours of the felts. Over sew one edge using the first colour, then using the other colour form a cross-stitch to finish the edge. Finish other edges in the same way. Sew the points in place. Add beads if desired. To make a bag, use **Copymaster 50** to provide a pattern for the parts, make up using cross stitches and fix the covering with Velcro®.

Activity 74: Jumper collage
Cut out the shape of jumper (say 20 cms by 20 cms) from thin card and apply the chosen coloured wool with glue to make up a miniature jumper. Discuss qualities of materials that are suitable for clothes. Make a list: soft, warm, etc.

Activity 75: Making and using dyes
Collect samples of raw wool, cotton, and fabrics, natural dyes from blackberries, cold water dyes (Dylon®) and dyesticks. Work with your children to find out how to make dyes from natural materials that will stay colour-fast. Try different approaches, try to dye unwashed fleece, try washed fleece, record the results. For more information about dyeing please refer to the Textile skill section on page 126.

Activity 76: Dolls' costumes
Make up simple clothes for dolls by using **Copymasters 47** and **48**. These give basic shapes for most types of garments. Obviously some changes may have to be made to ensure a good fit, nevertheless the shapes can be used as simple patterns and will be a good starting point. Give each child a copy of the Copymasters. Pin them to two layers of felt. Help to cut and fix the shapes together either by sewing or using glue. For older children sequins will give extra colour.

Trace pattern, cut out, pin to fabric, make up garment.

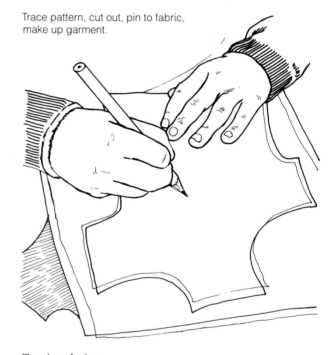

Tracing designs

Activity 77: Pasta jewellery
Make a collection of different types of uncooked pasta, include spirals, fan shaped and macaroni. Paint with PVA paints and thread together or fix onto a safety pin as a brooch.

Activity 78: Make up, masks and hairstyles
Use panels of cardboard from cartons. Draw a rough outline of each child's face in the centre of a panel, cut an opening for the whole face. Make a basic flat mask for a robot, flower or animal and colour it. Use face paints to make-up using co-ordinating colours to match the masks.

Activity 79: Paper strip weaving

Provide your children with 30 cms squares of coloured sugar paper and contrasting colours cut into strips about 3 cms wide. Cut parallel lines in the square of paper. They should be 3 cms apart and finish 3 cms from the edges of the square. Get your children to weave the strips through the cuts in the square. Fix the ends with glue.

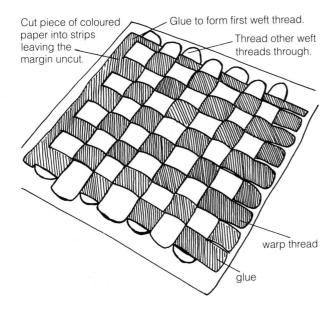

Cut piece of coloured paper into strips leaving the margin uncut.

Glue to form first weft thread.

Thread other weft threads through.

warp thread

glue

Activity 80: Woven patterns

Use the **Copymasters 40** and **41** woven pattern sheets for colouring exercises. These patterns will allow children to think about what happens when they are weaving. They can plan designs before actually weaving. Two scales of patterns are included to suit the dexterity of different aged children.

Activity 81: Simple weaving on card loom

Take a piece of card that is serrated as in the diagram. If you use a small square about 10 or 15 cms square young

children will be able to get quick and good results. Tie and wind the warp as shown. This needs to be fairly tight. Secure with Sellotape® on the reverse side. To avoid the problem of 'waisting' do not use a continuous weft thread, instead cut about 250 lengths of weft about 15 cms or 20 cms long (depending on the size of the square used). Using a turned up tip needle work from one side. Thread the first strand, over and under alternate warp strands. Make the protruding edges equal; continue until the card is complete. Each alternate thread of weft will pick up different warp threads than the previous one (where the previous one went over this should go under). Make sure to push the weft threads well down on each other using the needle, level up as each piece is completed. Remove the work when complete by gently prising the warp loops over the notches. It will be necessary to stitch to secure the weaving along the edges that form the fringes.

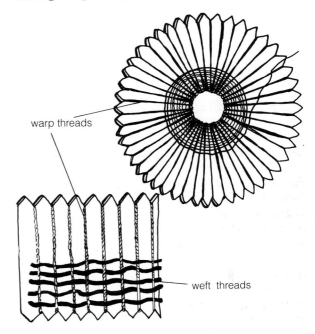

warp threads

weft threads

Simple card loom

WATER

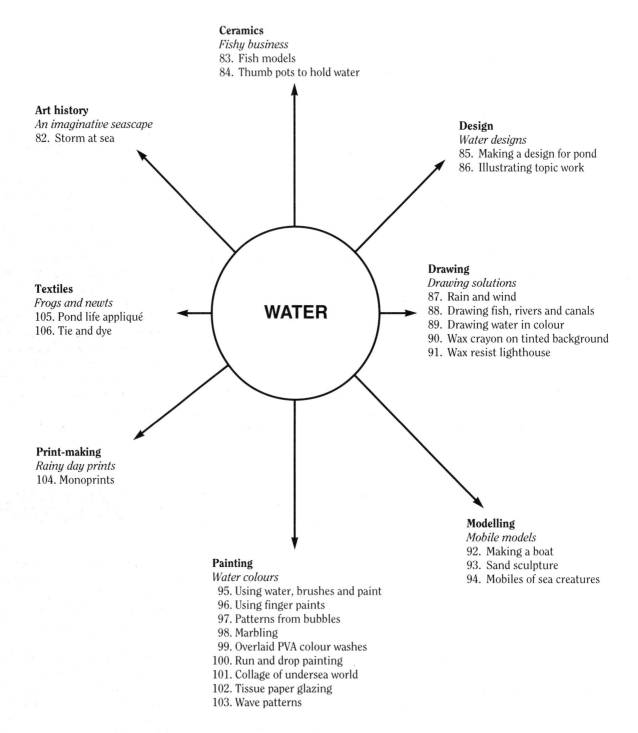

Ceramics
Fishy business
83. Fish models
84. Thumb pots to hold water

Art history
An imaginative seascape
82. Storm at sea

Design
Water designs
85. Making a design for pond
86. Illustrating topic work

Drawing
Drawing solutions
87. Rain and wind
88. Drawing fish, rivers and canals
89. Drawing water in colour
90. Wax crayon on tinted background
91. Wax resist lighthouse

Textiles
Frogs and newts
105. Pond life appliqué
106. Tie and dye

WATER

Print-making
Rainy day prints
104. Monoprints

Modelling
Mobile models
92. Making a boat
93. Sand sculpture
94. Mobiles of sea creatures

Painting
Water colours
95. Using water, brushes and paint
96. Using finger paints
97. Patterns from bubbles
98. Marbling
99. Overlaid PVA colour washes
100. Run and drop painting
101. Collage of undersea world
102. Tissue paper glazing
103. Wave patterns

CROSS-CURRICULAR LINKS ▶

Design and technology Designing and making a boat or raft to float and carry one lego man involves the choice of materials (including waterproofing materials), applying previous knowledge, fixing, folding, etc.
Drama and dance Puppet and mimed stories and poems, rhythmic movement of various sea-creatures
Environmental studies Importance of water to global health, ways water can be used, sporting activities and safety
History Of transport on water, water supplies; carriers and early supplies such as from London Bridge
Language Listening, imaginative and reportive writing

Mathematics Measurement
Music Making water music and sounds equivalent to aspects of water, Debussy's *La Mer*, Mendelssohn's *Fingels' Cave*, Little April showers song from Snow White. Singing in the rain; The Pastoral by Beethoven, Yellow submarine
RE Stories from Bible, baptism, ceremonies from other religions
Science Origin of life in water, changes in state: solid, liquid, gas, the water cycle, conversation about floating and sinking good language development

ABOUT THIS TOPIC ▶

General points
Water is a popular infant topic. As a material it needs to be used progressively as children grow. Its use should not disappear as children move up the school. Water can be introduced in an exploratory way by seeing how equipment such as funnels, jugs and tubes can be used. Children can be asked to predict whether various materials will sink or float. Such an approach holds openings for a wide range of art activities to be introduced.

Displays and resources
As always, a stimulating environment is a basic requirement for a successful topic. Besides examples from the work of artists as given below, try to collect and display some of the following. Examples of algae, sets showing the germination of seeds (such as broad beans, conifers, rye and sunflowers), amphibians including frogs, toads and newts, mounted specimens of fish and their

skeletons, coastal, oceanic, pond, river and lake birds, comparative fresh and salt water displays including: crayfish, tadpoles, shrimps and whelks, hermit crabs, jellyfish, lugworms, starfish, barnacles and other crustaceans, sea shells, models of cetaceans, otters and turtles. You may also be able to get multi-cultural artefacts associated with water, such as gourds. Different ceramic and metal containers plus examples of domestic plumbing and fittings and bottles can be useful. Obviously you will not be able to get all of the following but try to borrow a few models. These may include bridges, canal locks and narrow boats (plus painted canal ware), hydroelectric power stations, watermills, north sea oil rigs, shipping (Bell's Comet, Cutty Sark, SS Great Britain, lighthouses) and amphibious dinosaurs. Historical artefacts such as washing dollies, scrubbing boards, old swimming costumes, water carriers and yoke will all be useful.

STARTING POINTS ▶

There are tremendous opportunities to collect a variety of images of water. Many artists have contributed their own visions of subjects relating to water and you should be able to have help from your library and museum service in getting examples. A selection of those listed below plus posters, photographs and videos will provide a rich and stimulating background to the topic. They will open the door to discussions on such subjects as reflections, power, tranquility, clarity, rainbows and storms. You may be lucky enough to live near the coast, a river, watermills or canals. If you can, arrange a trip, remembering to prepare well for it. Preparation may well include a close focus upon particular aspects of water; reading stories and poems and making worksheets to set tasks.

The list of works by artists given here is quite long. It contains all kinds of images from which you can choose. They will start a lot of discussions.

Boudin (1824–98) *Beach scene, Village by the stream*; Canaletto (1697–1768) *Venice, Regatta on the grand canal*; Capelle (1624–79) *Coastal scenes, River scenes*; Cezanne (1839–1906) *Bathers*; Claude (1600–88) *Embarkation of the Queen of Sheba, Narcissus*; Corot (1796–1875) *Evening on the lake, Seine near Rouen*; Cotman (1782–1842) *Seashore*; Cuyp (1620–91) *A river scene*; Degas (1834–1917) *A beach scene*; Derain (1880–1954) *The pool of London*; Dufy (1877–1953) *Deauville, Drying the sails*; Gainsborough (1727–88) *Sunset carthorses drinking at a stream, The watering place*; Guardi (1712–93) *View on the Venetian Lagoon*; Hobbema (1638–1709) *The Haarlem Lock, Amsterdam*; Hockney (born 1937) *A bigger splash*; John (1878–1961) *Washing day*; Leonardo (1452–1519) *The deluge*; Loutherbourg *Battle of the Nile*; Lowry (1887–1976) *The pond*; Monet (1840–1926) *Flood water, River scene, Beach at Trouville, Water lily pond*; Nash (1889–1946)

Dead Sea (Totes Meer); Oldenburg *Soft drainpipe*; Pasmore (1908–) *Quiet river, Chiswick*; Rembrandt (1606–69) *A woman bathing in a stream*; Ruisdael (1628–82) *A landscape with a waterfall and castle on a hill, A pool surrounded by trees, A waterfall, Two waterfalls*; Spencer (1891–1959) *Swan-upping at Cookham*; Turner (1775–1851) *Seascape with storm coming on, Pilate washing his hands*; Van de Velde (1591–1630) *Dutch man of war, other vessels in breeze*; Wallis *Schooner under the moon*; Whistler (1834–1903) *Old Battersea Bridge*; Wouwerman (1619–68) *Seashore with fishwives offering fish to a horseman*; and stories and poems such as *The little mermaid*.

WATER ACTIVITIES

An imaginative seascape

Activity 82: Storm at sea

As a warm up activity you can give a slide show of a good selection of the ways different artists have depicted water. Choose a few pictures by Turner and while you are showing them tell the story of how Turner was determined to show what it was like to be caught in a storm at sea. Ask your children to suggest ways to show such an experience realistically (it may be that some of your children have been on ferries during windy weather). Now explain that Turner had himself strapped to the mast of a ship as it headed into a storm and used this experience as a starting point for painting. Follow up this discussion by setting the task of painting a picture based on the idea of being at sea in a storm. There are a number of ways that your pupils may approach this subject.

Give each child a piece of A3 sugar paper but let them choose the colour. Explain that it is not always necessary to use brushes to apply paint. Fingers, sponge and other tools can be used instead.

Another approach is to squeeze or splatter paint direct from the tube or bottle of paint. Dry powder paint can also be dropped onto wet or damp paper with interesting results. Your children's storm at sea paintings using this splattered paint can be combined with cut out pieces of marbled paper. For further information about marbling please see below or refer to the Print-making skill section on page 119.

You need
Reproductions of paintings, paper, powder paints, brushes, bowls for marbling, straws, marbling colours, glue.

Fishy business

You need
Illustrations or drawings of fish, an aquarium from which to make drawings, **Copymasters 51** and **52**, clay, blunt knives, scrap material to texture surfaces, board, rolling pin, glazes, brushes.

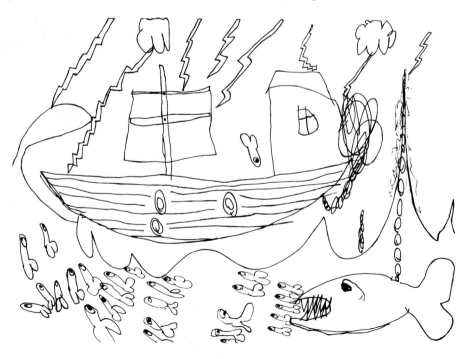

Storm at sea

Activity 83: Fish models

Copymasters 51 and **52** contain a variety of different outline drawings of fish. Your pupils can use these or make their own similar simple drawings from studying fish in the aquarium or the mounted specimens. Discuss the way fish move and the kinds of shapes that their bodies make. Give each child a small lump of clay. Let them roll it out on their board to a thickness of about 7–8 mm. The rolled out clay should be slightly bigger than the outline drawing of the fish that the children are going to use. Using scissors cut out the paper outline of a fish to produce a template. Carefully lay this on to the surface of the clay slab, trace around the outline with a pointed modelling tool. Remove the paper template and using the blunt knife cut the outline of the fish cleanly, removing the excess of clay and put this scrap back in the clay bin or storage bag. Now that the outlines of the different fish have been made, your pupils can make marks for the eyes, fins, scales and mouth.

If you do not intend to fire the pieces your pupils can colour their fishes by using water-based paints and then, under very close supervision, varnish them if required. If you wish to glaze the fish you will need to biscuit fire them. After this, glaze is applied and the pieces refired. To make sure that your children get somewhere near the results they want carry out tests before working on the fish. For further information see the Ceramic skills section on page 92.

Activity 84: Thumb pots to hold water

Examine and discuss examples of domestic pottery. Include some mugs which your pupils use at home. Talk about how the wet clay is transformed into a solid object that can hold water. Is the glaze important? Does it make the pots waterproof? Which pots are porous? (Flower pots).

The task is to make a small mug with a squeezed out handle that can hold water. Give each child a small lump of wedged clay (free of air bubbles). Get them to form the lump into a small mug-shaped vessel. They should use their thumbs until, with regular pressure of the fingers, they produce a thick pot. Keeping the wall of the pot relatively thick, gently squeeze out a simple solid handle with which to hold the mug. Now, with care, gradually squeeze the wall of the mug until its is about 6 mm thick. Once the mugs have been dried and biscuit fired, the inside and outside can be glazed. The mugs should now hold water. (If you refer to the Ceramic skills section on page 89, you will find information about pinch and coiled pots).

Water designs

You need
The opportunity to design a pond for your school, paper, **Copymasters 17** and **18**, paints, pencils, felt tip pens.

Activity 85: Making a design for pond

Having a pond in the school grounds can be an enormous advantage for scientific environmental studies. Quite a number of schools designate small patches of land as conservation areas. With a pond, the value of such areas is greatly enhanced. Pond dipping, using just a net and notebook, can produce an excellent combination of art and science. As children approach Key Stage 2 they can draw upon their experiences of visiting lakes, rivers and canals to form opinions about the kind of habitat that they would like to design for the school. If your school does not have a pond think about the possibility and involve your pupils in designing one. You can demonstrate the value of using grid sheets for simple mapping exercises. Make a map of the proposed area, use **Copymaster 17** or **18** grid sheets, number the grids along their axes to make a scale plan. Explain how this small plan can be scaled up, use a chalk grid on a blackboard for this. When your plan has been scaled up as a group design it can be mounted as a mural. Your children can make up the various elements: plants, animals, amphibians, tadpoles and birds, all of which can be drawn in and coloured. This activity may well be

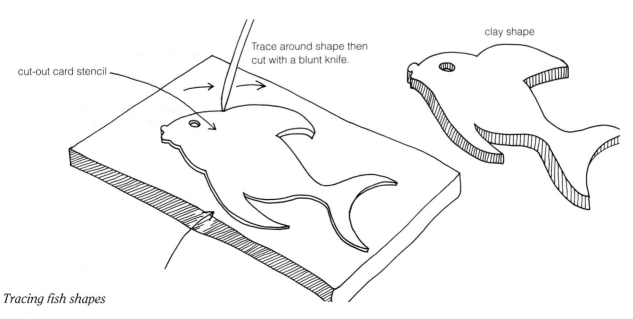

Tracing fish shapes

followed up by making a 3D model of the pond area using papier mâché and eventually you may construct a real pond and stock it with live creatures that started their lives in your classroom. Many other themes and activities may be derived from making a pond: precious things, summer collage, pressed flowers and simple weaving.

Activity 86: Illustrating topic work

Do not forget the tremendous value that the art activities can have as illustrations or designs for stories such as Jonah and the whale and Moses dividing the sea, or their own poems. Children can also produce cartoons of various elements of videos such as 'Yellow submarine'.

Drawing can also play an important function when recording play activities and scientific experiments. Such experiments might include: recording their careful observations of how to make a boat that will float and the development of frogs from tadpoles. Your children also may draw pictures of things that hold water: buckets, cups, aquaria and even mouths.

 Drawing solutions ▷

Before you start

You will need to judge the capabilities of your children and match them with activities and your expectations. As children approach Key Stage 2 you can involve them in more demanding tasks. At whatever age they happen to be you should try to encourage a love of drawing in all its forms.

Activity 87: Rain and wind

Read a story or poem that includes strong images of rain and wind to your children. Get them to paint a thick coat of paint onto a sheet of paper; use two different colours, one for the sky the other for the land. Now give the children a range of coloured chalks. These can be

used to draw streaks across the wet surface for rain and wind. Other colours can be used to draw houses and street lamps. The lines and marks of the chalks will absorb a little of the colour of the painted areas and will not smudge. This extends the use of chalks and pastels. Take care not to tear the damp paper by drawing too roughly.

You need
Paper, paints, brushes, chalks.

Activity 88: Drawing fish, rivers and canals

If you are able to visit rivers or canals then your children are very lucky; through drawing and painting they can make friends with their local landscape. Felt tip pens, pencils (soft and coloured) and wax crayons can all be used to good effect with a small sketch pad when working out of the classroom. Making observational drawings does not mean that you are asking every child to produce pictures of brooks and streams ripple by ripple, rather they should be gathering visual information for further work in the classroom. Try to direct your children's attention to specific visual features of water. For example the water near the banks of canals or rivers is invariably darker (and easier to see through) than water in the centre of the river. Also reeds below the water surface appear to bend. Using pencil to explore the different elements of the picture first can be good practice; when children are happy with the sketch they can then work over with fine felt tips. Crayons are best used by young children. If you have an aquarium, studies of fish can be made using coloured pencils or felt tip pens. Date the pictures.

You need
Sketchbooks, felt tip pens, pencils, crayons.

Activity 89: Drawing water in colour

Discuss the ways that water can be drawn, photographed or painted. Examine a selection of illustrations of water, photographs and copies of works of art. Let your pupils choose a favourite picture to work from. Ask them to make their own version using a variety of coloured drawing materials that can be blended together to produce different colours that imitate the way colours merge and blend when looking at water. Pastels, chalks and water-soluble coloured pencils can be obtained in a good range of colours. Your children can smudge chalks and pastels easily with their fingers to mix different colours. Using oil pastels on tinted papers can be very effective as the pastels blend together easily. Water-soluble pencils can be used dry and wet on smooth or rough papers. Get your children to try out the colours, blending them together with a wet brush on scrap paper, before tackling their chosen subject. You will have to fix the chalk and pastel drawings when they are complete to stop them smudging.

You need
Chalks, pastels, water-soluble coloured pencils, smooth and rough papers, tinted and white papers, brushes and plenty of illustrations of water.

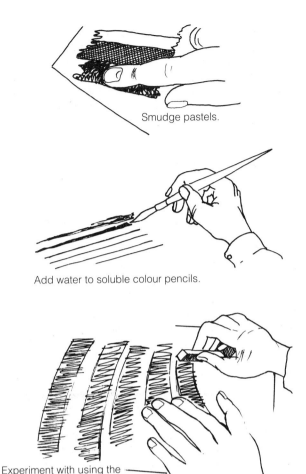

Smudge pastels.

Add water to soluble colour pencils.

Experiment with using the
sides of pastels and crayons.

Using pastels and water-soluble pencils

Wax resist lighthouse

Mobile models

Activity 90: Wax crayon on tinted background
Give each child a piece of tinted paper, blue or
blue–green is the most effective, and some white wax
crayons. Set the task of making a line drawing of a
model or imaginary boat set on the sea.

You need
Tinted papers, white wax crayon.

Activity 91: Wax resist lighthouse
Another simple exercise that emphasises strong linear
designs is to use candles as a drawing medium. Give
your children pieces of tinted sugar paper to work on
with pieces of clear candle. Ask them to make drawings
of lighthouses or versions of drawings made on their
trips to the river or canal bank. Keep the pictures simple
and when the drawings are finished brush over the
drawings with coloured ink. The wax resists the ink and
will remain the colour of the paper while the remainder
of the paper absorbs the ink and thereby produces a
strong silhouette drawing.

You need
Tinted sugar paper, clear wax candles, water-based inks
and brushes.

Activity 92: Making a boat
Children can be asked to design and make a boat or raft
to float and carry one Lego® man. This activity may
involve two approaches, one based on the children's
own imaginations, the other on the use of **Copymaster
55**. First discuss the kinds of boats that are contained in
the pictures that you have collected. How can metal
float? How can a ship made from wood sink? After
careful consideration and observation ask your children
to design a boat. Get them to make drawings of their
designs. Use junk materials to make up their designs,
waterproof (use wax polish or candle grease) and test
them to see if they can float when loaded with a Lego®
man. Compare the results of their own design with
results obtained by making up the boat on **Copymaster
55**. How can the children make the copymaster ship
float better? Wax over the card? Use some ballast in the
hull to make it stable?

You need
Copymaster 55, junk materials, glues, wax for
waterproofing, paint to decorate the ships, Lego® men,
a large enough sink or bowl for testing.

Activity 93: Sand sculpture
This classroom activity uses the immediacy of drawing
or carving into wet sand as a starting point for
sculpture. Use a small cardboard box (a shoe box) and
half fill it with damp sand, smooth down the surface and
then use fingers, modelling tools or press objects into
the surface to make a relief carving in the sand. Emphasise the drawn image by exaggerating the lines and cuts
into the sand so that they are quite pronounced. Now
mix up sufficient plaster to make a cast from the sand

carving. Refer to the Modelling skill section on page 111 to find the information about how to mix and use plaster. Carefully pour the plaster onto the sand carving. The plaster needs to be about 2–3 cms thick. Let the plaster harden and when cool remove it from the sand. When the plaster is well cured wash it and dry before colouring.

You need
Wet sand, old shoe boxes, plaster, objects to press into the sand, modelling tools, paint.

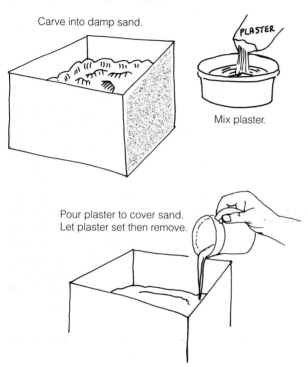

Carve into damp sand.

PLASTER

Mix plaster.

Pour plaster to cover sand.
Let plaster set then remove.

Sand carving

Activity 94: Mobiles of sea creatures
The outlines of a variety of sea creatures can be made in a number of ways. **Copymasters 51–4** contain simple outline drawings of fish, a crab, seahorse, octopus, lobster and shark. Your children will need to decide how big each type of creature should be for the mobile. These outlines can be freely drawn at the size required onto pieces of white painted corrugated cardboard. You will probably have to cut out the shapes which can then be painted, strung and hung. Alternatively some shapes, such as the octopus could be printed by pressing a glove onto a pad of paint and then pressed onto a piece of card. Star shapes can be cut out and printed in a similar way for starfishes. Cut out the shapes and finish painting with brushes, string and hang from the cane. Coloured polythene and acetate can also be used, giving a transparent feel to the mobiles. Further information about hanging mobiles can be found in the Modelling section on page 111.

You need
A supply of corrugated cardboard sheets (paint these with white emulsion on both sides before using in class), paints, canes, cotton or gut, scissors and craft knives (for your use), **Copymasters 51–4.**

Sea creature mobile

Water colours

Before you start
It is often necessary to demonstrate how to do things. You can save a lot of time and materials by teaching the whole class simple things such as how to hold and use a paint brush. Children do not need 'to reinvent the wheel' in order to learn from their own experiences. Make sure that good materials and tools are available and your pupils will develop their manual skills quickly and will recognise the need to select the right equipment and materials for specific work. Explain that it is the lubricating quality of water that allows paints to be mixed and used and that it is the proportion of water to paint that is crucial when using different methods of application.

Activity 95: Using water, brushes and paint
Pupils need a variety of brushes: small, fine ones for detailed work, medium size hog hair brushes for bolder work and ranging to house-painters' brushes for group work on murals.

Show your children that holding a fine hair brush is rather like holding a pen but with the brush being held more by fingers and thumb rather than cradled in the joint between thumb and index finger. Show how larger brushes are cradled in the joint between finger and thumb. House painters brushes are normally held like an ice-cream cornet. Brushes should not be held like daggers as they will quickly be destroyed.

Explain that the relationship between the brush type and the quality of paint is important and that a fine brush needs to be loaded with liquid or watery paint to allow a point to be formed and for easy application. Hog hair brushes and house-painters brushes usually require a more creamy consistency of paint. Demonstrate how to load brushes from paint pots. Using a medium size hair brush, pick up some liquid paint from

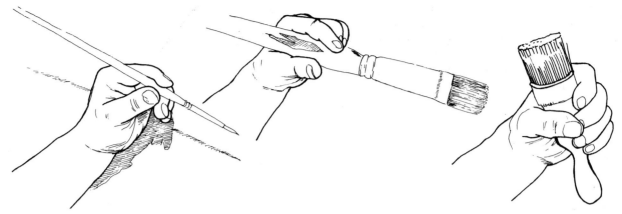

Holding paintbrushes

a paint pot. Try to paint with it a series of graceful curving lines. Now try again but this time take care to remove excess paint from the brush by wiping it on the inside of the pot. Get a good point to the brush and paint the lines anew. Show a range of different results from different consistencies of paint.

You need
An easel, large sheets of paper, a range of good clean brushes, paint mixed to various consistencies, water and paint pots.

Activity 96: Using finger paints

While playing with fingerpaints should be free and fun, the value of the experience is enhanced when preceded by discussion about making marks, lines and designs. Show how it is possible to use all parts of the hand and forearm, brushes (nail brushes and art brushes), leaves, feathers, sponges, lolly sticks, plastic scouring pads and many types of scrap materials to generate a very exciting visual language. Add water to the paints and make new experiments. Demonstrating in this way will ensure that your pupils do not simply think of finger paints as being for reception class children. Finger paints and action methods continue to be used by older children and even professional artists.

You need
Water, finger paints, paper and an easel for demonstration.

Activity 97: Patterns from bubbles

This is a method of producing water colour patterns in a similar way to marbling. Use a small quantity of washing up liquid and mix in a spoonful of water-based paint, pour the mixture into a shallow dish and, using a straw below the surface, blow as many bubbles as possible until they are above the edge of the dish. Now carefully lay a piece of paper over the bubbles. The impression of the coloured bubbles will transfer to the paper. You can try numerous variations of this; for example carefully pour one colour and detergent mixture at one end of the dish and another at the other end. Blow carefully to produce a mixture of blended and pure colours. These patterned sheets can be cut up and used as parts of collages or used to cover books.

You need
Washing up liquid, ready-mixed water-based paints, paper, mixing pots, shallow bowls.

Activity 98: Marbling

This is a simple and creative way to use the resistance of water to oil colours to produce attractively patterned paper. Have everything ready before you start. You could use straws to drop colour onto the surface of water but as the colours are oil-based you need to be careful to avoid spoiling your pupils' clothes. Dropper top bottle sets of marbling colours are newly available and reduce the potential of messing up clothes.

Float marbling inks on water, mixing carefully to form patterns.

Lay sheet of paper carefully on surface.

Remove paper, flatten, dry and display.

Making marbled paper

35

Float one or two drops of colour onto the surface of water contained in a large shallow tray. The colours will tend to swirl around. They can be guided and moved by very careful movement of the surface with special combs (if you are too rough the inks will sink and the results will be washed-out and poor). Your pupils will be able to see how the inks disperse and choose the time when to drop a sheet of white paper onto the surface. After a few moments remove the sheet and lay it face up to dry on some newsprint. This activity can be progressed as children move through your school and on to Key Stage 2.

You need
A large shallow dish (approx. 60 cms × 40 cms by 5 cms deep), dropper topped inks, marbling comb, paper.

Activity 99: Overlaid PVA colour washes
PVA water-based paints are extremely versatile. Give your pupils clean white paper, a limited number of PVA colours and a medium size brush. It is important that the paints are watered down so that they are transparent without being too washed out. Use a ruler to run a series of parallel lines across the paper about 4 cms apart. Now paint a series of bands of colour to fill each of the pencilled in strips. Use reds, yellows and purples. Let the paint dry out completely. Now draw a series of parallel lines to intersect the first series and use blues, greens and oranges to overlay the first set while occasionally leaving some squares unpainted. The PVA paint is impervious when dry so the overlaid colours will mix like glazes and result in a super range of transparent tints and broken colours.

You need
Watered down PVA colours, brushes, pencils, rulers, white paper, mixing dishes or palettes.

Activity 100: Run and drop painting
Get your pupils to soak a piece of good quality white paper and lay it on a board. Mix up some colours so that they are of a light, creamy consistency. Raise one edge of the board and pour a little paint in the centre. Let it run right across. Repeat with other contrasting colours until nearly all of the surface is covered. Lie the board flat and let the painting dry. On another piece of soaked paper carefully drop small quantities of powder colour. Both the run and dropped painted sheets can be used as backgrounds for further painting or as part of collages. Be careful about choosing the right colours to suit the subject of the work. While paint is still wet it can be blown through straws to give different effects.

You need
Watered down wet paint, powder colours, paper, straws and boards.

Activity 101: Collage of undersea world
This subject can be based on views of your aquarium or from stories of mermaids, sunken treasure and King Neptune. Now is the opportunity to draw together marbled paper, bubble patterned paper, and other results from previous experiments. This can be a group or individual activity. First of all get your pupils to make

a plan of their picture and collect together all the materials that they will need. Use marbled paper and the bubbled paper as the background. Make up the main figures by sticking sequins and small pieces of fabric to the surface.

You need
Marbled paper, bubble printed paper, scrap fabrics, sequins, glues.

Activity 102: Tissue paper glazing
This is an extension of Activity 101. The subject can be the same whilst the technique is completely different. Use a blue background piece of sugar paper. Cut out a lot of sea creatures and sea weeds from variously coloured tissue paper. Onto the background paper stick a few pieces of lighter ordinary paper. Now using a watered down PVA glue paint over the areas to which you are going to stick tissue paper fish or creatures. Stick them down and build up a whole underwater world. When the PVA glue has dried out it will be transparent and give the tissue paper an extra feeling of translucency as if underwater.

You need
Tissue papers, sugar papers, PVA glue, brushes, scissors.

Activity 103: Wave patterns
Look at the way Hokusai (*Crest of the great wave of Kanagawa*) produced pictures of waves, examine the template of waves on **Copymaster 56**. Talk about simple patterns and silhouette pictures. Use the **Copymaster 56** wave. Take two pieces of different coloured paper (blue and light yellow are a good combination to start with). With paper clips fix the template to the front sheet and trace around the design. Remove the template and cut out the design from both blue and yellow sheets at the same time, the paper clips will hold them together. Doing this will produce positive and negative shapes based on wave patterns. Your children can now experiment with arranging the waves on yellow or blue backgrounds before sticking them down. Patterns can be mirrored, repeated, overlapped or used to give an impression of reflection. **Copymaster 56** can also be used as a stencil when paint can be stippled through to produce a repeat pattern.

You need
Sheets of paper in contrasting colours (include blue in the selection), glue, pencils, scissors, brushes, paper clips, **Copymaster 56**.

 # Rainy day prints ▷

Activity 104: Monoprints
Discuss the drawings that were made on the banks of the river or look out at the rainy weather. Talk about all the ways that water has been used in different activities to produce different effects. Choose and mix a range of colours that will suit either the rainy day or closely match the colours along the riverbank. Using clean

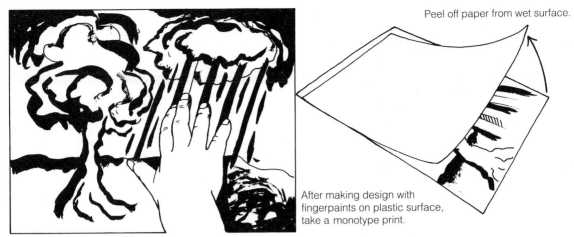

Peel off paper from wet surface.

After making design with fingerpaints on plastic surface, take a monotype print.

Monotype of rainy day

trays (big enough to allow the paper being used to fit), ask your pupils to place the mixed colours carefully in roughly the right positions for their pictures. Now using their fingers, brushes and, if necessary, a little water, make pictures on the bottom of the tray. The pictures should closely match their feelings about a rainy day or recall their visit to the river bank. When finished and still wet, place a clean piece of white paper onto the picture and rub it down gently onto the paint. Remove the picture, which you will notice has been laterally inverted. Try different monotype prints on differently coloured paper.

You need
Finger paints, clean trays, water (a little to keep the paints wet for printing), brushes, white and tinted papers.

Frogs and newts ▷

Before you start
Using dyes with young children means that you have to be careful with spillages. Use only non-toxic dyes. If you

need to heat ingredients make sure that you do this yourself. Protect your work surfaces with newsprint and polythene sheets.

Activity 105: Pond life appliqué
Observational drawing is a vital ingredient of National Curriculum art, and close study of tadpoles, frogs, newts and weeds provides an ideal opportunity to develop this skill. Provide magnifying glasses to study the miniature forms of life with greater accuracy. Your pupils draw-ings will be as rich in emphathy as they are in detail or texture. Encouraging this natural feeling for fellow creatures will build your pupils' confidence. Use a stout piece of straw board as a support for the appliqué. Choose two or three transparent fabric scraps of suitable colour as background. Alternatively your pupils can prepare a special tie dyed background as described in Activity 106. Now get your children to trace some of their drawings of pond life onto thin card. Cut the card shapes out and use as templates to transfer the shapes to scraps of fabrics. Cut out the designs from the fabrics and apply with glue to the background. Use freely draped scraps to stand for swirling seaweeds, stick sequins and shiny materials (Mirriboard® holographic sheets) as eyes and scales.

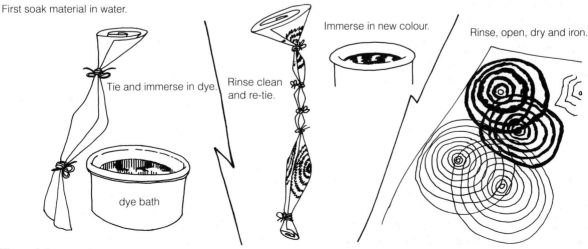

First soak material in water.

Tie and immerse in dye.

Rinse clean and re-tie.

Immerse in new colour.

Rinse, open, dry and iron.

dye bath

Tie and dye

37

You need
Sheets of straw board, scissors, glue, brushes, scraps of fabrics, sequins, shiny materials such as Mirriboard®.

Activity 106: Tie and dye
Plain white cotton fabric or silk can be hand dyed or printed in many ways. Tie and dye can be used successfully as backgrounds for appliqué. Silk can be tie dyed and later painted using silk paints. First take a piece of fabric, bunch it and tie it along the whole length wherever it is desired that dye does not penetrate. As a background to a pond life your pupils will probably need a random and rich design. To achieve this tie the fabric in many places. Vary the tightness of the knots. After dyeing the first colour, rinse and wash according to the manufacturers instructions and repeat with other colours. When finished, dry and iron the fabric to use as a background for appliqué work.

You need
Fabric (cotton), cold water dyes, buckets, string, an iron.

CIRCUSES
AND FAIRS

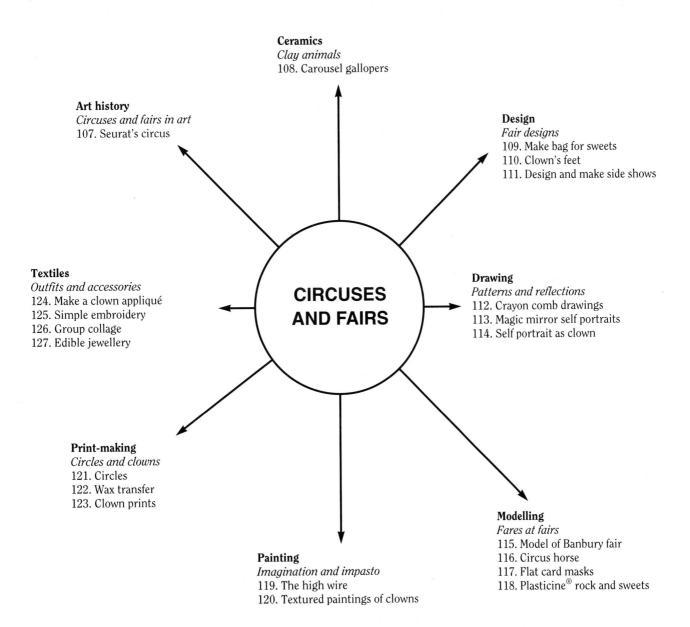

Ceramics
Clay animals
108. Carousel gallopers

Art history
Circuses and fairs in art
107. Seurat's circus

Design
Fair designs
109. Make bag for sweets
110. Clown's feet
111. Design and make side shows

Textiles
Outfits and accessories
124. Make a clown appliqué
125. Simple embroidery
126. Group collage
127. Edible jewellery

**CIRCUSES
AND FAIRS**

Drawing
Patterns and reflections
112. Crayon comb drawings
113. Magic mirror self portraits
114. Self portrait as clown

Print-making
Circles and clowns
121. Circles
122. Wax transfer
123. Clown prints

Modelling
Fares at fairs
115. Model of Banbury fair
116. Circus horse
117. Flat card masks
118. Plasticine® rock and sweets

Painting
Imagination and impasto
119. The high wire
120. Textured paintings of clowns

CROSS-CURRICULAR LINKS ▶

Design and technology Design and make a big top, raise and fit out with modelled animals, make acrobat toy

Drama and dance Carnival, parade of animals, role-play

Environmental studies Care and conservation of animals, open spaces

History Of fairs, circuses, use and abuse of animals

Language Listening and reading, imaginative and reportive writing

Mathematics Measuring, counting for catering requirements

Music Circuses and fairground, Sergeant Pepper

RE Cruelty to and caring for animals and people, fairness, cheating, deceit, religious significance of fairs

Science Change of state of materials, water frozen so deep and solid that it can support great weight, London frost fairs

ABOUT THIS TOPIC ▶

For all aspects of fairs and circuses the importance of colour, style, exaggeration, and an appreciation of fun and nonsense is very clear. For infants it is this that is important. The colour, flamboyance, distortion, music, movement, animals and performance are the vital elements that can launch a variety of exciting art activities.

Displays and resources

The visual strengths of the topic can be grouped into main elements that include: simple strong two- and three-dimensional shapes (spirals, circles, cones, triangles and squares), colour, design including the various flamboyant alphabets and signs and paintings, performance and role-play, make up, costumes and masks, distortion and lighting. Collect together all kinds of resources to add to your display.

STARTING POINTS ▶

Colour and light Collect brilliant images of 'flamboyant style of painting', slides of fairground images, images of circuses and animals and circus folk, ornate alphabets.

Fairs

Banbury fair, London frost fairs, plus Goose fairs and the most famous Widdecombe Fair, gingerbread fairs.

Forces and energy

Fairground rides, raising big top, acrobats.

CIRCUS AND FAIR ACTIVITIES ▶

C17, 38, 57–61

Circus and fairs in art ▷

Before you start

Try to show famous paintings of circus and fair activities. Picasso sympathised with the life of travelling circus people and other theatrical people. He painted many pictures of troubadours, acrobats and harlequins. Seurat painted a wonderful swirling rhythmic acrobat on horseback in a circus. A number of British painters have recorded fairs and circuses. Samuel Colman painted a detailed picture of St. James's fair in 1824. The

particular style of painting fairground rides and signs is called 'flamboyant'. It combines swirling lines and brash colouring. Collect together as many images as you can to add to your display. A slide show of fairground images and pictures from other sources could get this topic off to a good start.

Activity 107: Seurat's circus

Show Seurat's painting of the circus and show how he used little dots of colour to make his pictures. Give your children straws, colours and paper. After sketching an outline (or use **Copymasters 57–9** as templates) paint a picture using the end of the straws to make dotted coloured images.

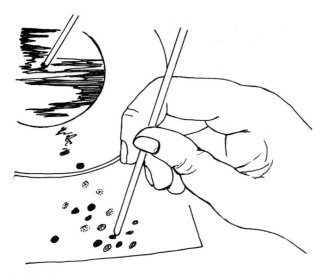

Using straws

 ## Clay animals ▷

Activity 108: Carousel gallopers

Different kinds of animals and birds feature in the most famous of fairground rides, the carousel. Collect as many images of animals and roundabouts as you can. Use them in your display. Your children will be happy working directly with clay, shaping, rolling and pinching it to form horses, swans and ostriches. Try to help them include a feeling of movement in their animals. **Copymasters 57–9** contain simple outlines of a number of animals. These can be used as templates or as a stimulus for your pupils to make their own designs for gallopers on the roundabout. To use them as outlines first roll out some clay into a slab about 2 cm thick. Having already cut out the animal shape place this onto the clay slab. Draw carefully around the template, remove it and then cut out the shape using a blunt knife or modelling tool. This flat clay shape can now be modelled and finished as desired, either freestanding or as a plaque. Besides using the copymaster versions get your children to make their own drawings as a basis for animal templates or draw directly into clay slabs.

Drawing into clay

You need
Clay, rolling pins, clay boards, modelling tools, illustrations and **Copymasters 57–9**.

 ## Fair designs ▷

Activity 109: Make bag for sweets

Ask your pupils to bring in all kinds of containers, boxes and bags for sweets. If they are able to bring any that originated at a fair or circus so much the better. Before starting to design bags for sweets get your children to look at and make coloured drawings of pop corn, licorice allsorts, peanuts (in their shells), chocolates, jelly babies and flying saucers. Use magnifying glasses if necessary to examine colours and shapes closely.

Another part of the design problem will be the technical matter of making a design for a bag that can actually hold the sweets. A good way to come to understand what may be involved in this is to take apart existing bags and cartons. Once the flat nets are seen it is possible to understand how flaps, edges and openings are made. **Copymaster 61** contains a number of simple nets for bags and containers that can be used by your children as templates. The children should choose what kind of decorative image they will use and what size of bag or container they will design. How many sweets will it hold? Once these decisions have been made it is time to choose the materials.

Remember the importance of hygiene. The most likely materials will be either card or paper. Will a carton need lining? Once the material is chosen, draw the net on the sheet material, making sure that tabs and openings are marked. Cut and crease. It is best to decorate the container before assembling it. Once the decoration (painting, drawing or printing) is complete make up the container and fix with glue. Add the bags to your display and compare with manufactured products.

You need
Examples of bags, paper, paints, greaseproof paper, thin card, glue, scorers, scissors, craft knife and cutting mat, safety rule, **Copymaster 61**.

Activity 110: Clown's feet

The challenge is to make an enormous pair of shoes that would fit a circus clown and could still be used to walk in. If you have a collection of different shoes on display it will be possible for your children to make a list of the common features and make a description of what would be the best design for a clown's shoes. Look at the way shoes are constructed: the sole, uppers, tongue, laces and fasteners. Do an imaginary X-ray drawing of a clown's feet when wearing the shoes. How big should they be? How can the feet be stopped from flopping about inside? Is it possible to make the shoes from cardboard boxes? Is it possible to make one by folding and fixing card? Perhaps papier mâché could be used? Can a pair of old, ordinary shoes be used as a basis for the extended clowns shoes?

Try tracing around the child's feet and folding the paper up and carefully creasing it over the feet in such a way that it can be unfolded and cut along the creases. This rough net can be stuck onto an extended sole of thick card which can then be built up with papier mâché to make the clown's shoe. Allow to dry and decorate.

You need
Shoe boxes, old shoes, paper, tracing paper, pencils, papier mâché, paint.

Activity 111: Design and make side shows
Using cardboard boxes, tubes, junk and balls, design and make a fairground side show. Making a side show will involve designing it so that prizes can be won. Children need to decide what constitutes a win. Do the balls have to be guided into baskets, channels or fall through holes to score points? Besides the technical side of this activity your children will have to decorate the show in a suitable manner, with colour, style, lettering and, for older children, battery-operated lights. For younger children it would be best if you are able to prepare the cardboard boxes by painting them with white emulsion prior to the lesson. They will then be able to make bright decorative designs more easily. **Copymaster 60** contains a decorative or flamboyant alphabet that can be used as a visual stimulus.

You need
Cardboard boxes, junk, glue, tubes, balls, paints and tables to stand the games on, **Copymaster 60**.

Patterns and reflections ▷

Activity 112: Crayon comb drawings
Curves, ellipses and sweeping lines are important visual elements of fairs and circuses. After you have shown and discussed images of animals and acrobats performing

in the ring of the big top, give each child some tinted paper and crayons to work with. A technique which is worth trying for the ring and other large curved shapes is to make thick crayons into combs and use them for drawing the shapes. Choose two or three thick bright crayons (remove any paper) and cut a series of V grooves along one side as in the diagram. When the crayons have been prepared in this way, they can be held firmly and used to draw sweeping series of parallel lines. Combs are particularly suitable for decorative work. Once this first stage is finished, your pupils can use white and coloured crayons to draw animals and acrobats in the normal way. The whole design can be completed by carefully

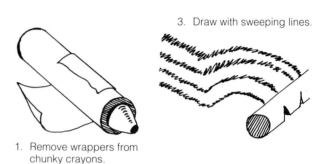

3. Draw with sweeping lines.

1. Remove wrappers from chunky crayons.

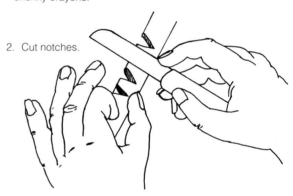

2. Cut notches.

Making crayon combs

Side shows

choosing a number of coloured dyes and painting with these over the whole surface of the paper. Using a bright yellow dye over the ring area and darker colours in the crowd will produce a varied lighting affect. The wax crayons will be unaffected by the dye and retain their original colour.

You need
Chunky crayons, sharp knife, tinted paper, dyes and brushes and illustrations.

Activity 113: Magic mirror self portraits
A hall of mirrors is a favourite place for children in the fairground. The distorted faces and bodies can be a wonderful subject for drawing. Using old shoe boxes and Mirriboard® you can make small concave and convex mirrors for your children to do drawings from. Give each child the opportunity to work from the mirror, initially using fine felt tip pens.

You need
Old shoe boxes, scissors, Mirriboard®, paper and felt tip pens.

Activity 114: Self portrait as clown
This is a simple imaginative activity that will be enhanced through role-play. If it is possible to use makeup and clown props, then your children can see what they look like in the mirror and will be able to make much better drawings.

You need
Paper, paint, brushes, face paints, mirrors.

Fares at fairs

Activity 115: Model of Banbury fair
Read and discuss the famous Banbury fair nursery rhyme:

As I was going to Banbury,
Upon a summer's day,
My dame had butter, eggs and fruit,
And I had corn and hay!
Joe drove the ox, and Tom the swine,
Dick took the foal and mare,
I sold them all – then home to dine,
From famous Banbury Fair.

What other things might have been sold at Banbury fair? Make a list and write a description of a stall at Banbury fair. Give the children a range of materials including clay, papier mâché, junk materials, paint and scraps of material. Set the task of making a stall at Banbury fair complete with awning, wheels, produce and perhaps a figure of the fair merchant. Small models can be made or, as a group activity, a large version can be produced for the home corner.

You need
Cardboard boxes, sheets of cardboard, clay, fabric scraps, brushes, paint, glue, scissors and craft knives and safety rules.

Activity 116: Circus horse
This activity involves making a costume for two children to play the part of a circus horse. The body is constructed by bending a number of pieces of thin basket making cane into circles that can pass over the shoulders of the children easily. A larger series of elongated hoops will be needed to accommodate the shape of the horse's shoulders to bottom as shown in the diagram. The body of the horse is made up by glueing and sewing calico to the hoops and allowing the material to drape onto the floor. The head of the horse, can be made from two cardboard boxes cut and joined together, with ears fixed on and the features painted carefully. The part of the fabric around the neck of the horse, can be drawn together by sewing with a thick thread around the opening and gently pulling until it is secure and will not slip down over the shoulders of the

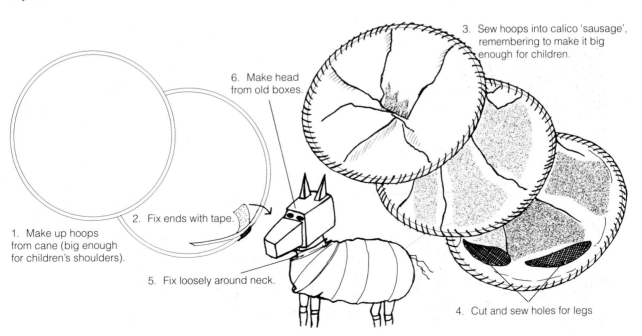

Making the horse

front part of the horse. A mane of raffia can be fixed to the neck of the horse.

You need
About seven metres of cane, card, string, scissors, glue, two and a half metres of calico, large needle, raffia, paints, brushes.

Activity 117: Flat card masks
Flat card masks are simple to make and can be used to portray all kinds of characters, including monkeys, lions, clowns and harlequins. Use panels of card cut from cardboard boxes. Get each child to cut a face shape, a little larger than their own face from a piece of card. Cut holes for eyes, noses and the mouth. A nose made from a piece of scrap card can be fitted to the basic mask shape. Look at pictures of animals to see what sort of nose it should be. The masks will be finished depending on the subject. For a lion, either yellow string or raffia can be stuck over the surface and the rest painted or yellow paper cut and curled around a pencil can be stuck around the edge of the mask and over the painted front surface. Details such as a mouth, the shape of the muzzle and whiskers can be painted on. A monkey may be finished using different scrap materials, whereas a clown will simply need to be painted with a bald head and ears fixed. A good way of finishing the masks to be used is to stick a piece of broom handle to the back with adhesive tape.

You need
Sheets of card, felt tip pens or pencil, scissors, scraps of fabric, paints, brushes, glue and pieces of broom handle and adhesive tape.

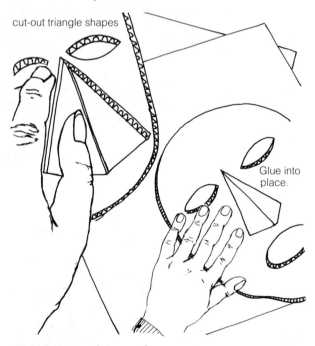

cut-out triangle shapes

Glue into place.

Making a nose for a mask

Activity 118: Plasticine® rock and sweets
Using clean bright Plasticine® your children can make sweets to fill their sweet bags or cartons. Roll out slabs of Plasticine® and lay on top of each other and press the sandwich down. Cut out pieces so that they look like licorice allsorts. Chocolate eclairs, nut clusters and other sweets can be made by pinching, squeezing and pressing plasticine together. Before placing in a bag your children could make small paper sweet wrappers for the sweets that will be sold at the fair.

You need
Plasticine®, paper, rolling pins, blunt knives.

Imagination and impasto

Activity 119: The high wire
Discuss the exciting acts that are often found in circuses. Lion taming, knife throwing, trapeze and high wire acts. Get your children to make a list of things to include in their chosen pictures. Encourage your children to think about light and shade in the circus ring, the floodlights and dark shadows of the crowds.

You need
Brushes, range of paints, mixing dishes, tinted papers, pencils and illustrations of various fairground activities.

Activity 120: Textured paintings of clowns
Adding thickener to paints will increase its texture. Provide your children with acrylic colour. This paint includes an adhesive and it is ideally suited to absorbing other materials such as fine sand, to give extra body and texture. Whatever extender or texturing material you add, must be mixed thoroughly with the paint using a palette knife and a mixing tray. Thickened or textured paints used to paint the face of a clown, can be combined with other materials to make a collage. First, paint a light pink or white oval shape for the face. A triangle cut from coloured card can be used for the hat. When the face is dry, use thickened acrylic paint to paint red lips, blue eyebrows and crosses for the eyes. Then using clear PVA, stick shiny materials, sequins, buttons, off cuts or wool and scraps of fabric to decorate the hat, supply the hair and provide eye-popping pupils. When dry, mount as part of your display.

You need
Acrylic paints, sand, sawdust, extenders, brushes, fabric scraps, buttons, sequins, tinted card and paper and scissors and mixing dishes.

Circles and clowns

Activity 121: Circles
The landscape of a fairground is often dominated by big wheels and other circular or curved rides. Give each child a piece of stout card cut from an old cardboard box. Using thickened PVA medium, get the children to draw designs based on circular and curved motifs from the fairground by dripping onto the card. Let the PVA dry and then ink up the surface of the design carefully

Circles of the fair

with a sponge loaded with colour. Place a sheet of newsprint or lining paper over this printing plate, and smooth down carefully onto the raised and paint covered surface of the design. Remove the paper carefully to see the print. Try prints on different coloured paper such as blue and black. Alternatively, designs can be made by sticking down pieces of cut string onto the cardboard base.

You need
PVA medium and thickener, sheets of cardboard, paints, sponge, lining paper and tinted papers, string and scissors.

Activity 122: Wax transfer
Give each child a small piece of paper (A4) and get them to fold it in half. On the top surface, cover it completely in a thick layer of coloured pastels or chalk. Choose the colours carefully to suit the subject, which may be a circus horse, clown, side show or view of a fair. Use blues in the rough areas where the sky might be and

bright colours where there might be light. It is important that at this stage large, undefined blocks of colour should be used to cover the whole of the folded paper. Carefully shake off any dust and first cover this chalk surface with a yellow or pink crayon. When this is complete, cover again with black crayon so that no chalk shows through. Now refold the paper so that the black surface is inside and covered by the other half which has not been coloured. On this clean surface, get your children to make their design or drawing, using a biro or pencil, pressed firmly as they draw. Make the drawings decorative. Use **Copymasters 57–9** to help with drawings of animals. When finished, open out the folded sheet to reveal three images: the original, a transferred image that will reveal the design in silhouetted chalk and a third image that will be a reversed design on the back of the surface on which the original drawing was made.

You need
A4 sheets of paper, crayons, chalks or pastels, pencils and biros.

fold over · CRAYON · thick crayon · press hard with pencil · open out

Transfer drawing

45

Activity 123: Clown prints

Draw and cut out the individual elements of a clown's head. The face shape, the individual crossed eyes, a great swelling mouth and a bulbous nose, hat and a little hair. Using a sponge roller and a tray of light coloured paint, ink up the face shape and press onto a piece of tinted paper. Using different colours for the different parts of the face, add to the original impression until the complete picture is finished.

You need
Tinted paper, rollers, mixing trays, card, pencils, scissors.

Outfits and accessories

Activity 124: Make a clown appliqué

Use **Copymaster 62** as a template for cutting out the basic shapes for a clown's head. Cut out the basic head, eyes, nose, ears, mouth and hair from coloured felts chosen by your children. Glue or sew pieces in place, use buttons and sequins to finish off the clown.

You need
Different coloured felts, buttons, needles and thread, glues, scissors, **Copymaster 62**, glues, PVA paint.

Activity 125: Simple embroidery

This is an extension of Activity 122 and is suitable for older children. Use **Copymaster 42**. Draw the simple shape of a clown's face on to it using felt tip pens. Keep the design small (10 cm × 15 cms). Transfer the design to Binca® and using large needles and coloured silks or cottons use running and cross stitches to make up the children's own designs of a clowns' faces.

You need
Copymaster 42, Binca® and needles, silks, cottons, and scissors.

Activity 126: Group collage

Make a list of all the elements that make up a circus: the tent, horses, ringmaster, acrobats, seals, lions, balls, clowns, crowds. Working in pairs the class should produce designs for each piece on large pieces of paper and then make up the designs using scraps of cloth, shiny materials, coloured paper, glue and paint. Bring all the pieces together. Discuss the final arrangements for the composition and assemble all elements as a large wall mounted collage. What sort of background would be most suitable? Which colours?

You need
Scraps of cloth, paper, glue, paints and scrap materials.

Activity 127: Edible jewellery

Get your children to collect various edible items that can be used to make up jewellery. Hula hoops, string licorice and other threadable bits and pieces can be combined to make an attractive necklace. What is more, they will produce a lot of amusement if they are used during a drama day as one of the clown's tricks: 'If you don't watch out I will eat my necklace'.

You need
Hula hoops, strip or string licorice, other threadable snacks.

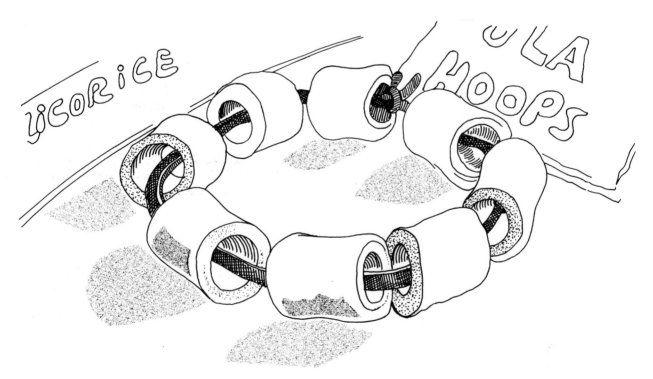

Edible jewellery

46

TRANSPORT

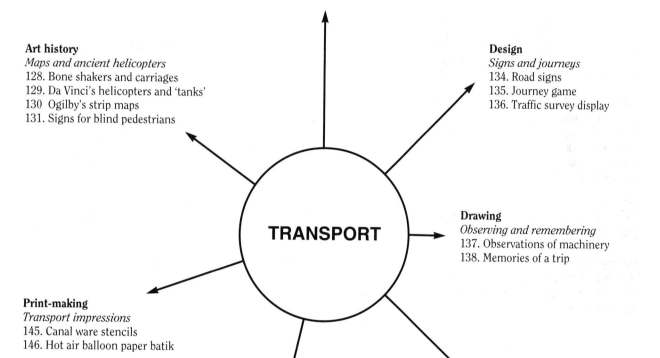

Ceramics
Clay fliers
132. Balloon basket
133. Plane and aviators

Art history
Maps and ancient helicopters
128. Bone shakers and carriages
129. Da Vinci's helicopters and 'tanks'
130 Ogilby's strip maps
131. Signs for blind pedestrians

Design
Signs and journeys
134. Road signs
135. Journey game
136. Traffic survey display

TRANSPORT

Drawing
Observing and remembering
137. Observations of machinery
138. Memories of a trip

Print-making
Transport impressions
145. Canal ware stencils
146. Hot air balloon paper batik

Modelling
Model journeys
139. Cow jumped over the moon
       mobile
140. Play vehicles for infants
141. Junk planes and parachutes
142. Boats and lorries

Painting
Abstracts and photographs
143. Photo-collage
144. Abstract shapes

CROSS-CURRICULAR LINKS ▶

Design and technology Design and make vehicles to do specific tasks, wheels, aeroplanes, boats, design a traffic control system for going in and out of classroom.

Drama and dance Famous journeys, famous engineers, role-play

Environmental studies History and construction of roads, canals, airports, maps, journeys to school

History Civilisations with and without the wheel, story of flying, ships, bicycles. Famous journeys such as Hannibal's

Language All areas

Mathematics Measurement of distance, time and speed

Music Popular songs about journeys and ways of travel: Baccharat 'Planes and boats and trains', Honeggar 'Pacific 321', John Paynter 'Underground Music', Chatanooga Choo-Choo, Themes from Star Trek, 'I am Sailing', 'I saw Three Ships' and 'Runaway Train'.

RE The journeys of pilgrims, methods of travel

Science Flight, floating, sinking, balance, buoyancy

ABOUT THIS TOPIC ▶

General points

This topic could stem from either historical or technological starting points. In either case it is important to set the context in an appropriate way for infants. Your children's own personal experience of travel in all its variety must be the very important centre of activities.

Your own environment will to a large extent define what you can cover. A historically based topic will tend to be much more wide and general than one that is set within a technological perspective of problem solving. Activities based on real experiences are so valuable that you are advised not to make impossible demands on your children's imaginations as these are no substitute for a well prepared visit. Besides the activities detailed below there are many others worth considering, for example, wall friezes of transport through the ages, kites, hot air balloon displays, designing and making strange vehicles for future travel, printing tickets and making ticket machines, using cogs and wheels for press printing patterns, fantasy journeys through time

and space. Transport is full of opportunities for art and design activities.

Displays and resources

Make up notices that show important dates and other information about transport to include in your display. Cover land, sea, air and space travel. From your library or museum service you may be able to borrow some of the following models: Hannibal aeroplane, Vickers Vimy or Wright Flyer, suspension and other bridge types, canal locks, canal ware, railway models, Stephenson's *Rocket* and realia, bicycle models, trams, hansom cabs, Bell's Comet, USS *Constitution*, *Cutty Sark*, SS *Great Britain*, Great Western, lighthouses, HMS *Victory*, Apollo rocket and moon probes. For drawing you will find that bits and pieces of machinery, such as railway track indicators and old tram ticket machines and ticket racks are particularly stimulating. Posters, story books and relevant information books, will all enhance your children's education.

Stephenson's Rocket

STARTING POINTS

Probably a good way to start the ball rolling is to discuss with your children:

● How they came to school
● Their most memorable journey
● Famous journeys
● Fantastic journeys of life and literature.

In such discussions it is important to celebrate the everyday as well as the excitement of flying and going on ships. Not everyone has a car and it is only a minority who have been to an airport, so it is necessary to be sensitive or children may feel disadvantaged.

TRANSPORT ACTIVITIES

C60, 63–70

Maps and ancient helicopters

Activity 128: Boneshakers and carriages

The direct and uncomplicated way that Thomas Bewick represented everyday forms of transport such as carriages and coaches can be a useful link with making drawings of contemporary vehicles. He made finely balanced black and white images, produced from wood blocks. Your children can see how black lines on a white background can show texture, tone and shape. Try to have models of forms of transport in your display. Bring in bicycles (perhaps your museum will lend you a penny farthing or a boneshaker).

Give your children black wax crayons, white chalk and a piece of A4 paper and biros. Fold the clean piece of paper in half. Cover one side of the folded sheet first with a thick coat of chalk, then cover this with thick black wax so that no chalk shows through. Now fold the paper so that this chalk and waxed surface is inside. Using the Biros get your children to make a drawing using only line. The drawing will be from observation of a bus, plane, bicycle, carriage or other transport model. Make sure that your pupils press firmly when drawing. When the drawing is complete lift the folded top part to reveal the transferred drawing below. This (or the white

on black version on the underside) can be cut out and fixed on **Copymaster 63** which contains a drawing made by Bewick and space for your pupils' work.

You need
Copymaster 63, chalks, crayons, paper, biros.

Activity 129: Da Vinci's helicopters and 'tanks'

Copymaster 64 contains impressions of Da Vinci's incredible designs for a helicopter and space for your children's work. Get your children to make their own designs for futuristic forms of transport by air and land. What will the machines be called? How will they move? What colour will they be? Where will the people or robots sit?

You need
Copymaster 64, felt tip pens, pencils.

Activity 130: Ogilby's strip maps

Try to have a collection of different types of maps for your children to examine. With older children use **Copymaster 65** to demonstrate how a journey can be mapped as a strip, just showing the road travelled on and the junction of cross-roads. Ogilby's type of maps show features such as hills drawn so as to show ascent or descent from different directions. While only the main route is shown with the intersections, churches, villages, and other features such as woods and rivers are

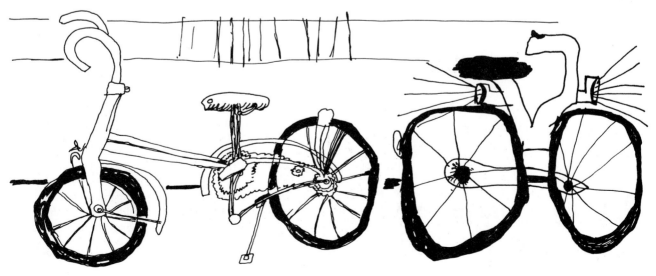

Child's drawing of bicycle

49

also shown. What happens to compass bearings along the route? Get your children to make their own strip maps of their journeys to school (or a small part of it). Ask them to design and colour cameos as part of their maps using relevant local features (designing symbols for trees, traffic lights and crossings).

You need
Copymaster 65, water-soluble coloured pencils, felt tip pens, pencils.

Activity 131: Signs for blind pedestrians
Give your children Plasticine® and set them the task of making a simple sign to tell blind people when to cross the road. Simple words such as: 'cross now' and, 'wait until beep' made in relief may be enhanced by the addition of textures to the Plasticine®. Test the signs when blindfolded.

You need
Plasticine®, texturing materials such as sand or small grit, card.

 # Clay fliers

Activity 132: Balloon basket
Roll out some clay to about 1 cm thickness. Cut out a net, comprising the base and four sides to make up a basket for a hot air balloon. Before assembling the slabs and fixing them together, press the surfaces of the clay with basketwork. Now join the parts together using slip. Model balloonists to go in the basket with small pieces of clay. Dry, fire and glaze. For further information refer to the Ceramic skills section on page 90.

You need
Clay, slip, rolling pin, clay boards, basketwork, glazes, hessian or similar to work on.

Activity 133: Plane and aviators
Using a small lump of clay make a pinch pot with thick walls. Gently squeeze this so that it is oval shaped rather than spherical. Roll out some clay and cut triangular shapes for wings and tail-planes. Fix with slip. Make a little seat to fit inside the plane. Fix with slip. Now make a pilot and co-pilot. Seat and fix them. Dry, fire and glaze.

You need
Clay, clay boards, slip, glazes.

 # Signs and journeys

Before you start
The following three activities depend upon your children being familiar with the traffic around your school

and should follow a thorough reconnaissance and note taking trip around the school. Draw a map of a brief walk in the surrounding area of the school. Make notes both whilst on the trip and from memory on your return.

Activity 134: Road signs
Make a list of the road signs found around your school. Discuss the symbols used and the colour combinations. What style of lettering is best? What about using the flamboyant alphabet of **Copymaster 60**? Discuss the merits of the simple alphabet on **Copymasters 69** and **70**. Which colour combinations add to legibility, which impair it? Do some colours signal danger? Some safety? Get pairs of children to cut up 35 cm diameter pieces of card and make up their own 'Children Crossing' sign for use by a lollipop lady or man. Try out different combinations of colours for letters and background: yellow and white, black, red, blue, grey and their own choices. When the signs are complete test them out in the playground. Which ones are the best? Test for legibility at 10, 20, 30, 40 and 50 metres. Present the results in a graphic poster.

You need
Sheets of card, paint, brushes, **Copymasters 60, 69** and **70**, mixing trays or palettes.

Activity 135: Journey game
The object of the game is to travel safely to and from school. Use the children's strip maps of their journeys to school as a starting point for designing and making the game (see Activity 128). Each game will have a start (the home) and a goal (the school). Features that could be included along the way might be traffic lights; crossings; shops; strangers (say 'no' to strangers); policemen; lollipop women or men. The games could have penalties and advantages built in. Manufactured dice could be used or children can make their own spinner dice. Children will need to make their own counters using clay or card and then shape them according to the method of travel to school.

You need
Map of journey to school, paper, felt tip pens, pencils, rulers, clay, illustrations, dice.

Activity 136: Traffic survey display
Set up a 15 minute traffic survey. Include such questions as 'Was it busier in the morning or afternoon?' 'What kind of traffic uses the main road?' 'Were there more people or more cars?' 'What kinds of vehicles did not come on to the main road at all?' 'How many vans used the main road?' 'Were any bottlenecks caused?' 'How many people were there altogether?' It is best to allocate one vehicle type per child. Make symbols for each category. Design and present survey findings in an attractive way.

You need
Paper, paints or coloured felt tip pens, pencils, rulers.

	Type	9.00 to 10.00	10.00 to 11.00	11.00 to 12.00	12.00 to 13.00
1					
2					
3					
4					
5					
6	other				

Survey poster

 ## Observing and remembering

Activity 137: Observations of machinery

Children are often given a piece of machinery such as springs, cogs, coils and wheels to draw. Observational drawings can be more than mere records of what has been seen. If you wish to go a little beyond represent-ational drawing, give your children subjects which are likely to involve them in posing questions and research.

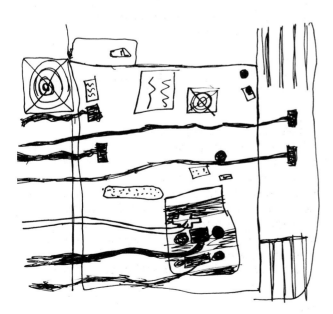

Drawing of machinery

Occasionally provide objects that cannot be understood immediately (things that you will have to look for in illustrated reference books). This can start with quite young children. Old railway items such as track indica-tors can encourage truly exploratory drawings. These sorts of gadgets seem to pose questions like: 'What were they for?' 'Why was this bit like this?' 'What is this for?' 'Perhaps that was for …?' Let children open boxes and poke around inside safe pieces of equipment. Let them explore things through their drawings.

You need
Pieces of transport machinery, paper, pencils, felt tip pens, rulers, reference books.

Activity 138: Memories of a trip

Working from memory is an important way of building artistic skills. Look at and discuss illustrations of air, sea, land, rail and space transport. Talk about trips that your children have been on. Many will have been to airports, bus stations and ports, on double decker buses, trains, ferries, cars, narrow boats and dinghies. Write down what they remember about specific journeys: 'What was the weather like?' 'What was the time?' 'How did they travel?' 'How fast did they go?' Use the written accounts as a stimulus to drawing from memory. Let your children use water-soluble coloured pencils or pastels for a change. There are a number of different brands available. All can be used both dry and wet and on a variety of different papers. Test the pencils before doing the drawing. Do a few lines of different colours alongside each other and then blend them together with a wet paintbrush. For young children it is advisable for the paper to be used dry and only wetted when the drawing stage is complete. For older children get them to work on dampened paper with pastels or work directly with a pencil or pastel that has been dipped into water before use.

You need
Soluble coloured pencils, water, brushes, paper, pencils, felt tip pens, crayons

 ## Model journeys

Activity 139: Cow jumped over the moon mobile

Discuss strange or crazy journeys. Recite the nursery rhyme 'The cow jumped over the moon'. Make a list of all the elements in the nursery rhyme: the cow, moon, little dog, spoon and dish and plenty of stars. Give the children panels of corrugated card (cut from cartons and ready painted white), plus some drawing paper. Using soft pencils and working in pairs, get the children to sketch out all the characters from the nursery rhyme. It is important to keep an eye on the size of the designs. They will need to be seen clearly from a distance so they should not be too small. The cow and moon will need to be bigger than the other parts of the mobile. Once you are all happy with the drawings, cut out the shapes from the sheets of card. Get the children to paint the shapes on both sides. When the paint has dried use cane and

51

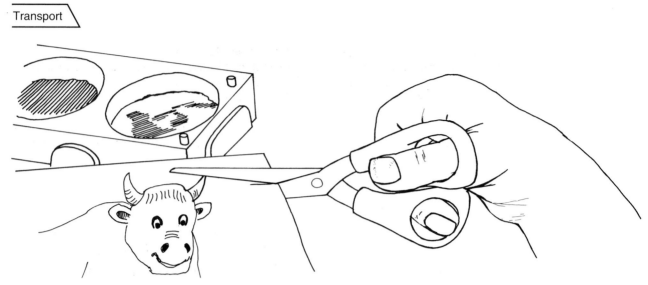

Cutting out cow shapes

nylon gut to string and hang the mobile. Include the nursery rhyme as part of the mobile.

You need
Nursery rhyme books, paper, tinted paper, thin card and sheets of cardboard ready painted white, pencils, paints, brushes, mixing trays, string or gut, canes.

Activity 140: Play vehicles for infants
Diagram shows how easily and simply infants can transform a couple of cardboard boxes into make-believe cars and other vehicles. Just open out and fit the boxes together and fix a paper plate on a tube for a steering wheel. If you can get hold of large cartons (from chest freezers), then more sophisticated vehicles can be made. For example, coaches ready to be held up by Dick Turpin can be created for role-play with the addition of cardboard wheels, cut out windows and doors.

You need
Cartons, paint, brushes, craft knife, scissors or safety snips, glues or adhesive tapes.

Activity 141: Junk planes and parachutes
To reinforce the need to plan a sequence of activities first get your pupils to design an aeroplane to be con-structed from specific pieces of junk that they have selected. Then, using only these specified items, they are to make, fix and paint the model according to their plan. Once this is complete discuss the use of para-chutes, the ultimate method of survival for pilots. What kind of shape should the fabric for a parachute be? Round? Square? Oval? Where should the parachute be folded and fixed to the Lego® man? Will an old hanky work better or worse than a piece of polythene? Test the designs by throwing the Lego® men up into the air in the playground. The pilot should be able to fall safely to the ground supported by the parachutes.

You need
Egg cartons, tubes, polythene, string or cotton, straws, sticky tape, glue, thick and thin card, paper clips, scissors, crayons, paper, paint and brushes, a Lego® man.

Activity 142: Boats and lorries
The ability to move between two- and three-dimensional work is indicative of a child's mental development. Including progressive activities will aid this develop-ment. For example, simple mathematical solids made from nets can be used for all kinds of structures. **Copy-masters 29 a** and **b** and **55** contain the nets of a house

Infant in play car

and a boat which are very basic geometric shapes. **Copymaster 66** is a net of a slightly more complex form, the template for making a lorry. Copy the designs from the copymasters onto thin card. The templates can be cut easily by young children using scissors. Then they are scored and fixed to make up the designs. Scrap materials can be added later to change the basic ship into a galley or paddle-steamer. Before trying to float the boat, remember you will need to waterproof the surface with wax polish and use some ballast to ensure the buoyancy of the ship. Older children can make up the lorry design from **Copymaster 66**.

You need
Copymasters 29, **55** and **66**, card, glue, wax (furniture polish), paints and brushes, scissors and craft knives, safety rule.

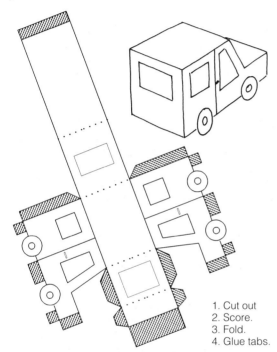

1. Cut out
2. Score.
3. Fold.
4. Glue tabs.

Making up the lorry net

Abstracts and photographs

Activity 143: Photo-collage
Collect lots of illustrations from newspapers and magazines of as many forms of transport as possible. Sort the pictures and cut them out carefully. Give each child a piece of tinted paper as a background support for the collage. Ask the children to draw either a plane, fire-engine, steamer, space ship, car, horse or lorry as their subject. Draw an outline picture of the chosen subject on a separate piece of drawing paper. Cut out the shape and carefully trace the outline on to the tinted paper. Choose cut out magazine illustrations and fit and glue these to fill the outline on the tinted paper.

You need
Lots of illustrations, tinted background paper, glue and brushes.

Activity 144: Abstract shapes
Give each child a large piece of sugar paper, paints and brushes. Talk about the shapes found in all kinds of vehicles. First get the children to use black to paint strong, even lines to make up squares, rectangles and circles. Then, when the design has dried, use other chosen colours to fill in the spaces between the black lines.

You need
Sugar paper, brushes, paints, mixing trays.

Transport impressions

Activity 145: Canal ware stencils
Canal ware is often painted with floral designs in bright colours on deep green enamel pots, dippers and jugs. **Copymasters 67** and **68** provide a number of simple stencils that can be used to produce similar designs to those painted by old butty men. Carefully cut out the designs and wax the edges of the paper to stop the stencil immediately becoming sodden with paint. Use tinted paper as a background and sponges loaded with colour to produce stencilled pictures. Use pinks, whites, reds and yellows on different parts of the stencil to produce multi-coloured results. Let each colour dry before moving on to the next.

You need
Canal ware, books, **Copymasters 67** and **68**, pencils, sponges, paints, mixing trays.

Activity 146: Hot air balloon paper batik
Draw thickly on paper with wax crayons a scene including the bold shapes of a number of hot air balloons. Divide the landscape up with strong lines of colour showing the individual network of fields. Cover the whole surface of the paper with crayon. Scrunch up the drawing, dunk it in a bath of coloured dye, flatten it and allow it to dry.

Hot air balloon

53

LIVING THINGS

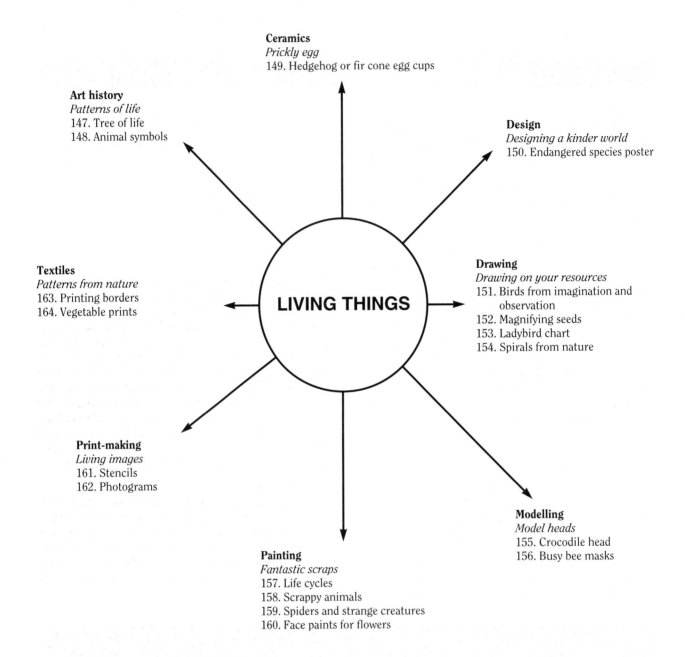

Ceramics
Prickly egg
149. Hedgehog or fir cone egg cups

Art history
Patterns of life
147. Tree of life
148. Animal symbols

Design
Designing a kinder world
150. Endangered species poster

Textiles
Patterns from nature
163. Printing borders
164. Vegetable prints

LIVING THINGS

Drawing
Drawing on your resources
151. Birds from imagination and observation
152. Magnifying seeds
153. Ladybird chart
154. Spirals from nature

Print-making
Living images
161. Stencils
162. Photograms

Modelling
Model heads
155. Crocodile head
156. Busy bee masks

Painting
Fantastic scraps
157. Life cycles
158. Scrappy animals
159. Spiders and strange creatures
160. Face paints for flowers

CROSS-CURRICULAR LINKS

Design and technology Design and make system for feeding pet mice or gerbils
Drama and dance Plenty of role-play and dance opportunities
Environmental studies Exploring ponds and local environment
History Roles of animals
Language All forms

Mathematics Measuring growth of pets, weighing, presenting information in simple graphs
Music The flight of the bumble bee, 'Frog chorus', 'Never smile at a crocodile', 'How much is that doggy?', Cats musical, Carnival of the animals, 'Daddy's going to take me to the zoo tommorow'.
RE The ark, symbolism, kindness, cruelty
Science Growth, animals as food and sources of energy

ABOUT THIS TOPIC

General points
Living things is a topic that should give young children opportunities to grasp fundamental ideas and most importantly, to wonder at the variety of life and the beauty of patterns, shapes, colours and textures that make up the natural world. The topic should reinforce the innate empathy that young children have for their fellow creatures.

When introducing this topic to the young children, place it in the context of the school, its environment and your children's homes and gardens as much as you can. Patterns, spirals and growth shapes are important visual characteristics of living things and have for many years inspired artists. Look at the arrangement of veins in a leaf, branches on a tree, the way fern fronds uncurl as they grow, or the regular spiral shape of nautilus shells. In the arts living things have been represented in cave paintings, the arts of Egypt, Greece and Rome, medieval manuscript, tapestries and carpets, European and North American bedspreads and wallhangings, paintings, ceramics, drawings, woodcarvings, print-making, films and videos.

Displays and resources
The importance of direct experience as a basis for much of your work with children makes it vital that you have a rich collection of resources to support your living things topic. For art activities, first hand and secondary source materials, such as those suggested below, may be used independently as they are interesting and stimulating things in their own right. They can provide valuable stimulus for close observational drawings and paint-

ings. It is likely that they will be most effective when linked together and used in conjunction with relevant reference books. Resources can be linked together loosely under such headings as:

- Colours in nature
- Patterns in nature
- Shapes in nature
- Changes in nature
- Lines and spirals of nature.

First hand resources
Try to borrow models, specimens, posters, pictures, books, and slides from your local library and museum service. These might include: botanical specimens, and cereals, algae, apple blossom, fungi, germination displays, specimens of seeds and roots, displays of the four great plant groups, human anatomical models, zoological specimens, amphibians, fish, birds (food chain set), nests, eggs and feathers, invertebrates, insects, bees, beetles, moths, butterflies; aquatic life: fresh water and sea water sets, shells (section through nautilus shell); mammals: baboon skulls, badgers, bats, models of cetaceans, deer, foxes, hares, rabbits and reptiles; fossils of leaf fronds, sea urchins and sharks' teeth.

Secondary source material
Models of dinosaurs, ceramics, sculptures, needlework, illustrations and original prints and paintings of: Noah's ark, Adam and Eve, weird and strange animals, Cretan bulls, dolphin mosaics, horses on Roman coins, William Morris designs, flamingos, peacocks, falcons, owls, toucans, cockerels, ducks, camels, horses, leopards and dogs.

STARTING POINTS

School environment Make a point of listing as many of the kinds of life that exist within the school grounds as possible. Check ponds, undergrowth the brickwork with magnifying glasses
The seasons Spring is a good starting point as plants and young animals are in abundance. Design and make an incubator for chicks
Pets Collect information about the types, colours, shapes and behaviour of your children's pets

Art history The celebration of plants that is a hallmark of the work of William Morris, is rooted in some wonderful pieces of earlier embroidery and tapestries. English and Persian carpets and hangings and the crewel bed spreads of the USA are often based on natural forms worked into symmetrical flowing designs. These floral forms have strong links with the geometric designs of Islam. Other sources worth considering are the animal imagery of South America, the Greeks,

Stubbs, and Thomas Bewick and the botanical drawings of P.J. Redoute. If you can, show the Disney masterpiece, *Fantasia*, as it shows mythical and historical life forms

Stories and fantasies Print up large versions of famous simple poems, read about mythological creatures

LIVING THINGS ACTIVITIES

 ## Patterns of life

 ## Prickly egg

Activity 147: Tree of life
Copymaster 71 is based on 'The fruiting tree' design from the early 17th century. The original shows many fruit, cherries, pears, lemons and acorns, grafted on to one tree and flowers, birds, leaves and many animals (including a unicorn) united in a fluent celebration of life. Only part of the design is shown. Discuss the idea of symmetry and get your children to complete their version of the picture and colour it.

You need
Copymaster 71, fine felt tip pens, pencils, water soluble coloured pencils.

Activity 148: Animal symbols
Talk about how different cultures have represented animal life. Show a variety of pictures including Chinese dragon designs, hieroglyphs and fossils. Look at simple shapes and discuss how they may be used to produce pictograms of animals. Give your children cut up strips, triangles, circles, semi circles and arcs of coloured sticky paper. Using dark background paper, make up simple abstract forms based on animals. **Copymaster 78** contains the seven pieces of the tangram which you can make and use in a similar way.

You need
Sticky coloured paper, illustrations, dark background paper, scissors, **Copymaster 78**.

Activity 149: Hedgehog or fir cone egg cups
Give each child a small lump of clay and a ping-pong ball. Press the ping-pong ball into the lump of clay and form a rough body shape with the ball half immersed. Work on the clay adding spikes or copying the shape of the fir cone, pull and shape the nose and feet or the stem of the fir cone. When complete, carefully remove the ping-pong ball and let the egg cup dry and then fire and glaze it. Do not make it too thick. If you use slips for colouring then finally use a transparent glaze after biscuit firing.

You need
Clay, ping-pong balls, clay boards, fir cones, mounted specimen of hedgehog (or good photographs), glazes, kiln.

Making a hedgehog egg cup

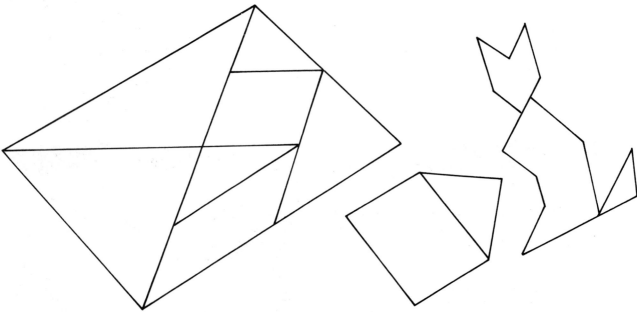

Tangram and symbolic animals

Designing a kinder world

Activity 150: Endangered species poster
Discuss the problems that face our world and identify species that face extinction. Look at the interrelation between environments and plants and animals. Ask your class to make a poster that draws attention to the problems and suggests some answers.

You need
Books, paper, pencils and paints or coloured pencils, brushes.

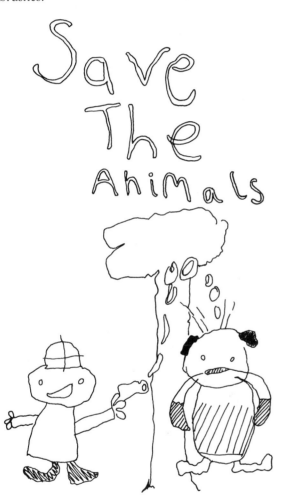

Drawing on your resources

Activity 151: Birds from imagination and observation
For this activity you need to have a collection of mounted specimens of common or garden birds. The activity falls into two distinct phases and will allow you to cover important elements of the National Curriculum in a most interesting way.

Introduce the first session by talking with your children about the kinds of birds that they can see around the school or at home. These are likely to include, jays, starlings, blackbirds, magpies and crows. Make sure that you do not have any illustrations, books or any source materials about birds as this first phase will rely entirely on the children's memory. Ask questions about the colours of the birds, what differences there are between males and females and what shape the birds are. Get your children to draw pictures of the common birds, using coloured pencils and felt tip pens. Ask them to name the birds and estimate how big they are by drawing a simple scale on the bottom edge of the drawing.

For the second part of the exercise, borrow mounted specimens of the birds that your children have already drawn from memory and imagination. Try to provide specimens that are not enclosed in glass or perspex cases and let your children examine the birds closely before they do any drawing. Provide the same materials as for the first drawing and ask your children to make accurate studies from the specimens, measuring and naming in the same way. When the second drawings are complete, compare them with the first versions and discuss with your class. This activity can be extended further by using books alone as a source for drawings of the common birds. You will probably find that drawings made from memory are 'birdlike', schematic, and show a strong empathy for birds. Drawings from specimens will be much more detailed with texture and three

Comparative bird drawings

57

dimensions in evidence, whilst drawings copied from books look flat with colours that can be completely inaccurate, relying as they do on the often poor colour reproduction in books.

You need
Mounted birds, books, paper, pencils, coloured pencils, felt tip pens, rulers.

Activity 152: Magnifying seeds
Use magnifying glasses and microscopes to study the surfaces of seeds and insects. Record patterns, bumps and scratches on the surfaces and use the drawings to help classify and name the seeds and insects by looking at reference books. Use **Copymaster 77** for this activity.

You need
Magnifying glasses and microscopes, seeds, insects, pencils and felt tip pens, **Copymaster 77**.

Activity 153: Ladybird chart
Use a piece of A2 paper and draw a large circle in the centre. Get your children to study the various stages of development of the ladybird. Use magnifying glasses and felt tip pens and coloured pencils to make drawings of each stage on small pieces of paper. Start with drawings of the mating phase and work around the stages until the ladybird has matured through bright yellow to the fully grown adult in red and black. When the drawings are complete cut them out and glue them to the life cycle chart naming the phases and using arrows to complete it for classroom display.

You need
Magnifying glasses, felt tip pens, pencils, coloured pencils, scissors, A2 sheet of paper, specimens to study.

Activity 154: Spirals from nature
Many fossils, nautilus shells and opening ferns have strong spiral patterns. Get your children to study these spiral patterns and make drawings either using candle wax or silver crayons on white paper. Keep the drawings clear and simple using lines to build up the patterns without filling in large areas. When the drawing is finished, brush dark coloured ink or dye across the whole picture. The wax will resist whereas the unprotected paper will absorb the colour. The result will

be a bright contrasting drawing against a dark background.

You need
Source material from your display, wax crayons or candle wax, paper and cold water dyes or inks, brushes.

 # Model heads ▷

Activity 155: Crocodile head
Give each child a panel (about 20 cms by 40 cms) of thin card plus a supply of old egg cartons. Get them to draw out the shape of a crocodile's head on the card. Each child will need to cut about 30 or so tops from the egg cartons and flatten them out. Cut a further set of mountain ranges from the egg cartons. These should be much more complete as they will be used for the teeth. Two sets of teeth, each three peaks long, are first fitted and glued in place along the bottom edges of the crocodile's face (as in the diagram). The remaining flattened out pieces of egg boxes are stuck over the remaining areas of the face except for the eyes which are left uncovered. Finish by painting around the base of the teeth a suitably bloody red, the scales a slimy green and the eyes yellow, white and pink.

You need
Paints, brushes, glue, pencils, egg cartons and thin card.

Activity 156: Busy bee masks
A class of 30 children will need 15 balloons to make them a mask each. Blow up the balloons fully. Tie the balloons firmly with string and thread this through a tube and tie the end of the string to the base of the tube. While making the masks the tubes will simply act as a convenient handle to hold. Using watered down PVA, a brush and strips of torn newspaper cover the whole surface of the balloon. Build up about eight layers of newspaper, occasionally allowing it to dry out before proceeding. When sufficient layers have been built up let the basic mask shell dry out thoroughly and remove the tube handle. Paint the whole surface with white PVA paint and allow to dry. Cut the balloon in half through chin, ear, top of head and completely around so to make

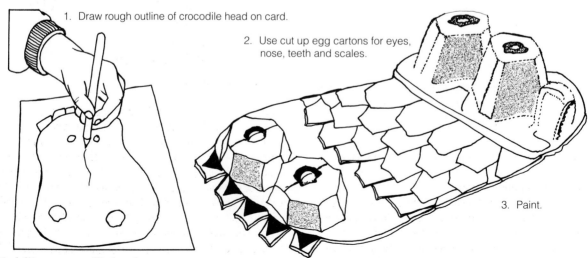

1. Draw rough outline of crocodile head on card.

2. Use cut up egg cartons for eyes, nose, teeth and scales.

3. Paint.

Modelling a crocodile head

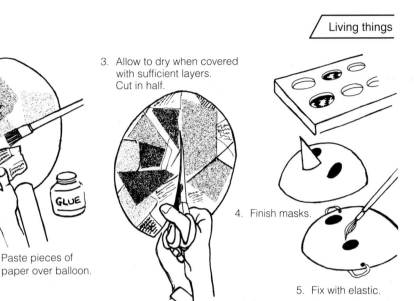

1. fix tube to base of balloon with string.

2. Paste pieces of paper over balloon.

Stick with masking tape.

3. Allow to dry when covered with sufficient layers. Cut in half.

4. Finish masks.

5. Fix with elastic.

Making a balloon mask

two basic masks shapes from the one balloon. Mark the position of the eyes and nose and cut out carefully and then paint the face in a series of black and yellow stripes. Fit with elastic and the masks are ready. Additional antennae and protruding eyes can be fitted by using various junk materials.

You need
Round balloons, newspaper cut into strips, watered down PVA, brushes, paints, scissors, string, cardboard tubes.

 ## Fantastic scraps ▷

Activity 157: Life cycles
Paintings from imagination can be stimulated by reading poems:

Caterpillar by Christina Rossetti
   Brown and furry
   Caterpillar in a hurry,
   Take your walk
   To the shady leaf, or stalk,
   Or what not,
   Which may be your chosen spot.
   No toad spy you,
   Hovering bird of prey pass by you;
   Spin and die,
   To live again a butterfly.

Or, poems may be used to illustrate your children's own imaginative writing, for example, 'A day in the life of a ladybird'.

You need
Paints, brushes, mixing trays or palettes, pencils.

Activity 158: Scrappy animals
Collect and sort various scrap materials. Put rough, soft, hard and smoothly textured materials into different groups. Place a pad of sponge loaded with paint in a tray. Use this pad to cover the surface of the scraps with paint. Get your children to try out the different

materials with which to apply paint onto paper. After experimenting for a while set your children the task of making pictures of lions, butterflies, parrots or leopards on tinted paper using a variety of different materials to apply paint.

You need
Sponge, tray, paints, scraps of materials, tinted paper.

Using scraps to paint

Activity 159: Spiders and strange creatures
Give your children pieces of black paper and a range of liquid colours. Place the paper on a board. From the centre of each piece of paper dribble lines of bright colour to the edges of the paper so that they end up with a series of radiating lines like the spokes of an umbrella. Using fine brushes connect up the spokes with a series of concentric circles or polygons to produce a spider's web. The web can now be finished with images of spiders and flies. Similarly, using black paper, first fold each sheet in half. Working only on one side of the sheet

drip and pour different colours. Fold over and press, the opened out sheet will be covered by a symmetrical abstract pattern that can be changed by additional brushed paints to produce images of strange beasts. Try drip painting half a crab on one side and then folding over.

You need
Liquid paint in squeezy bottles, black paper, brushes, palettes.

Spider's web painting

Activity 160: Face paints for flowers
Using **Copymaster 79** and trace the outline of a face shape onto a sheet of card (ready, painted white from cartons). Draw petal shapes radiating from a distance of 5 cms from the outline. Cut out the flower head, also cut out the shape of the face. Stick a rod or other suitable piece of wood on the reverse to act as a handle. Paint the petal shapes, add cut out tinted or crêpe paper

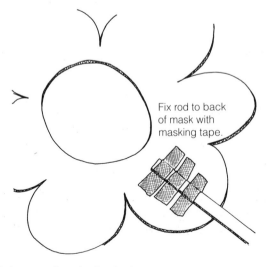

Fix rod to back of mask with masking tape.

Fixing a rod to the back of the mask

and add to the background of the petals. Use face paints to match the colours of the flower.

You need
Card sheets, **Copymaster 79**, paint, brushes, sticky tape, wooden handle, face paints, glues, tissue, crêpe or tinted paper, scissors and a craft knife.

Living images

Activity 161: Stencils
There are a number of copymasters that can be used to produce stencils for this topic. **Copymasters 57–9** contain simple animal outlines, **Copymasters 72–5** can be coloured in a number of ways to give impressions of stencilled patterns. **Copymaster 76** is a simple pattern based on seeds and leaves. All of these can be copied onto thin card and cut out to produce stencils. To make the stencils, waterproof over the edges with wax from a candle. You will have to help with some of the cutting out. Use stencil brushes or pads and dyes to produce a range of stencilled images. Use softly coloured paper and pastel tints of paints to make delicate combinations.

You need
Copymasters 57–9, **72–6**, card or greaseproof paper (for border stencils), candle wax, pencils, craft-knives, scissors.

Activity 162: Photograms
If you have a darkroom then your top infants will be able to begin to do photography by making simple photograms. A photogram is an image made on photographic paper without using a negative. Normally it is a design in greys and white on a solid black background.

To make dramatic pictures from living things (or once living) all you need are a few props, photographic paper and developing and fixing solutions. Collect leaves, grasses, feathers and wings of flies and butterflies. Under suitable darkroom safe-light conditions arrange a selection of objects onto a piece of photographic paper (with the emulsion facing up). Place a piece of scratch free perspex or plate glass over the whole arrangement. Either switch on the enlarger to expose the paper on the baseboard or switch on the normal light for 1 or 2 seconds. (You will probably need to experiment to find the best exposure time.) Now process the paper in the normal way, ensuring that you produce a good solid black and also retain a clean white in some areas of the picture.

Extending this technique you can sandwich a fly's wing or section of feather in the negative holder of the enlarger. Place this back in place and switch on. Your children will be able to focus the image on the baseboard. Switch off. Take a small piece of photographic paper and place it under the enlarger lens on the baseboard. Make a test-strip and process as usual. Choose the best exposure time, again make sure that you will produce a full rich black when the paper is fully developed. Make a full print from the image projected from the collection in the negative holder.

Pictures produced in this way will allow close examination of highly magnified parts of living organisms. Take care when handling chemicals.

You need
Photographic paper, developer and fixer (stop bath as well if possible), three or four photographic dishes of suitable size, photographic tongs, thermometer, protective clothes (rubber gloves perhaps), an enlarger (not essential) or desk top light, sheet of perspex or plate glass large enough to cover the paper fully, safe-light, feathers, grasses, leaves, insect wings and tweezers.

Photogram

Patterns from nature

Activity 163: Printing borders
Make sure your children wear overalls. Cut an old cotton sheet into pieces approximately A3 in size. Discuss the kinds of shapes that can be found in nature. Choose a design to print (the sycamore on **Copymaster 76** is a good subject). Take strips of greaseproof paper long enough to print the whole length of fabric and wide enough to accommodate the height of the pattern with at least 5 cm spare on top and bottom. Fold the greaseproof paper like a concertina. Each double fold should be wide enough to take the pattern. Draw half the shape of the leaf on one folded edge as shown in the diagram. Cut the shape out through all the folds of paper. Open out and iron the paper so that it is flat once more. Lay the pieces of ironed fabric out on the table and place the edge strip pattern in place on top. Sellotape® to the table so that it will not move. Make up a dye pad in the following way: take a piece of chipboard about 8 cms square (large enough to cover the cut patterns) and wrap around a couple of pieces of scrap cotton to make a soft pad, sellotape in place. Coat the pad with dye and press directly onto the open areas of the pattern to make the border. As the pattern has been sellotaped in place your children can add more dye to the pad and reprint if the first impression is too light.

You need
Cotton to decorate, scrap fabrics, dyes, chipboard pieces, Sellotape®, greaseproof paper, **Copymaster 76**, pencils and scissors.

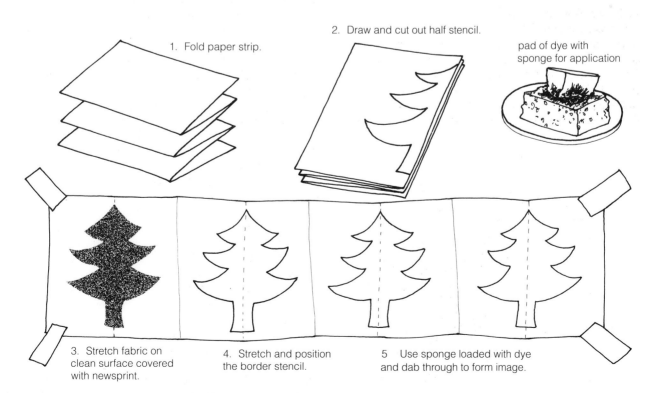

1. Fold paper strip.

2. Draw and cut out half stencil.

pad of dye with sponge for application

3. Stretch fabric on clean surface covered with newsprint.

4. Stretch and position the border stencil.

5 Use sponge loaded with dye and dab through to form image.

Cutting and printing a border stencil

Activity 164: Vegetable prints

Make a dye pad as in Activity 161 but big enough to accommodate sections of vegetables and fruits. Choose vegetables and fruit that can be handled easily by your children. Cabbages can simply be cut in half and printed directly, other items such as potatoes can be cut in half and have simple motifs cut into the surface. Cut apples and oranges can be quite effective. Before working on fabric try out patterns on newsprint. When ready to print on the fabric (cotton or silk) press the potato, apple or cabbage onto the dye pad and then press into place on the fabric. Repeat, making sure to keep inking up the printing surface and adding a little dye frequently to the pad.

You need
Vegetables and fruit, dyes, fabric, dye pad, a knife.

COLOUR

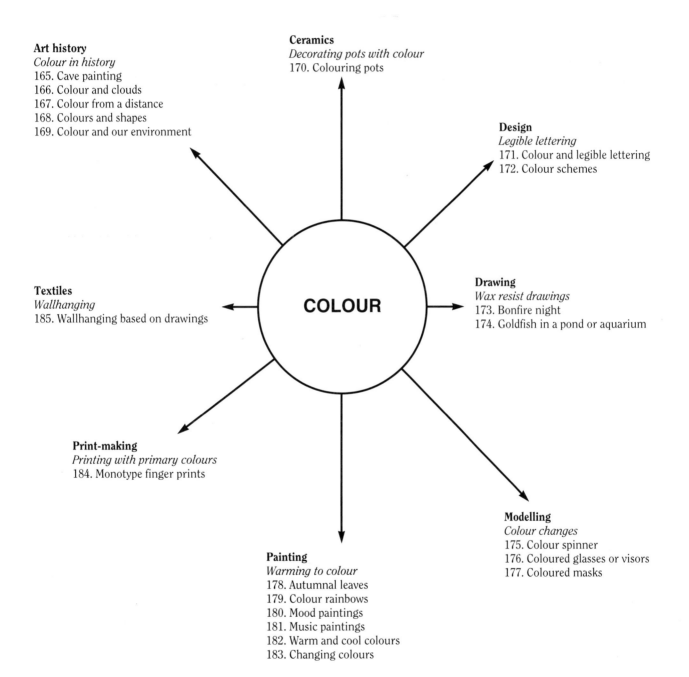

Art history
Colour in history
165. Cave painting
166. Colour and clouds
167. Colour from a distance
168. Colours and shapes
169. Colour and our environment

Ceramics
Decorating pots with colour
170. Colouring pots

Design
Legible lettering
171. Colour and legible lettering
172. Colour schemes

Textiles
Wallhanging
185. Wallhanging based on drawings

COLOUR

Drawing
Wax resist drawings
173. Bonfire night
174. Goldfish in a pond or aquarium

Print-making
Printing with primary colours
184. Monotype finger prints

Modelling
Colour changes
175. Colour spinner
176. Coloured glasses or visors
177. Coloured masks

Painting
Warming to colour
178. Autumnal leaves
179. Colour rainbows
180. Mood paintings
181. Music paintings
182. Warm and cool colours
183. Changing colours

CROSS-CURRICULAR LINKS

Design and technology Designing and making houses, vehicles, lighthouses
Drama and dance Firey colourful dances of China
Environmental studies Colours from natural materials
History The search for valuable minerals, black tulip
Language Descriptive languages
Mathematics Colour patterns, charts (data collection), sequencing patterns, popularity of colours survey, cars, most popular colour
Music 'Yellow submarine', *Firebird*, *Pastoral suite*, Pictures in an exhibition, Firework music
RE Joseph's coat of many colours
Science Types and uses of materials

ABOUT THIS TOPIC

General points

Colour, colour and light or colour and shape are popular topics at Key Stage 1 which, of course, have enormous science potential. Colour is a topic that is inherently progressive and can be revisited often at different levels from reception right through to Key Stage 3. You will find more information about colour in the basic skills section of this book, under painting. Only a few key points are introduced here.

Vocabulary

Names of colour were originally related to the source of the pigment. As new colours were developed so did the need for an increased accurate vocabulary: cave paintings were rendered in only five colours (yellow, orange, red, brown and black) and now we have over 7,000 named colours in the UK. Our environment has given us the colours that we use, whether they are derived from earths, flora, fauna or minerals. For everyone, starting as young children, it is necessary for us to have a good vocabulary of colour so that we may be able to think in colour and communicate our thoughts. One simple way is to use adjectives with the primary colours, for example a dull, bright, lively, deep or light red. When discussing colours with young children it is important to use words such as tone correctly.

Displays and resources

It is essential that you prepare a lively and useful display that can be added to and changed as the topic progresses. One approach is to prepare a 'colour environment'. This will include brightly coloured natural and made objects, bottles, leaves, fabrics, books with brightly coloured jackets, paintings, prints and posters, prisms, colour charts from DIY stores. It is a good idea to take familiar objects such as bottles and paint them with bright opaque colours (PVA). When dry these make excellent features for colour demonstrations. Ideally the classroom should be capable of being blacked out and then illuminated by coloured lights. (The best way is to use three or four strong directional lights that are projected through theatrical quality coloured acetates. Try cyan, magenta, yellow and a bright green).

Alternatively you may gather images of the use of colour and examples of natural sources of colour or ask your children to bring in objects for single colour displays, starting with violet and changing every week until you have covered the whole rainbow of colours. Remember that the displays can give your children a real experience of colour.

STARTING POINTS

Colour is a topic that can be introduced during any term, depending on where you start. It is, of course, particularly suited to run through the autumn term because of the range of natural colours and the proximity to Christmas. Also, should you wish to black out the classroom for colour displays it is much easier when there is not so much light coming in through cracks around your blinds.

- From your display
- Stories and poems (nursery rhymes), featuring autumn, winter and summer plus direct references to colourful subjects
- How colours were first made and used, grinding and mixing colours from natural materials
- Painting from landscape, still life, portraits, mixing from primaries, warm and cool colours
- Colour from other cultures, batik work
- Colour of festivals, Chinese New Year, Caribbean festivals
- Colour of food
- Colour and shapes, tessellations, spinners
- Colour and the artists: explore how famous artists have used colour
- Colour and our environment, rural and urban; churches, buildings, natural and made building materials, signs and symbols, lettering and legibility.

COLOUR ACTIVITIES

 Colour in history ▷

Before you start

Colour is a major element of most visual arts. You can find interesting and exciting ways to make links between the practical work that children undertake and art history. The National Curriculum requires that at Key Stage 1 children should make connections between their own work and that of other artists. A suggestion from the National Curriculum is that children should paint pictures of flowers and look at the work of William Morris and others, eventually making patterns of repeated units by printing.

Activity 165: Cave painting

Look at illustrations of the cave paintings at Lascaux and discuss the magic nature of art and how the colours were made. Get the children to collect berries, earths and charcoal. Using a pestle and mortar grind these into powders or juice mixing with a little PVA to produce paints. The children can then make their own cave paintings using a good range of colours. Use **Copymaster 82**: Colours I have made, to keep examples of colours made by your children, including details about how they were made and written descriptions of the colours.

You need
Illustrations, samples of natural sources of colour, clear medium PVA, mortar and pestle, paper, brushes, **Copymaster 82**.

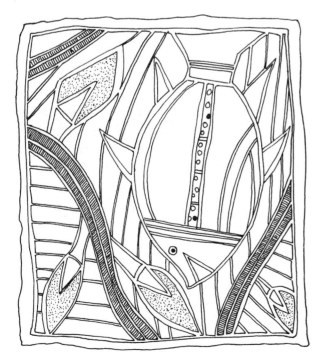

Aboriginal art

Activity 166: Colour and clouds

Show examples of work by artists, such as Constable, Corot and Turner. Discuss how they used colour to paint clouds. Get your children to look at the painted clouds.

You need
Good illustrations of the artists' works, photographs of clouds, opportunity to look at clouds. Paints, paper and brushes.

Activity 167: Colour from a distance

Work by Van Gogh is very often shown to children as a stimulus to seeing colour. Van Gogh's painting of his friend the postman is a particularly good example of a direct and free use of colours. Look at other expressionist paintings and get your children to do their versions of the paintings.

There are other ways to use and mix colours. You may wish to follow up work on colour by copying the way that other artists worked such as Seurat, who was an impressionist (a pointilliste, in fact).

Having already done some experiments with colour mixing in previous topics, show the children enlarged details of work by the Impressionists and look at the surface of a colour TV or monitor through a magnifying glass. Pure colours are mixed by putting them closely together, so that seen from a distance, dots of blue and red, for example, would appear to be purple. Get your children to do some dotty pictures using **Copymasters 80 and 81**. What size coloured dots appear to mix best from a distance? At what distance? Make the word colour using contrasting colours on each sheet. Which one can be seen most easily?

You need
Posters, illustrations, paints, brushes, paper, **Copymaster 80 and 81**.

Activity 168: Colours and shapes

Islamic patterns and Mondrian's paintings are excellent for linking colours and shapes together. Ask children to use **Copymasters 19–24** and **80–85** for colour and shape exercises. Get them to mix and use colours to fill the shapes as they see fit. Show them examples of Mondrian's work and discuss how he dealt with similar problems of colour and shape. This can be linked to work on stained glass windows which also use flat areas of colour combined to form a picture. Use **Copymaster 11**. Use the Islamic patterns and **Copymaster 25** for composing abstract colour tessellations.

You need
Illustrations of Mondrian's pictures, Islamic patterns, felt tip pens, paints, brushes, **Copymasters 11**, **19–24** and **80–85**.

Activity 169: Colour and our environment

Explore the environment around your schools: the landscape, churches, buildings, natural and made building materials (include stained glass), signs and symbols, lettering and legibility (colour backgrounds). Get your children to make abstract pictures in a similar way to Activity 168 using the colours that they find in the houses, grass, sky and shops.

You need
Sketchbooks, colours, paints and illustrations.

Decorating pots with colour

Activity 170: Colouring pots
Each child needs a lump of clay of about the size of a tennis ball. Children will instinctively enjoy squeezing and playing with clay and you should give them opportunities to be free and undirected. Here you set the task of making a primitive pot by hollowing out a cavity in the ball of clay using the thumb. Children should squeeze the wall as they build it to make it thinner. With practice they will be able to make a stout bowl or pot quickly and, later on, using this simple technique they will be able to make different types of pots. Let the pots dry out. When they are dry, discuss with the children what sorts of colours and patterns would suit the pots they made. Get them to make sketches before using poster paints to decorate their pots.

You need
Clay (or self hardening clay), poster paints, and brushes.

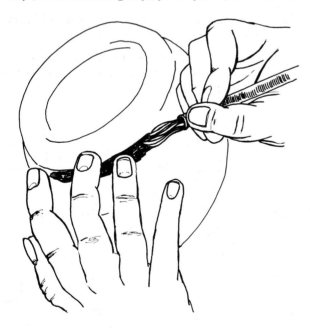

Legible lettering

Activity 171: Colour and legible lettering
Introduce the activity by discussing the need for legible signs, road signs and other warnings. The task is for the

children to experiment with colour and then to make a sign that can easily be read at a distance. Colour combinations will have to be tried out. Ask your children what they think white lettering on a yellow background would look like. What about red on green? The finished signs can be discussed and the best ones put on display. Discuss with the children whether certain colours may be better than others for different purposes. It is possible that some colour combinations are very legible but could be disturbing to some people. The copymasters contain different style typefaces for use with this activity. Get your children to try out different combinations of colours on copies of the typefaces.

You need
Paper, paint, brushes, pencils, rulers. Examples of coloured lettering and signs to be included in your class display, **Copymasters 60**, **69** and **70**.

Activity 172: Colour schemes
Introduce the idea of what a colour scheme is. For example, a colour scheme for autumn might be red and gold, and a misty scene might be blue and grey. Ask the children to design and make a room in which their favourite toy can hold a party for two or three of its friends. The way the room is coloured and laid out is very important. Will it be restful? Will it be a disco? Make sure that the doors and windows will be a suitable size for the dolls. Tables and tablecloths, curtains,,

armchairs, pictures or posters, should have a well thought out colour scheme. This mini project should be a lot of fun. When the interiors are finished, the children can discuss each other's work and perhaps think of improvements. Use **Copymasters 86** and **87** to try out colours that harmonise and those that clash.

You need
Cardboard boxes, fabrics, wallpaper samples, monotype prints (done previously by children), tissue paper, glue, paint and brushes, **Copymasters 86** and **87**.

 ## Wax resist drawings ▷

Before you start
Wax crayons are often used by very young children. They give instant strong marks and can encourage a bold and colourful drawing style. Their water resistant quality can also form useful links with batik and they may be used for encaustic painting and print-making. You should be careful, however, not to allow the ease and cheapness of the media to get out of hand. It is important to encourage the appropriate materials to be used for the right purpose. Many fine, detailed studies started in pencil or felt tip are obliterated by drawing over the top with thick, stumpy crayons. The best work in crayon is likely to be that which has been pushed beyond simple line drawings. The activities described here use the qualities of the crayons as a starting point.

Bonfire night can be a good subject for drawings in wax crayons, as can the study of fish in aquaria. If you are going to set either of these subjects for your children, please ensure that you prepare them for the work. Ask them to take special note of the way the colours look and to do the drawings either directly from the aquaria or after seeing fireworks on November 5th.

Activity 173: Bonfire night
Get the children to make crayon drawings of firework displays on bonfire night. Make sure that the crayons are applied firmly. Once drawing with crayon is complete let the children make up and choose their own colours for the backgrounds, using powder paints or ready-mixed water-based paints. Apply the colour quickly over the whole picture. (If areas are left untouched it will be possible to do another colour stage.) If the crayon is not thick enough you may find that it does not resist the water paint very well. In such cases run the finished picture under a tap until the desired effect is achieved. Let the finished picture dry out face up on newspaper. This process can be repeated with further layers of wax drawings and staining if necessary.

The colours of bonfire night can be effectively shown by a combination of bright wax crayons combined with a black wash or water-based paint. (As a background black always makes colours stand out more brightly.)

You need
Wax crayons, paper, water-based paints or dyes, illustrations of firework displays, night scenes, lights at night, books, scissors.

Activity 174: Goldfish in a pond or aquarium
Show Matisse's famous picture of swimming goldfish. Get the children to make observational drawings of fish swimming in a pond or aquarium. Use the same approach as for the firework displays in Activity 173 with the exception that for such subjects as swimming fish your children will need to use a light blue or green wash as a background.

You need
Wax crayons, paper, water-based paints or dyes, illustrations of Matisse's goldfish, books, scissors.

The results from these drawing activities can be very good starting points for fabric pictures based on the same theme. (See Activity 185.)

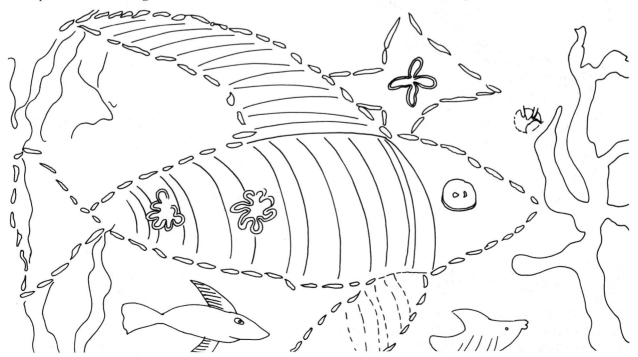

Colour changes ▷

What you need
String, scissors, card, paints, Sellotape®, coloured cellophane, squared card, **Copymaster 88**.

Activity 175: Colour spinner
Use the template provided on **Copymaster 88**. Stick one copy to both sides of a ready cut circle of stout card. Carefully colour the labelled sections on both sides and allow to dry. Then pierce the two holes as marked and thread a length of string through. Tie the ends together and spin. If the colours are fairly accurate then, when viewed spinning, all colours will tend to give a white impression.

Activity 176: Coloured glasses or visors
Cut out the shapes for the glasses frame, trap the cellophane between the two rims and use glue and Sellotape® to fix together. These glasses can be made with a whole range of different coloured 'lenses'. They can be used to paint pictures of everyday sights made magical. Alternatively, the children can make bands of card to fit their heads to which they can fit a coloured visor of cellophane. These options include good problem solving opportunities.

A colour visor

Activity 177: Coloured masks
Make a simple flat mask as described in Activity 117. Give your children five or six bright colours, brushes and plenty of clean water. Get them to choose one colour and to paint a line about 1 cm thick around each hole cut for eyes and mouth. Follow this with a contrasting colour butted up to the first lines. Continue until the whole mask is painted.

 # Warming to colour ▷

Before you start
For all painting and messy activities it is important that the tables are protected with newspaper, that the children wear protective clothing and that paint is dispensed carefully and in small quantities. Remember to leave plenty of time at the end of the session to clear up.

Activity 178: Autumnal leaves
The well tried exercise of painting autumnal leaves should not be ignored. This can be a class exercise giving you the degree of control that is useful when technical matters are being taught. Make sure that the leaves are big and well coloured, and that the children use good quality paper and decent brushes and paint. Make sure that the children draw the leaves first, then carefully explain the way that colours are mixed. It is worth explaining for example, that brown cannot be mixed directly from only two primary colours. It can be mixed from red and green. Green is not a primary colour but can be mixed from yellow and blue, which are primary colours.

Prior to starting work with leaves you may wish to use some 'warm up exercises'. A good one is to ask the children to paint a small circle (1 cm) in either pure red, yellow or blue, in the centre of a piece of A4 white paper (rather like the masks in activity 177). Thereafter any colour mixed from the basic palette can be painted in a series of concentric circles until the whole of the paper is covered. Do not leave gaps between the circles. Avoid using black as this can have a deadening effect and and turn everything to mud.

You need
Paper, paints, finger paints, felt tip pens, brushes, pencils.

Activity 179: Colour rainbows
Using **Copymasters 89** and **90**, get the children to mix a little red gradually into a bright yellow and paint a section at a time until the bright yellow is replaced by a bright red at the other end of the rainbow. Do this for the following pairs of colours: red and green, blue and orange, yellow and purple.

You need
Paper, paints, finger paints, felt tip pens, brushes, pencils. **Copymasters 89** and **90**.

Activity 180: Mood paintings
Discuss with the children what particular feelings they have about colours. Discuss their emotions, happy and sad feelings. Ask children to paint pictures that emphasise the importance of colour, to illustrate the following feelings: happy, sad, angry, satisfied, love, hate, jealousy, loneliness.

The paintings are best when kept to a small scale and are most effective when kept as abstract designs. This is because children can concentrate on the meaning of colours or combinations of colours.

You need
Paper, paints, finger paints, felt tip pens, brushes, pencils. **Copymasters 91** and **92**.

Activity 181: Music paintings
Choose some colourful music. Try to avoid the usual choices. Include things like 'Rhapsody in blue', 'Yellow submarine', 'I can sing a rainbow', 'Blue bayou', 'Green grow the rushes', 'Little white duck', 'By the light of the silvery moon', 'Blue Hawaii', 'Pink panther', 'Black is black', 'Yellow rose of Texas', 'Bluebells of Scotland', 'Blue suede shoes', 'Red sails in the sunset', 'Green green grass of home', 'Ebony and ivory', 'Roses are red', 'Greensleeves', 'Itsy, bitsy, teeny, weeny, yellow, polka dot bikini', 'When the red red robin' and 'The lady in red'. Discuss the music and make some notes. Ask the children to paint pictures that include bold and soft colours to represent their feelings about the music.

You need
Paper, paints, finger paints, felt tip pens, brushes, pencils.

Activity 182: Warm and cool colours
Using **Copymaster 93**, and the three primary colours plus white ask the children to mix 12 different warm and cool colours to complete the picture.

You need
Paper, paints, finger paints, felt tip pens, brushes, pencils, **Copymaster 93**.

Activity 183: Changing colours
Ask your children to test a range of colours, including browns, oranges, greens and blacks. With a bucket of water and strips of blotting paper (2 cms by 10 cms) you can find out what colours are composed of. Put small blobs of colour roughly in the centre of the strips of blotting paper. Dip the pieces a few centimetres into the water and hold there for a minute. Watch the colours change. Greens often break down into blue and yellow. Try black fountain pen ink.

You need
Bucket of water, strips of blotting paper, various water-soluble colours.

Printing with primary colours

Activity 184: Monotype finger prints
Young children are amazed by the number of colours that can be mixed from primaries. One exciting exercise is simply to apply small quantities of finger paints to different points on a formica or perspex sheet. The three primary colours can be mixed by drawing them into each other and then carefully applying a little white. This can be mixed to give a variegated range of colours and tints. Once the picture has been completed on the surface, a permanent record can be made by laying a piece of newsprint onto the wet paint and taking a monotype print. When the primary colours are mixed they produce secondary colours of orange, purple and green.

You need
Perspex sheets (approximately 35 cm × 25 cm), finger paints, newsprint, newspaper.

Wallhanging

Activity 185: Wallhanging based on drawings
Use the work done previously on firework night or goldfish as a starting point. Show some examples of quilts and wallhangings. Discuss how individual pieces can best be arranged so that the colours balance in a pleasing overall composition. Make viewers that are 20 cm square. Ask each child to select a small section from their original drawing that they particularly like. If they are working from the brilliant colours of fireworks then the explosive colours need to be shown, if from the aquatic world of fish then it may be the soft and gentle tints of blues, pinks, golds and greens that need to be included. Once the children have made their selection get them to trace the outline of the picture carefully, making a note of the colours in each section. Now they should try to find the right kind of scraps to make up

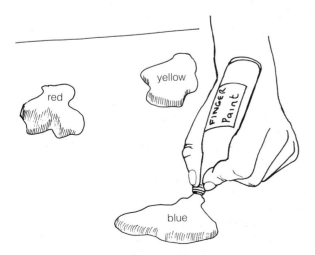

Monotype printing

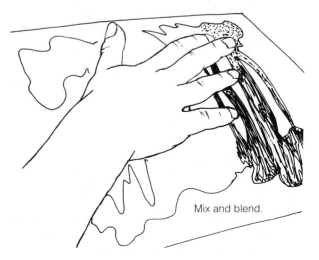

Mix and blend.

69

their own individual panels. They will need to look for colour, size, shape and texture. When they have found what they need they can cut out the individual traced shapes and pin these to the right colour and thereafter cut out the fabrics. It is a good idea to have a background in a suitable colour upon which to fix the cut out shapes, either black (or dark blue) or light shimmering blue/green. Combine all the sections together on one large wallhanging.

You need
A range of coloured fabrics, scraps of tissue paper, square pieces of backing canvas for children to work on (approximately 20 cm square), a piece of canvas to support all children's work when finished (approximately 1.6 metres by 0.8 metre) which is sufficient for a class of 32 children.

MATERIALS

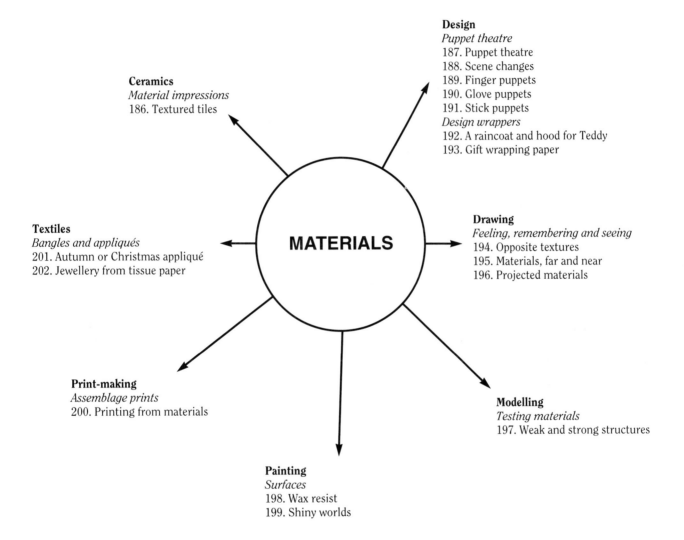

Ceramics
Material impressions
186. Textured tiles

Design
Puppet theatre
187. Puppet theatre
188. Scene changes
189. Finger puppets
190. Glove puppets
191. Stick puppets
Design wrappers
192. A raincoat and hood for Teddy
193. Gift wrapping paper

Textiles
Bangles and appliqués
201. Autumn or Christmas appliqué
202. Jewellery from tissue paper

MATERIALS

Drawing
Feeling, remembering and seeing
194. Opposite textures
195. Materials, far and near
196. Projected materials

Print-making
Assemblage prints
200. Printing from materials

Modelling
Testing materials
197. Weak and strong structures

Painting
Surfaces
198. Wax resist
199. Shiny worlds

CROSS-CURRICULAR LINKS ▶

Design and technology Designing and making structures using different materials
Drama and dance Tin man from the Wizard of Oz
Environmental studies Natural and made materials
History Alchemy, discovery of atoms

Language Factual and reportive writing
Mathematics Comparisons
RE Water into wine, the transformation of materials
Science Insulation, durability, waterproofing, changes in materials

ABOUT THIS TOPIC ▶

General points

The scope of a theme like materials is potentially very wide. You could include everything from an atom to an asteroid, leather to plastic and silicon chips to potatoes. Try to ensure that you focus carefully upon what you want the pupils to cover otherwise you may end up with a mishmash of unrelated activities of dubious educational value. Try to be simple. Look at a comparison between natural and synthetic materials or those which are derived from animals or plants. You could look at those which change, those that are stable, those which are hard, or soft. Any of these approaches can be a good starting point for art activities.

Those activities linked to the design of a puppet theatre may be used as a topic in themselves. They will bring together the use of many kinds of materials, rigid, flexible and malleable. Probably the best time to tackle this series of puppet activities is during the autumn term as you approach Christmas.

Displays and resources

For imaginative and observational work alike it is vital that you provide a range of stimulating display materials and relevant books. For this topic it is a good idea to make a collection of natural and made things as examples of materials. These could include natural items such as leaves, wood, powders, pigments (from petals and earths of cochineal), coal, peat, earth, crystals, stones, shells, bones and skeletons from small animals, wool (include raw fleece if possible), snake skins, examples of furs and cotton. Made materials, on the other hand, could include plastics (range of products made from soft and hard plastics types), building materials based on clay such as bricks, tiles, fine porcelain and rough earthenware pottery, sandpaper, wood shavings, sawdust, mirrors, metals, fabrics, papers and cards. Arrange with your library and museum services for collections of relevant books and artefacts to enhance your displays.

STARTING POINTS ▶

- Consider differences between made and natural materials
- Use questions in the displays to stimulate discussion
- Try to add to and change your display(s) as the topic develops
- Discuss what materials can be found in the classroom, the school, the home. Make a list. What is the smallest piece of material that your children can find? A grain of sand? A grain of salt? A speck of pollen? What happens when small things are examined under a microscope?

- Make lists of materials in pairs of opposites. For example: hard and soft, rough and smooth, shiny and matt, heavy and light, absorbent and waterproof, natural and made, woven and continuous
- Divide the class into groups. Choose which contrary pairs they will concentrate upon and make up collections to match their pairs of material types
- Ask questions about what materials are used to make toys
- Follow up the art history activity in the previous topic on Colour. Make your own colours and dyes.

MATERIALS ACTIVITIES ▶

C39
94–6

Material impressions ▷

Activity 186: Textured tiles

Get your children to make two or three small clay tiles. They should not be bigger than 10 cms square. Using a range of different materials make impressions in the tiles. Dry, fire and glaze them. Add the finished tiles to your display with a description of how they were made.

You need
Clay, materials for pressing, glazes, brushes.

Puppet theatre

Before you start

As Christmas approaches children become more en-thralled with stories, particularly those to do with the nativity. A very positive way to work with materials of all kinds is to produce small puppet theatres (for example, a nativity theatre) complete with the main figures, changes of scenery and props.

Class organisation

Divide the class into groups of four or five children. Read the story of the journey to Bethlehem and consider the kinds of clothes that Mary, Joseph, the shepherds, angels and wise men might wear. Get your children to produce their own designs for the clothes of the main characters (including the animals). Ask them to con-sider the various scenes on the journey. What might the places have looked like? Do some imaginary drawings of the countryside and the stables and crib.

You need

Try to make a small collection of puppets including shadow puppets from Bali, Greece and Turkey and finger, glove and stick puppets. **Copymaster 95** contains a traditional design for a shadow puppet.

To make the theatres, each group will need a cardboard carton (approximately 45 cms wide × 40 cms deep × 35 cms high); paints; coloured paper (previously produced by monotype printing, marbling or commer-cially produced); felt tip pens and brushes; scissors and a craft knife (naturally you will have to assist when using the knife, as young children should not handle dangerous tools); water-based brown tape for reinforc-ing joints and openings (this tape is better than masking tape as it takes water-based colours better).

For the glove and finger puppets you will need felt or cotton; felt tip pens; scissors; glues (water-based clear drying PVA); wool; sequins; buttons; lace and sewing equipment.

For the stick puppets you will need Plasticine®; Modroc® or clay; 20 cm of 5 mm dowel rod or giant lollysticks; fabrics for the costumes (robes as well as undergarments); wool for sheep; wool scraps for hair; metal foils for crowns; water-based PVA glue; paints and felt tip pens; scissors and a sewing machine (to be used by the teacher).

Activity 187: Puppet theatre

Give each group a carton. Get them to work out where to cut out a window (with an equal border in one long side) and also in the bottom of the carton. Strengthen the window (the proscenium arch) and the opening in the base with brown adhesive tape (water soluble). Carefully paste the decorated paper over the outside of the theatre walls. Line the inside with coloured paper (blues or light grey).

Activity 188: Scene changes

Make a number of scene backdrops as needed. They include the escape, the inn and the stable. These can be hung in place as shown in the illustration. Design and make a curtain that can be pulled back easily from the sides.

Making the puppets

There are no rights and wrongs about making puppets. There are endless varieties for very young children. It is sensible to limit the possibilities and the following approaches will work well.

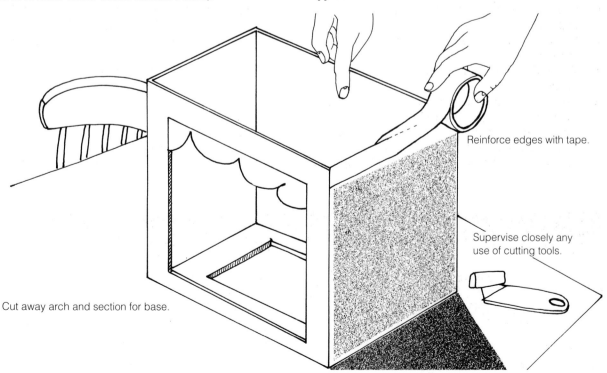

Reinforce edges with tape.

Supervise closely any use of cutting tools.

Cut away arch and section for base.

Making the puppet theatre

73

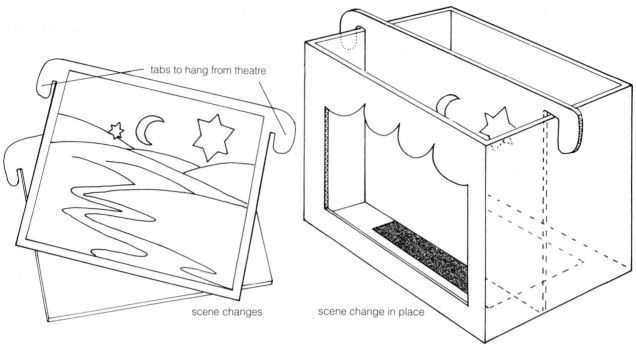

tabs to hang from theatre

scene changes   scene change in place

Making scene changes

Naturally the puppets must be the right size for the theatre and be capable of being operated. Your children will also have to think about the colour and design of the clothes, the making and finishing of the faces. Will the angles have wings? How will these be made? Such questions will give you a chance to extend the range of materials to be used. Perhaps the wings should be transparent? Perhaps they should be made from feathers (clean down).

Activity 189: Finger puppets
The simplest finger puppets are those painted on to the ends of fingers with face paints. Finger puppets made from fabric scraps may be a good alternative to the normal glove puppet as the theatre could become rather crowded if too many children have to operate puppets at

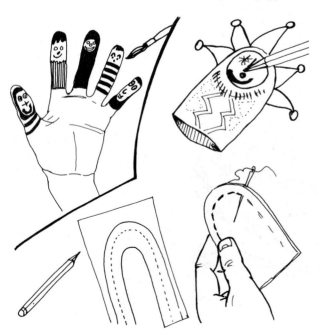

one time. Using finger puppets will allow one or two children to operate up to five or six characters at one time. Use the pattern on **Copymaster 94** and transfer to a piece of thin card (card is better as the template will last for future use). Cut the pattern out and lay it onto pieces of material, tracing the outline. Cut out and follow the method given below for glove puppets. Take care with very young children not to allow them to put small items in their ears, mouths or noses. For this reason you may have to intervene to fix eyes and other features really securely to the puppets. (Make sure to use safety eyes, etc.)

Activity 190: Glove puppets
With very young children it is advisable to fix the clothes with glue. You may wish, however, to help make up the basic gloves using a sewing machine. Transfer the pattern from **Copymaster 94** onto thin card. Lay the cut out pattern onto the fabric, trace around it and cut out two identical pieces. Mark the seam as shown and carefully apply glue from a fine nozzle along the line and then place the second piece on top to fix and dry, or stitch along the marked seam line. Then turn the glove inside out. The individual figures can then be finished according to the children's own designs.

Activity 191: Stick puppets
Although stick puppets are often used with older children there is no reason why young children should not produce attractive, if somewhat basic, stick puppets.

The best option is to use a self-drying, modelling compound such as Modroc® for squeezing the rough shape of a head and body onto the giant lollystick as shown in the illustration. Try to resist the temptation of interfering in this process. (There are few worse things to do to a child than to take over and pretty their sometimes clumsy but genuine efforts.) Once the body and head are dry and well fixed to the stick the children

Flatten rolls.
Sandwich lolly sticks with glue.
Paint and finish.

can carefully paint the heads to make the various characters. Afterwards pieces of fabric can be fixed around the neck using glue (or you can help stitch them). Use metal foils for making up crowns.

Operating the theatre and puppets
Probably the easiest way to operate the theatre is to set it up as shown in the diagram. This arrangement will allow children to crawl underneath, hidden by the hanging curtain and to operate either the glove or stick puppets from underneath.

 ## Design wrappers ▷

Activity 192: A raincoat and hood for Teddy
A class discussion about the weather and what it is like to be cold and wet can be linked to the suitability of

various materials as protection against the cold and wet and how to make up weatherproof garments. Make lists of good and poor materials for keeping warm and dry. Discuss the ways that materials can be combined to make new ones that have different qualities. Make lists of waterproofing materials. Discuss and experiment with reversible and irreversible changes in materials – ice and water, wax as a solid and liquid (wax crayons melt at a very low temperature and can be used to apply to pieces of fabric to test for waterproofing).

Invite your children to bring their favourite soft toys, such as teddy bears, to school. Set them the task of designing and making a raincoat and hood for the chosen toy. To do this they should:

● Measure their toys with tape measures and make patterns with thin paper (relating solids to flat areas)
● Test their paper patterns to see if they are the right shape and size for making up the garments
● Transfer the patterns to the chosen material, pin and use chalk to outline
● Cut out the shapes
● Consider whether or not to colour the individual pieces of fabric and waterproof them before making up the finished garments
  – Use potato prints to pattern the coats
  – Use felt tip pens to decorate the fabrics
  – Use Brusho® to dye the fabrics
● Make up the coats and hoods (depending on the age and ability of the children you will have to intervene when needles and thread are used, alternatively glue and velcro can be used).
● Dress the teddies up and have a fashion parade and of course test for waterproofing.

You need
Fabric scraps (old sheets, shirts), polythene, clear laminating plastic, elastic (for the hood), velcro (for coat fastener), metal foils, card, wax crayons, candles, Brusho®, felt tip pens, squared paper, thin pattern paper (tissue paper), scissors, pins, needles and thread, and

Position theatre to straddle two tables, allowing access from below.

75

glue, soft toys, photographs of raincoats and books and magazines with patterns for raincoats and hoods.

Activity 193: Gift wrapping paper

There are many ways of introducing repeating pattern designs. This method is very simple and can produce some stunning results. It combines a variation on Japanese paper dyeing and simple block printing.

Step one Take a sheet of newsprint paper and fanfold it as in the illustration. Make sure that each crease is nice and sharp. Prepare some small quantities of Brusho® dye in the 'Christmas' colours that the children have chosen. (You may also like to experiment with dyes from natural sources such as onion skins, blackberries, flowers or you may wish to use made dyes from sources such as coloured tissue paper).

Step two Hold the folded fan of paper firmly so that the edges are in close contact with each other. Apply Brusho® either along the edge of the creases or by dipping the edges carefully into a dish of Brusho®. When the first dip is dry apply a different colour to the other creased edges. In this way irregular lines of colour will be dyed across the whole of the paper. When dry unfold and refold in the other direction and repeat the process with different colours. If you use one darkish colour and one light colour for each direction then you should end up with a fairly regular rectangular design. When dry open out the paper.

Step three Measure the light area at the centre of the rectangles and make up simple potato blocks of Christmas trees or similar festive motifs. Potato print in the light area to complete the wrapping paper design.

There are many possible variations that can add sparkle to the paper. These can involve more complex folding and dyeing of the paper. Try folding the first strip into triangular shapes (see diagram), or potato printing onto different kinds of papers.

You need
Examples of wrapping papers and the types of material used in their manufacture (shiny and matt surfaces), a collection of books and magazines about gifts, potatoes, water paints for potato printing, brushes, Brusho®, newsprint, photographic dishes.

Fold newsprint into strip.
Touch alternate edges in different colours of Brusho®

Open when dry.

Feeling, remember-ing and seeing

Activity 194: Opposite textures

Using your collection of materials, the children can classify them in terms of their texture. At the start, relatively crude differences will be noticed, e.g. smooth and rough, soft and hard. As you progress words like 'ribbed' and 'woven' may be used. Make a note of all the words and include them in your display. Get your children to choose two or three pairs of contrasting materials from your collection or display. Each child should think about 'opposites' and look for objects which are the softest, roughest, smoothest, most rounded or scratchy. Using their chosen media children can try to make the feeling in the form of a picture. To do this they should select pencils, Biros® or charcoal as they feel will suit the textures of the materials they have chosen. They may of course use combinations of media to draw the different objects.

The children can take rubbings of the different surfaces of materials using soft pencils or wax crayons. For this it is useful to use a thin paper such as newsprint and materials with a pronounced textured surface such as the long grain of timber.

Secretly, you can select different comparative pairs of soft/hard, smooth/rough objects and place them one at a time into feely boxes. Doing this can enhance the need for children to think before drawing and this is a valuable lesson in itself. Good combinations include: fir cones and wool; sandpaper and a plastic cup; leather gloves and a string bag. Children will be able to draw pictures to represent their feelings as they experience them directly.

The children's drawings can be either attempts to represent the objects realistically or the making of visual equivalents to the feelings of furriness or prickliness.

Use **Copymaster 39** to record your children's efforts. Photocopy one per child: children can do rubbings, drawings or paintings of the softest, roughest, smoothest, rounded or scratchy objects on display.

As children grow you can use feely boxes to stimulate drawing from memory. Objects can be felt thoroughly for a few minutes and then in one, five or ten minutes children can be asked to recall their impressions on paper and later to make a study from looking at the same object. Use **Copymaster 96** to make drawings of 'I feel, I remember, I see'.

You need
Pencils, wax crayons, pastels, charcoal, felt tip pens, Biros®, A4 paper (white and sugar), magnifying glasses, feely boxes, visual resources, photographs, posters plus a range of artefacts that include pairs of opposite textures as **Copymaster 39**.

Activity 195: Materials, far and near

Select a few different materials to study. For example, an old knitted jersey, a furry toy, a toy lorry, heavily grained wood, a collection of pebbles and a broken brick. Make sure that your children have objects available that are made from materials which will reveal extra interest when viewed closely such as feathers and crystalline solids. Get your children to do two drawings of the same object, one when placed on a table in front of them, the other when viewed through a magnifying glass. Ask your children to think, look and observe the qualities of the materials before deciding whether to use pens, pencils or charcoal. Emphasise the relationship of shapes and texture within the rectangular shape of the drawing area. Note where lines coincide and intersect.

Where children are studying complex objects ask them to use a viewfinder. This will help them choose the best view and also to select and focus upon the close up section for special attention. (Try to ensure that the ratio of sides cut as a viewer is the same as that of the drawing area.) This work with simple viewfinders can be built upon as children progress to include irregular shapes and to draw attention to familiar viewfinders such as windows, mirrors and spaces between houses.

You need
A variety of drawing media including pencils, charcoal, pen, felt tip pens, erasers. Cartridge paper (A3 sheets), magnifying glasses and viewing frames as described below.

Using a viewer

Activity 196: Projected materials
Take sections of materials, slice very thin and make up glass clad slides, project these onto a white screen. Children will be able to get to grips with the structure of organic/inorganic, made/natural materials. Suggested materials include: leaves, cucumber, beetroot, fly's wing, piece of feather. Drawings and paintings can be made directly from observation or by tracing outlines of images and finishing work after further observations.

You need
Projector (35 mm), glass slide mounts, craft knife, materials to be sliced, paper, felt tip pens, pencils, brushes and colours.

 ## Testing materials

Activity 197: Weak and strong structures
Pliable sheet materials such as thin sheet metal, plastic, card and paper can be made strong by folding or rolling them into three-dimensional shapes. These activities link well with design and technology.

Using **Copymasters 17** and **18** produce a number of gridded sheets of card. Ask the children to cut pieces of card 5 cms wide by 20 cms long. Get them to hold it out in front of them to see how much plasticine it will support at the far end before the card bends. Try the same with paper.

Using the same pieces of materials score the middle line on the strips, using the back of the scissors and the safety ruler. Fold the two strips into a 'V' shape and test how much plasticine it will support. Does it support more or less than in the first test?

Score two further lines as in the illustration and carefully fold the piece of card into triangular sections. Glue the overlapping strips, allow to dry. Now test to see whether the sections can support more weight than previously.

Make up different sections for use in making a model house. Which ones are best? Are some stronger than others yet still not the best for the job? Do some look better?

Write down reasons for choice.

You need
Paper, card, safety ruler, cutter and scorer, scissors, plasticine (for weights), glue (PVA), paper clips, **Copymasters 17** and **18**.

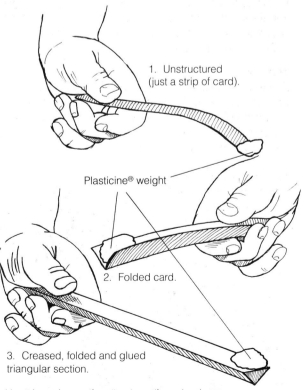

1. Unstructured (just a strip of card).

Plasticine® weight

2. Folded card.

3. Creased, folded and glued triangular section.

Use triangular sections to strengthen structures.

Making strong structures

Surfaces ▷   **Assemblage prints** ▷

Activity 198: Wax resist

This way of working will build upon previous experience of using wax crayons, reinforces concepts about the resistance of wax to water and is also a useful link to batik work.

The children use wax crayons to make a picture or design in which the crayon is applied thickly over the whole paper surface. When complete roll up the picture into a tight ball with the intention of crazing the wax picture surface. Now dunk the ball in water. Flatten and smooth out the damp paper. Use a strong mixture of Brusho® or paint and brush over the surface of the picture. The remaining wax will resist the paint while the paint penetrates where cracks have occurred and completely transforms the image.

You need
Wax crayons, paper, powder colour or Brusho®.

Activity 199: Shiny worlds

Discuss what kind of surfaces are shiny, quite shiny, not very shiny and matt. Ask your children to look at their faces reflected in various objects. Try a spoon, a window, a mirror. Do they look different, lighter, brighter, more or less colourful, bigger or smaller? Using shiny materials get your children to do a series of small drawings or paintings.

You need
A collection of variously reflective materials and images; include shaving mirrors, aluminium foil, spoons, pieces of different metals such as aluminium, brass, stainless steel, plastics and coloured bottles, drawing and painting materials, paints, brushes and paper. (Include pastels and coloured sugar paper for older children.)

Activity 200: Printing from materials

Direct surface printing is very exciting, the search for suitable objects to print from can be almost as much fun as making the print itself. Using a variety of materials make a series of prints or pictures or drawings. Some remarkable images of great beauty can be produced. Your children can also cut up some of these and use them as backgrounds to collages or appliqué.

Printing from a base Get children to select a range of materials and stick them to the surface of a sheet of board (for stability and ease of use). Encourage the children to take care in arranging (composing) the collection. Try to make sure that the materials are roughly the same thickness.

Printing from individual surfaces Make the same sort of selection but do not use a board to arrange a composition, merely take prints from each item in turn.

If you use leaves ensure that they are kept flat and do not dry out too much (or they will break under the pressure of printing). Using water-based inks means that you should ensure that all objects are dry or the ink will be diluted and may smudge and be patchy when printed. Dry your subjects with a sheet of newsprint or blotting paper prior to inking up.

Taking a print will involve your children in choosing colours carefully for printing. Help your children to roll out the ink or paint on the perspex sheet so that the roller has a fine even coat over all its surface and carefully apply the loaded roller to the individual materials or the assembly. Once all materials are inked carefully lay a piece of newsprint on top, gently but firmly rub the paper where it overlays the materials. The back of a spoon can be used or fingertips for rubbing the print onto the paper. When this is complete carefully peel the paper away and reveal the surface prints. Use the prints with a written account in your display.

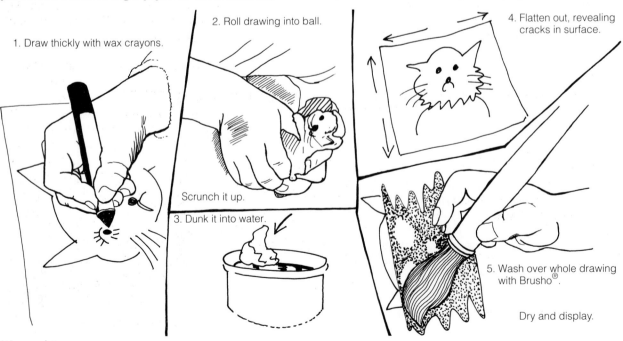

1. Draw thickly with wax crayons.

2. Roll drawing into ball.

Scrunch it up.

3. Dunk it into water.

4. Flatten out, revealing cracks in surface.

5. Wash over whole drawing with Brusho®.

Dry and display.

Wax resist

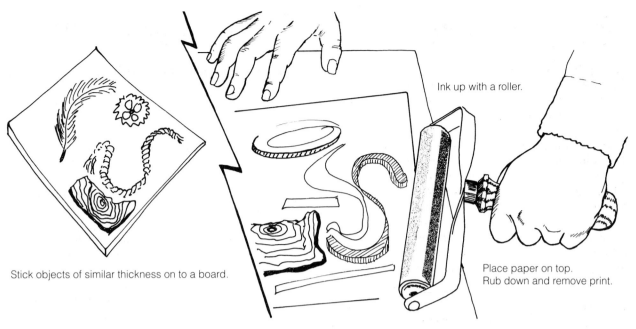

Stick objects of similar thickness on to a board.

Ink up with a roller.

Place paper on top.
Rub down and remove print.

Taking a print

You need
Pieces of perspex (30 × 25 cms) for rolling out ink rollers. Paints or printing inks, paper (newsprint). A collection of materials (include leaves, feathers, fabrics, screwed up and unfolded foils, tiles, pieces of bark and wood, ferns, textured wallpapers, doilies, string, string bags, rope, corrugated card). Thick strawboards or card for making composite prints.

Bangles and appliqués

Activity 201: Autumn or Christmas appliqué
Autumn is a good time to introduce the idea of using fabrics as an alternative medium to paint in the making of pictures. This is because the autumnal colours are so rich that using the colours of fabrics can heighten children's awareness of the brilliance and depth of the 'broken' colours of russets, golds, rusts and greens (surprisingly, there are few dull browns in the autumn landscape). Also with the approach of Christmas, imaginative work can have a new stimulus through children's own growing excitement combined with new techniques.

Collect a sufficiently good range of scraps and sort them into groups. Then every possible colour and tone, texture and effect can be produced through using fabrics. With very young children you should limit the size of the picture and it is a good idea to be very thorough in discussing and planning the pictures. Introduce the activity by either reading a story or poem about the time of year or arrange for children to make some observational drawings of seasonal landscape. Try to include unusual sources as they can be most evocative of 'mind pictures':

Make up small panels of cut fabric.

Join all sections together on wall hanging.

Draw and then trace sections of design.

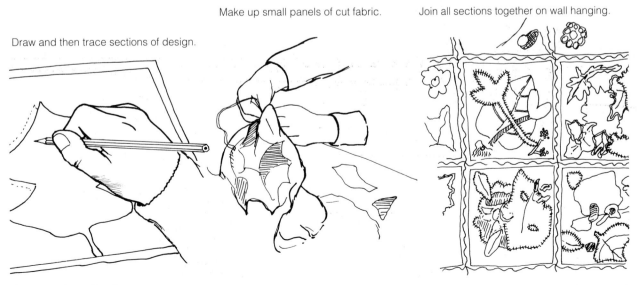

Autumnal appliqué

79

Down with the Rosemary and so,
Down with the Baise and Mistletoe,
Down with the Holly, Ivie, all
Wherewith ye drest the Christmas Hall.

Or,

Ivy, Ivy, I love you,
In my bosom I put you,
The first young man who speaks to me
My future husband will be.

From these beginnings the children will be able to move on to produce a collage or appliqué based on observation or from the imagination, using as many different materials as possible. It is important that the children should be encouraged to make a simple plan of their compositions before starting to work in the fabrics themselves. Now transfer their sketches to a stout piece of strawboard which will be the base for the appliqué. Select the materials and find the best ways to position things. The quality and freshness of the ideas, the simplicity of cut shapes, and a discriminating approach to colour and tonal values of the fabrics will enrich the children's artistic appreciation.

First cut and arrange the pieces then carefully glue in place. Fixing of fabrics can be a problem. Some (loose hairy fabrics) need to be sewn while others may simply be glued in place. When handling different materials, the children will have to be aware of all of their qualities, not just their colour and tone.

Felt tip pens can also be used to draw into fabrics that are plain. This will give the work extra richness.

You need
Fabric scraps, PVA, colours, strawboard, hessian, wool tufts, papers, pens, felt tip pens, scissors.

Activity 202: Jewellery from tissue paper

Get each child to cut a piece of cardboard about 5 cm wide and long enough to go over their hands when formed into a bangle. Add 2 cms to the length to ensure that there is enough material to stick firmly in places as in the diagram. Mark the position of the overlap then glue and fix in place, use paper clips to hold in place and push the bangle over a bottle (used as a former) to form a circular shape while it dries. When the joint is dry remove from the bottle and apply glue over the whole of the outside and on a 1 cm strip on the inside edges. Cover the outside with a strip of tissue paper and fold over strips to stick on the inside edges. While the bangle dries, the children can roll strips of tissue paper into thin strings that are then applied with glue over the surface of the bangle. Using different colours the whole of the surface can be covered in rhythmic lines. Take care not to apply too much glue as the colours of the tissue papers will tend to run.

You need
A piece of stiff card for each child, assorted colours of tissue papers, Gloy®, tape measures and rulers, pencils and paper clips, scissors, PVA glue.

ART HISTORY

INTRODUCTION ▶

With reception class children one of your first aims will be to make them more aware of their immediate surroundings and the visual qualities of what they see and feel around them. Activities that encourage discussion and comparison of aspects of the visual world should lead to the formation of likes and dislikes followed by the emergence of reasons for their preferences. By introducing an awareness of various kinds of works of art you can extend children's perceptual and critical skills. By making available a wide span of art from many cultures and periods you will provide the basis of a wider sensitivity and understanding of the value of art for different people.

By the end of Key Stage 1 your children are required to apply their knowledge of the work of other artists to their own work and to have knowledge and understanding of art. This includes art history and knowledge of significant exponents of different forms of art. A sensible and manageable approach to this is to surround your children with images from art of different periods and schools and to draw upon these as support for practical work. This approach should be well thought out and progressive. At this stage you should not make unreasonable demands on your children. It will be sufficient to provide opportunities to start the processes of understanding. For example you may wish young children to discuss and compare the shapes and symbols used in ancient and primitive cultures alongside work by Miro and Picasso. This would be logical and may encourage young children's confidence in their own work. This is because many elements from primitive and ancient art and contemporary work based on primitive art appear naturally in the work of children as they develop from simple schematic and symbolic drawings into more complex forms. Try to make the visual resources that you provide support and extend the stages of your children's development.

Displays and resources
Relevant and rich visual resources have a direct impact on the quality of children's work. An exhibition which is regularly changed is a vital ingredient for any primary classroom. You may be able to arrange with your local school library and museum service for a series of display materials to be delivered to you. Slide shows are received enthusiastically by children. Ask for examples of work by specific artists; librarians will do their very best to help. Whether or not this kind of service is available, you need to ensure that books, posters, works of art and natural and made objects are displayed in a relevant, logical and purposeful way. Contact your school library and museum services to get information about artists and craftsmen who may be relevant to your topics or could form a focus for study.

Comparison of child art and primitive

81

Art history and skill areas
Enjoying paintings, sculpture, drawings, ceramics and all kinds of art products should be linked to the practical activities that infants are involved in. This does not mean that works of art cannot be enjoyed for their own sake but it does mean that visits to art galleries or looking at a range of art works from your local museum service will be more valuable when linked to subsequent practical activities.

The command words in the National Curriculum Order do not call for formal study of art history at Key Stage 1. Children are required 'to discuss, look at and compare'. This chapter begins building knowledge, by including specific references to artists, schools and periods that can be studied effectively and linked to practical activities. The aim is to provide you with sufficient information and guidance so that you feel happy to impart that knowledge to your children. This part of the book makes a positive link between practical activities in particular skill areas and art history.

ART HISTORY AND DRAWING
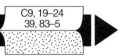

C9, 19–24
39, 83–5

When planning your teaching of Art history, you may focus on specific elements of the visual language. If you do then you can select examples of work that are particularly suitable.

Line
Selected drawings by Rembrandt, Guardi, Van Gogh, Klee, and from prehistory and the calligraphy of Japan will help extend your children's understanding and use of line in their work.

Shape
This is often a main element of drawings by Mondrian, Modigliani and Henry Moore. **Copymasters 57–9** contain outline drawings of animals; **Copymasters 83–5** also will be useful when dealing with shape and colour.

Tone
Work on tone can be supported by looking at work by Mary Cassat, Holbein, Seurat and Rembrandt.

Texture
The flicking, scratching marks of some of Van Gogh's drawings give marvellous impressions of texture as do drawings by the Japanese master Hiroshige and the carefully studied drawings of Albrecht Durer. **Copymaster 39** can be used to do work on textures.

Pattern
Islamic art (**Copymasters 19–24**), Escher and architectural drawings and designs for wallpapers and fabrics.

Space
Different views of space can be found in the drawings of Escher, Michelangelo and de Chirico.

Try to provide illustrations of drawings from imagination, observation and memory. For example your children could collect observational drawings of animals such as those by Durer. After looking at them and talking about them they can make their own drawings of the school pets.

Other activities could include:
- Doing drawings of themselves for people to look at in the future (**Copymaster 9:** 'When I'm 64').
- Thinking about the meanings in other people's drawings. Asking such questions as: 'What were they trying to convey?'
- Finding out about the techniques used by different artists.
- Comparing the ways people from different cultures draw.
- Examining different subjects portrayed in drawings.
- Examining the range of marks in other people's drawings, those made with different tools, cave paintings, stick drawings, sand paintings and inscribed surfaces.
- Looking at sketches, finished drawings and paintings.

ART HISTORY AND PAINTING

C82–5, 91,
92, 97

Link the different elements of the visual language with particular artists.

Shape
Mondrian (**Copymasters 83–5**) Matisse, Braque, Stuart Davis, Patrick Caulfield, Lowry

Colour
The Impressionists, Van Gogh, Constable. Discuss the way that colours are made. Where do they come from? What do their names mean? Which are the oldest colours? Which are the most modern? Use raw materials such as cochineal beetles, lichen and charcoal, ground up and mixed with PVA to make paints. Use **Copymaster 82** for this exercise.

Pattern
Lowry, Vasarely, Ernst, Braque, Picasso, frescoes from ancient Greece and Rome

Texture
See how colour and texture have been used to represent all kinds of materials and textures. The *Portrait of a woman* by Rogier van der Weyden, Dutch still lifes such as those by Willem Kalf, Japanese paintings of animals on silk; Ford Maddox Brown's *Pretty baa-lambs*; Anthony Van Dyck's *Charles I hunting* or any society painting with fabrics; furs and hair; Holbein's painting of Henry VIII (1537).

Space

Examine how paint has been used to show the world in different ways. The interiors of Vermeer, courtyard scenes of Pieter de Hoogh, landscapes of Ruisdael, Monet, Turner, Jan (Velvet) Breugel *The Earth* or *The earthly paradise* is particularly good, Pieter Breugel *Return of the herd*.

Line

Wall paintings e.g. Oryx and birds from Thera and calligraphy (**Copymaster 97** shows how simple lines can be very descriptive.)

Tone

Caravaggio, Rembrandt, Cassat.

Also:

- See how paint has been used to express feelings and attitudes. Include pastorals by Poussin, Claude, Watteau; soft and happy images by Renoir, excited images by Van Gogh, images of sympathy and concern by Picasso, (use **Copymasters 91** and **92** here)
- The different subjects covered: portraits, landscapes, animals and still life.
- Look at the different social backgrounds of artists, Lowry, *The potato eaters* of Van Gogh contrasted with the elegant social world of Gainsborough, for example.

Looking at the history of painting can lead to:

- Painting natural and made objects. A close examination of all kinds of subjects followed by trying to recreate those colours and textures.
- Colouring objects made from clay, card and fabrics.
- Paintings to convey feelings, memories or imaginary places, records of special events and imitation of the way other artists have worked.
- Imaginative play with costumes, portraits of children as Queen Victoria, Emperor Julius Caesar.
- Class collage of costumes through the ages, or a 'Roman' mosaic with sticky cut paper.

ART HISTORY AND PRINT-MAKING

It is believed that printing originated with the taking of rubbings from clay tablets of inscriptions in China. This could be a good place to start printmaking with your children. Get them to make up small clay slabs, suitably inscribed. Once the tablets are hard your children can relive the birth of printing by making their own rubbings from their printing blocks. You can take this historical perspective further by making up a printing block for demonstration. Get your children to make up a small, simple drawing of an animal on thin paper.

Paste the drawing face down on to a piece of lino. Rub away the back layers of the paper and oil the image so that it shows through. Carefully cut around the lines with a lino cutting tool. Remove all the unmarked lino leaving a simple outline drawing from which to take your print. This is thought to be the second stage in the development of printing.

Your children can also collect all kinds of printed images from the home and school which can be used in a number of different ways.

Do not tackle lino cutting until children are old enough and then close supervision of small groups is essential.

Make up clay relief tiles.
Allow to dry.
Take rubbings.

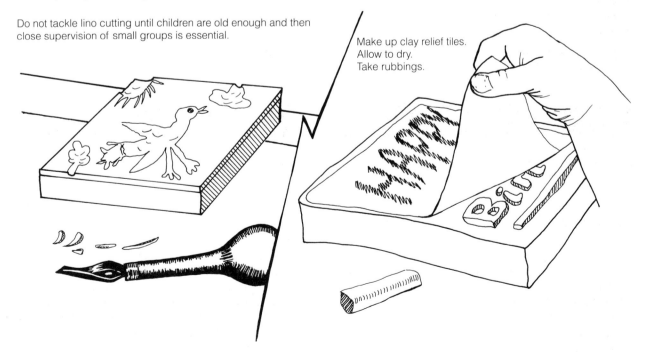

Rubbing a clay tablet and making up a printing block

- Discuss them and record why certain printed images are more popular than others.
- Look at books that contain early forms of print-making such as the animal woodblock prints of Thomas Bewick.
- Discuss samples of reproductions of William Morris's wallpaper and fabric patterns (use **Copymasters 72–5**). Ask whether the children like the wallpapers. Bring flowers into school. Can your children use them as models to make up simple stencils with which to print on fabric?
- Using black felt tip pens can children make drawings like woodblock prints?
- Children can look at rubbings they have made and discuss which are successful and which are not
- Children can make simple patterns by inking up textured surfaces.
- Make card printing blocks based on observational drawings.
- Stories can be used as a starting point and different printing techniques can be used as illustrations.

Some local authorities have collections of reproductions and contemporary prints for teachers to borrow. The printmakers listed below include those whose work is likely to be available only as reproductions and other contemporary printmakers whose original work may be available.

Shape
Matisse specialised in cut shapes and decorative stencil work, many modern Japanese prints. Original blockprints by Anne Marie le Quesne, lithographs by Yvonne Cole and blockprints by T. Ota.

Colour
Matisse, Albers, Ay-O (contemporary Japanese) and screen process prints by Chris Plowman.

Pattern
Vasarely and Bridget Riley.

Texture
Picasso, Braque and original prints by Chris Plowman, birds and animals by Coutu and Koster and landscape etchings by Robin Tanner.

Space
Reproductions of work by Escher and originals by B. Ingham and Brunsden.

Line
Bridget Riley, Bewick.

Tone
Rembrandt, Moore.

ART HISTORY AND MODELLING

C98–100

Your children can compare the different ways that animals and plants have been modelled in different times and cultures. Sculptures and models of animals and human beings from ancient and primitive societies can mean a lot to young children. Prehistoric, Chinese, Japanese, Mayan and early Greek pieces have such a 'feel' to them that children's empathy with living creatures is stimulated.

Provide collections of illustrations of:

- Cycladic
- Chinese
- Japanese
- Aboriginal
- South American
- African sculptures and

include medieval carvings and work by Gaudier Breska, Elizabeth Frink and Henry Moore.

Copymaster 98 contains drawings of examples of animal sculptures from different cultures. Give each child a copy and ask them to identify the creatures by naming them and then making up their own versions of the animals with clay. In a similar way, you can discuss with your children toys, buildings and sculptures. Examine the materials, shapes and textures that they can see and feel. Try to encourage a move from simple likes and dislikes to a position where your children can

explain, even if only simply, why they like or dislike particular sculptures or buildings. Get your children to draw their favourite sculptures and record the reasons for liking the piece.

Crucial to the linking of understanding and knowledge to the practical activities of sculpture and modelling is the handling and discussing of natural and made materials and objects, and the representation of things particularly in clay, card and scrap materials. The use of tools and materials will enhance the process of making models of things, places and personal memories of favourite pets or imaginative places.

The formal elements of sculpture to consider are shape, colour, space, form and texture. There are great opportunities for infants to see how simple shapes and forms such as pyramids, cubes and cylinders have been used since ancient times. Your children can use the same shapes and forms to make all kinds of models and sculptures. In doing so, they will understand and recognise these basic elements and extend their knowledge of how to use the best shapes for a particular job. They will be involved in the processes of sculpting, carving, folding, scoring, joining and gluing. Use **Copymasters 99** and **100** which contain nets for simple solids and which can be used for building more complex forms and models.

Examples of primitive sculptures

ART HISTORY AND TEXTILES

The earliest form of textile is supposed to be basket work made from coiled grasses. Baskets were essential as a convenient way to collect and store food. All kinds of materials, roots, bark, reeds, vines and leaves have been used in basket making for strength, pliability and colour. Changing these natural materials through sorting, drying and stripping off bark were important elements in a long process. Illustrations of domestic scenes of life in Egypt, Colombia, Greece, Rome and medieval England offer opportunities to discuss the problems of storing food and the pleasurable, rhythmic activity of basket making. You may be able to collect your own range of baskets or perhaps be lucky enough to have a basket maker come to your school to demonstrate their skill. Basket making is closely akin to making corn-dollies and these activities are particularly suited to harvest time.

Another route to explore the links between art history and textiles is through the history of costumes. Role-play and drama activities based on historical periods can be linked to simple practical activities such as weaving, using finger spindles and dyeing fabrics. Specific activities can include:

- Make up simple dolls (either historical or multi-cultural)
- Collect, sort and compare illustrations of various clothes
- Use **Copymaster 44** to colour and identify the country of origin of the costumes
- Look at different types of hats. For example those used to keep away the plague, hard hats for protection, baseball, space helmets
- Make up jewellery based on cowry shells. Use illustrations of Cretan, Minoan and Egyptian and jewellery which was often based on animals and insects and Bronze Age jewellery
- Make Greek chitons in either wool or linen. (Use old pillow cases with openings for head and arms) dye these and use a piece of old sheet as a cloak. Look at the illustrations on Greek ceramics and sculptures).

ART HISTORY AND CERAMICS

Most local museums have good collections of different kinds of ceramics including medieval tiles, clay pipes, pitcher jars and contemporary craft pottery. You may be lucky to find that your library or museum service has collections of contemporary ceramics available for loan. Try to avoid showing only samples of the craft pottery (such as work from the Leach family). To do so would present a very limited and a rather precious impression of what domestic pottery is all about. Do not ignore the early English tradition. Medieval English pottery tends to be rather crude, fun and well coloured. There are plenty of fun ceramics that you may be able to get hold of such as: knitted teapots, slip ware by Sasha Wardell, agate ware, colourful sculpted pottery, raku pots, urns and lustre ware. If you find it difficult to borrow examples locally, it may be worthwhile contacting the Crafts Council for help.

Use books, posters and other illustrations of the wonderful range of early ceramics including the highly coloured dolphin Cretan pieces (**Copymaster 101** contains a design from an ancient Greek platter). Do not ignore early Chinese and Japanese ceramics which contain an exciting range of colours, designs and patterns as a stimulus to your children's own work.

GLOSSARY OF TERMS ▶

Abstract art
Aesthetic appreciation of formal aspects such as line and colour rather than representational quality of work. Not a modern concept, examples are found throughout art history.

Action painting
Form of abstract expressionism often associated with Jackson Pollock. Similar to drip painting techniques used by infants.

Aegean art
25th–12th centuries BC Greece mainland and islands. Try to get images of Cycladic sculptures as these are very elegant and simple in form and interesting to infants.

Arts and crafts movement
Movement in England, starting approximately 1865. Ruskin and William Morris were central to this reaction against the growing industrialisation of crafts. They wished to make a return to more individual craftwork of high quality and reasonable prices.

Black-figured pottery
Like the red-figured pottery, this is ancient Greek. Featuring either black or red decorations on red or black backgrounds. This can be a good point of departure for infants when designing their own pots

Book of hours
Richly illuminated books of prayers. Excellent for linking with decorative alphabets and handwriting patterns.

Cruciform
Cross-shaped, as in the floor layout of churches. Use the shape drawn on a baseboard as a starting point for models of churches.

Dyes
Soluble colours used for colouring fabrics.

Earth colours
Paints made from earths such as red oxide, early forms of colours that can be made up using pestle and mortar in class.

Expressionism
Best known exponent is Van Gogh, his work stresses the intensity of feelings that are shown through a personal use of colour, shape and textures. Other artists include: Kokoschka, Munch, Rouault and Soutine. Introducing painting activities for infants by discussing particular feelings such as anger, fear, happiness can be very effective.

Fast colours
Colours that do not fade. You can easily set up some simple experiments by selecting a number of colours, painting them on sheets of paper and covering half of each sample and then placing all the samples in strong sunshine for a few weeks. Afterwards uncover the protected parts of the samples and compare with the unprotected elements.

Fauves
Group of expressionist artists including Matisse, Derain, Dufy, Marquet and Rouault, active from early 20th century.

Fresco
Mural painted directly onto fresh lime plaster. As children approach Key Stage 2 they can try painting onto small plaster animals with watered down PVA paints, building up colours slowly by overpainting.

Geometric patterns
Hellenic art (C870–700 BC) and Islamic art are full of rich decorative geometric patterns. Use the copymasters to build appreciation of tessellation and making abstract designs.

Greek art
Hellenic art

Greek pottery
Vital for understanding life in ancient Greece and for appreciating fine shapes and design.

Icons
Painted orthodox religious images usually on wood panels.

Illumination
The art of decorating manuscripts, often with large decorated leading letters of text. Try to introduce decorative alphabets in class or individual books.

Impressionism
Form of art that paid special attention to using pure colours to paint images (often painted outdoors) that celebrated light and atmosphere, Monet, Renoir, Pissaro, Sisley and Degas. Many of these were impressed by the work of Constable and Turner.

Objective art
Art that is the antithesis of abstract art, it includes cave paintings and all works that rely on representing subjects.

Op art
1960s art that uses patterns and colours to produce optical effects, Vasarely and Bridgit Riley are the main exponents.

Pattern
For infants it means either a plan for a painting or model, or the motif from which a repeated image can be made by painting, printing or rubbing.

Pigment
Fine colour powder without any extender, binder or medium. Usually defined by association with the source, such as earth colours. You can try to mix small quantities of real pigment with different binders such as egg white, linseed oil, PVA or even hot wax.

Prehistoric art
Most notable are the cave paintings of Lascaux in France and those of Altimara in Spain. The extreme magical importance of this art, to control elements of nature, can be compared with the more simple observations of nature which make up much of art. This sort of idea can be touched upon with infants by discussing stories such as the Magic lamp and even TV cartoon series such as Captain Planet that rely on rings with magical powers.

Primitive art
The art of Africa and other groups of people from non-westernised cultures. Typical art objects are masks, carvings and other religious objects from metal, wood, clay or textiles.

Proportion
The relationship of parts to each other and to the whole. Infants can trace around each other, marking the size of heads, eyes, arms, then measure and compare to see, for example, how many heads make a body.

Realism
Realistic representation of people, animals and scenes without distortion.

Surrealism
Art that is linked to dreams and the subconscious mind.

CERAMICS

WORKING WITH CLAY ▶

The basic skills in this section are general to many activities using clay but they are related directly to making, drying and decorating functional ceramic items such as pots and tiles. Information includes guidance on how to store and use clay, how to manage what could otherwise be a messy area of activities, simple making, decorating, colouring and finishing methods. Imaginative activities are not included here as you will find plenty in the topics, simple rules for 'how to do' are included. These technical activities can, of course, be used in a wide range of making tasks. They are supplemented by further information in the Modelling skill section.

MATERIALS AND EQUIPMENT ▶

You need
Plastic clay either, buff or red. This can be purchased. If you can get local clay so much the better. You may even be able to dig clay yourself, but remember that clay needs to be weathered and tested before it can be used. (See Bernard Leach, *The Potters Book*, for details on this). You will also need buckets for glazes, bowls, jugs, sponges, modelling tools, sieves and sieving brushes, brushes, canvas for making slabs on, damp cloths for covering partly finished work, wood for the frames, scrap materials with which work may be imprinted, glue. Plastic bins or polythene bags for storing clay and partly completed work, blunt knives and glazes and slips, wooden rolling pins (no handles) scrapers for leather hard clay. Old toothbrushes are excellent for scoring surfaces that are to be joined together.

Storage and the condition of clay
Clay needs to be stored in a cool, damp, frost-free place. It can be stored in a plastic dustbin and polythene bags. The best way to do this is to mix up enough plaster of Paris to form a 4 cm covering of the bottom of the bin, allow the plaster to set. Once set, put a couple of pieces of battening underneath a wooden base (see diagram) in the bottom of the bin. This will allow you to keep the atmosphere damp by pouring water over the plaster and storing the clay on the wooden plinth. Work that is underway may need to be covered with damp cloths while being stored. Clay must be in good condition before it can be worked. For general use it needs to feel plastic and of even texture. To check it roll out a thin

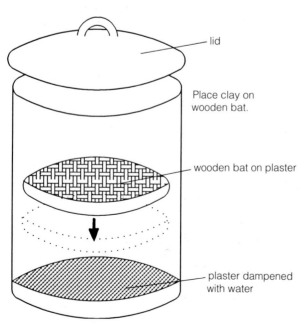

lid

Place clay on wooden bat.

wooden bat on plaster

plaster dampened with water

Plastic bin for storage

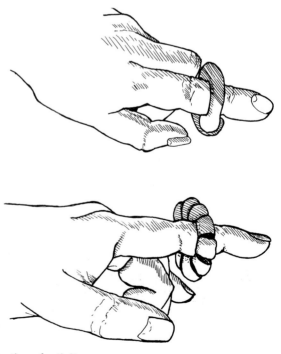

Testing plasticity

rope or coil, wrap this around a finger, if the surface is smooth it is ready to use, if the surface is cracked then the clay is 'short' and needs to be left for a while to settle. To check whether the clay is free from air bubbles use a wire and cut through; if there are air bubbles you will need to wedge and knead it until it is free from bubbles.

Managing claywork

Clay has the advantage of being cheap, versatile and great fun. Some teachers believe that it is inherently messy. It does not need to be any more messy than paint. Proper preparation and storage are of course vital. Ideally you need a small separate room or corner where water can be easily used and cleared up. The floor covering should be vinyl tiles. Do not work near carpeted areas. You will need stout work tables covered with hessian, canvas or cotton duck, or wooden boards on newsprint. Do not allow your children to work on plastic surfaces as these tend to produce a lot of flaked and dusty clay. Remember that silica, present in clay and glazes, is a health hazard. The over-riding health aim is to work in a dust free environment. Ceramics should not be worked with abrasives or brushed when thoroughly dried or fired, work when leather-hard. Take note of the technical information that accompanies products. Use damp cloths to wipe up dry clay or glazes. To complete clay processes access to a kiln is vital. When using plaster do not pour away excess down the drain! Use a tube in the waste hole to stop rubbish going down the drain. Fix it so that clean water runs away down the tube.

Activity 203: Thumb or pinch pots

Pinching is the most basic of all clay processes. Give each child a lump of clay about the size of a small orange. Get them to hollow out the ball with their thumbs until, with regular pressure of the fingers, they produce a thick pot or bowl about 7 cms wide. Now they can continue to work the pot from the centre of the base, gradually squeezing the walls until they are thinner. To keep the pots in good condition to work upon later, invert them so that the rims are rested on damp cloths. Making thumb pots can be a boring activity; similar skills will be developed if you ask your children to make a hollow cave in which some small animals can live.

Activity 204: Making a coiled pot

Coiling is merely a convenient way to build up walls, the coils are rarely left as coils. Get the children to knead a couple of handfuls of clay, form into a ball and roll it out on a flat surface to form a stumpy cylinder. Cut a piece and roll that out with both hands into a long cylinder about 1 cm diameter, care needs to be taken to make the 'ropes' or coils of clay smooth and without ridges. Make several coils of clay. Now coil up one roll to form a circular base of a pot about 10 cms diameter, get the children to flatten and smooth the coils to make a solid mass. Take another rope of clay and coil it around the edge of the base, round and up, each ring being pressed firmly on the one below to press out air cavities which might otherwise blow out in firing. Level off the top and use finger tips to smooth the inside and outside of the pot. The pot can be decorated by means of incised lines, coloured slip, glaze, or, if the pot is not going to be fired, ordinary water based paints can be used on the dry pot.

Activity 205: Making: slabs and tiles

Use square or rectangular frames made from 2 cm square wood. Restrict the size to a maximum of 10 cms square. This simple mould needs to be fairly strong so gluing and pinning are recommended. Place the frame on a board and oil or talc the inside of the frame. Place a piece of clay about the size of a tennis ball inside the frame and thump it until it has spread out then roll it to fill the frame to an even depth of about 2 cm. The surface can be built up or cut into to produce a

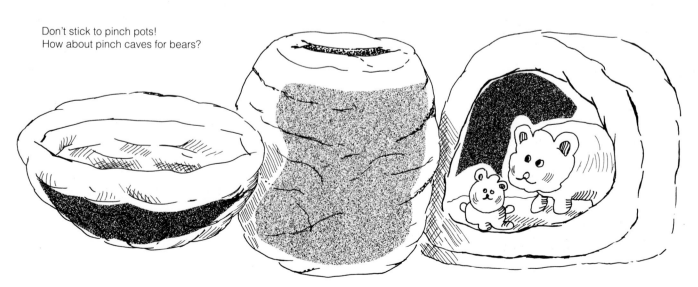

Don't stick to pinch pots!
How about pinch caves for bears?

Thumb pots or caves and animals made by pinching

89

The right way to join coils

bat of clay with
edges turned up
to receive first
coil of clay

The wrong way to join coils

straight walls to desired height

Do not place coils directly
above each other as the
walls will be weak.

the first coil flattened with
second coil applied

Coiled work, the right and wrong way to join coils, fixing to pinched base

patterned design or a picture for wall mounting (remember to poke a hole through for wall mounting). As a variation on this approach your children can build a relief picture to fit inside the frame and then press the clay over this to produce an imprinted tile. Tiles that have a relief design or pattern can, when dry, be used as a base for simple repoussé work. The tiles can be coloured by using slip or glazes and fired. Remove from mould and fire. Remember to slip before and glaze after biscuit firing.

Activity 206: Using slabs

Square or rectangular shapes can be built up by using flat slabs of clay about 1 cm thick. The slabs are easily and quickly made between two pieces of wood (lathes) 1 cm thick about 15 cms apart on a piece of canvas. Beat

or roll the clay in the hollow filling it completely, then use a rolling pin to flatten the top surface (lift the clay occasionally to release it for further rolling). When the clay is about 1 cm thick it is ready for use. You may wish to nail the lathes in place. Alternatively cut slabs with taut wire pressed flat on lathes.

Young children may only be able to make up simple low sided pots or sculptures from the cut up slabs. To cut the slabs it is best to transfer the shapes of the sides to the clay while still in the former, or on the canvas. Draw the five elements of a small open container as a net (remember the thickness of the clay in calculating the sides). Transfer the outline of this simple net on to the clay. Mark the surface with a tool to mark the outlines. Then cut almost all the way through the clay to the board. A blunt butter knife is suitable for this. Let the slab dry out a little to toughen up. To assemble the parts, roughen the edges to be joined and prepare a thin rope of clay. Apply a thick slip to the edges to be fixed. Hold one side against the base and work a piece of the clay rope firmly into the angle between the two parts. Press the edges well together, complete the other sides in the same way. This technique can be used for all kinds of slab work; making imaginary buildings, sculptures and decorated boxes.

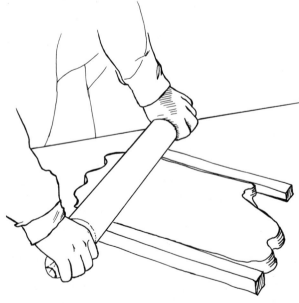

Making tiles by rolling

Roll clay out on to hessian.

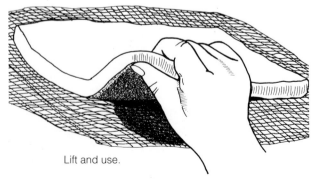

Lift and use.

Rolling clay and making tiles

90

Joining slabs

Activity 207: Texturing surfaces

Discuss how textures can affect the look of ceramics. Make an interesting display of visual textures and crayon rubbings from surfaces. Now you can show how clay can be used to 'take rubbings'. Roll out thick slabs of clay (or use damp slab pots), press, scratch and mark the surface all over, or press ready-textured objects into the clay. Beads, bark, hands, baskets or rough fabrics will make good impressions. Small samples of each textured surface can be cut and glazed to make pendants or a library of textures with notes about how and when they were made. Get your children to discuss how they have made their textures.

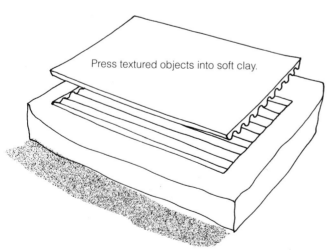

Press textured objects into soft clay.

Pressing clay

Activity 208: Drying work prior to firing

All ceramics should be dried carefully and slowly before they are fired. Do not try to hurry the process. A cupboard over a radiator is useful or a longish period in a warm room. The stage when clay can still be trimmed

and finished is called leather-hard. This means that the clay has dried and shrunk but still retains its original wet colour. If your children keep poking their work around while it is drying breakages will occur. Often it is quicker to make repairs after firing. Clay that has been dried is called greenware. Inspect the work before firing. Is it thoroughly dry? (If not it may explode!) Hollow forms need to have a hole pierced in them to allow the escape of hot air. Remember to pull a wire under pots to stop sticking.

Activity 209: Firing, loading the kiln

Firing is a very exciting time. After a piece of claywork has been thoroughly dried, it is fired at 1,000°C. This is called biscuit firing. Besides making the piece hard and resilient it also shrinks it by about 8 per cent. Pack the kiln carefully with a full load. 1080°C is the temperature for earthenware glaze firing. Make yourself familiar with kiln features and operations before firing your children's work.

Loading a kiln

Activity 210: Slip decorating and glazing

Work that is not going to be fired can be coloured by using water-based paints and then varnished if required. Coloured slips can be painted on to leather-hard clay. Glazing is a coating of glass applied to porous ceramics that is in the 'biscuit' state. Then it is fired again until it fuses into the surface. Glazing is by far the most exciting time, but it may also be the most disappointing. To carry out good glazing your children must have an idea of the finished colours so carry out test firings on a small piece of fired clay beforehand. The glazes need to be creamy for ease of painting. When firing you should raise the temperature of the kiln quite slowly and after firing cool it down slowly to avoid cracking the glaze.

GLOSSARY OF TERMS

Bat
A plaster, wood, or fireclay slab on which pottery is formed and dried. Fireclay bats may be placed in a kiln, plaster bats help absorb excess water.

Biscuit
Fired but not glazed ceramics, also called 'bisque'.

Bisque fire
The first firing, before glaze but after slip.

Body stain
Colour mixed into the body of the clay, i.e. not a slip covering or glaze. Can be used to make slips.

Brushwork
Fluid and calligraphic painted patterns can be very attractive. You could extend the work of handwriting patterns to decorating ceramics with considered abstract shapes.

Ceramic colours
Powdered metallic oxides used for glazes, and slips pale when unglazed, full colour after firing.

Clay
Available in a number of colours, called plastic when ready to use. (Some are better suited to different temperatures.)

Coiling
Method of forming pottery and forms by building up a series of 'ropes' of clay. Smoothed and finished by hand.

Combed decoration
Different coloured slips are applied in bands and then feathered to produce an attractive finish.

Earthenware
Opaque ceramics fired at about 1 100°C.

Firing
Process of exposing work to intense heat usually in a kiln. The heat permanently changes the chemical composition and physical nature of the fired substance be it clay or glaze.

Glaze
A thin coating that is fused to ceramics by firing in kiln. It is applied by dipping, spraying or painting. The most common glaze is a transparent one. Take care when making up glaze as it can be a health hazard. Add powder to a small quantity of water. Then add more water if necessary. Stir and sieve with 120 mesh sieve. Pottery is glazed ware.

Glost firing
The second firing, done to vitrify the glaze to biscuit ware. Biscuitware needs to be porous enough to absorb glaze.

Greenware
Ceramics that have been formed, allowed to dry but not been fired.

Hardening on
Process in which ceramics are heated to 320°C to burn off organic materials present in underglaze decorations. It is used to prevent blistering.

Kiln
A furnace for firing ceramics. Heat inside is measured by pyrometric cones observed through a peephole.

Kneading
After storage, wedged clay requires kneading prior to use, it makes it more pliable and of consistent texture.

Leather hard
Clay that has dried to the limit of shrinkage while still retaining its wet colouring, can be trimmed and finished in this state.

Lustreware
Ceramics decorated with metallic iridescent glazes.

Mould
Hollow container that is used in casting. The shape of the mould is given to clay or plaster.

Pinched
Method of shaping clay by pinching walls or parts with fingers.

Plastic
Pliable clay

Press
Method of texturing surface of clay by pressing objects into the plastic surface of the clay. Clay pressed into mould.

Pyrometric cones
Clay cones used to determine the temperature of a kiln that does not have a temperature gauge (pyrometer which operates above the range of mercury thermometers).

Scratch and sgraffito
Originally used by Italian potters in the 16th century. A coloured body was dipped or painted with white slip, allowed to firm and then engraved through the slip to reveal the design on the coloured base.

Settle
Maturing of clay as it becomes plastic, takes two–eight weeks.

Slab method
Method of making pots or sculptures. Rolled and cut slabs of clay may be bent into various shapes and joined to other slabs by slip or 'ropes' of clay pressed home into joints.

Slip and slip decoration
Creamy liquid mix of clay and water, coloured and used for decorative finish. Slips have a tendency to settle and often form lumps. Shake and sieve slips before use. If a piece is dipped in slip the resulting surface is delightful to work on, being smooth and silky. Then fire.

Slip casting
Slip poured into a mould made from absorbent plaster and rolled around to cover the whole surface will rapidly dry out. Pour out any excess then, when dry, add further coats of slip to thicken the wall. The slip cast will shrink away from the mould when dry and produce a perfect smooth cast. (Special casting slip is needed.)

Stencil
Paper stencils can be pressed against the dry clay surface and colour brushed or dabbed over them. Positive (or negative) paper patterns can be stuck to a damp surface which is then dipped into slip, when dry the paper is removed. Leaves can be used for this. It is advised that stencils are kept simple.

Wedge
To thump clay on a solid base until all air and lumps are removed. Cut through with wire to check for air bubbles.

DESIGN

ART, DESIGN AND TECHNOLOGY

Design forms a part of both art and technology. It can be thought of as a planning or hypothesising stage; a 'how to' stage. Young children very often feel happiest when making things in a direct and uninfluenced way. Their practical work apparently has no design stage. In fact their constant manipulation of clay or paint often teaches through trial and error which is a vital design process. Occasionally working on design as a separate activity will help develop your children's ability to think ahead before committing resources and time to the task.

The National Curriculum suggests that paying careful attention to the work of others is vital to the development of design skills in infants. It is through bringing well designed pieces of craft work, posters or objects in to your school that you can help your children to pose the questions that will enhance their critical awareness and improve their own practical work.

The processes involved in design are:

- Planning
- Drawing
- Scaling
- Tracing
- Cutting
- Scoring
- Painting.

When your children are involved in design they may well also may be concerned with:

- Observing and studying existing products
- Surveys of likes and dislikes
- Criticism. Asking questions such as: Is this poster a success? Can you read it? Do the colours suit the subject?
- Identifying needs or problems
- Imagining solutions to problems
- Finding resources
- Checking the suitability of materials
- Choosing materials and tools

- Drawing
- Scaling
- Visualising
- Thinking in 3D, moving from 2D to 3D
- Making
- Thinking about structures
- Making economical use of materials and time
- Changing qualities of materials through manipulation and processes
- Graphic design and packaging
- Testing and evaluation.

These may seem a little high flown for infants but you will find that almost all appear in the activities outlined later in this section.

Before you start
The activities given below should be introduced in such a way as to ensure that your children do things that have value and purpose. Do not involve them in pointless or staged design activities. Relate designs closely to the materials that are available for making the products. Wherever possible insist that your children select the materials they will use in advance and specify approximately sizes and colours for the finished work.

Besides the activities given below you may find these additional design suggestions useful.

- A moving teddy bear
- A junk robot with flashing lights
- A treasure chest
- A vehicle to cross a variety of surfaces
- A frog that jumps
- A peep hole environment
- Shadow puppets
- A buggy with wobbly wheels
- A box for Mrs Wobble's hamburger
- A protective package
- A special envelope
- A pair of shoes from cardboard.

MATERIALS AND EQUIPMENT

Paints, pencils, rulers, paper, squared and other gridded papers and card (copymasters include a number of different grids suitable for infants' work), rubbers, brushes, palettes and mixing trays, felt tip pens, scissors, illustrations.

Activity 211: Design and make a candlestick
Collect a range of illustrations and examples of old fashioned or multi-cultural lighting devices. Each child is to design and make a stable, decorated clay candlestick. Initially, give each child a piece of paper, rule,

pencils and source materials including candles and books. Choose a candle for the candlestick, measure it and draw it in profile onto the paper. Consider the height of the candle and how well it will need to be supported and the size of the hole (diameter and depth). Examine existing candlesticks. Can clay be used the same way as metal? What shape should the base be? What sort of decoration can be made? How much clay will be needed? How will it be made? Once the designs have been completed provide sufficient clay for each child and using rolling, cutting, fixing processes make up the candlestick. Make the size, candle hole and decoration as close to the design as possible. Dry, fire and glaze then test with candles.

Activity 212: Design and make a repeat pattern for a frieze

Look at the way simple motifs are used in wallpaper, printed fabrics and friezes. Some motifs will be abstract while others will be based on natural and made forms. Discuss with your children whether they will make an abstract design made up of simple shapes such as circles, stripes, squares and rectangles or one based on flowers, animals or perhaps a clown. Whatever they choose, the designs will have to be simple silhouettes. Give each child a piece of paper about A5 size, make their silhouette design for their motifs on the paper using a felt tip pen. Now give each child two strips of contrasting coloured paper, for example blue and orange. Choose one of the coloured strips and cut to form three A5 pieces. Hold them together and place the motif design on top. Hold the sandwich together with some paper clips and cut out using scissors. (You may need to help them with this.) When complete, arrange and glue down on to the other strip of coloured paper.

Activity 213: Design and make a stuffed fabric frog

Get your children to bring some soft toys into school. Compare them. Discuss which ones are preferred and

why. Set the task of designing and making a stuffed felt frog for themselves or a younger brother or sister. Give each child two pieces of felt about 25 cms square and a piece of paper the same size. Have available large-eyed needles, embroidery cottons, stuffing, buttons, sequins, scissors, chalk and pencils. First get your children to design the frog's shape on the paper. Take care to include feet and an identifiable head and mark rough positions for the eyes. Pin the complete drawing to a sandwich of both pieces of felt, cut out around the outline of the frog. Fix eyes (buttons) and make other decorations to the top piece of felt before joining together the two pieces. Using a suitable colour of cotton and with blanket stitch get your children to complete 75 per cent of the work necessary to join both pieces of felt together. Stuff and complete sewing.

Activity 214: Design and make a card for a special occasion

This suggested activity from the National Curriculum document is framed in such a way that it relies on children collecting and criticising various greeting cards as a starting point. Arrange a collection of cards to be put on display and make a simple class survey. Include questions about the fitness for purpose, aesthetic qualities, colour, graphic imagery of the cards. Get your children to measure the cards. Are they regular sizes? If so, why? Discuss with your children their favourite times of the year, birthdays, Christmas, Diwali, Easter, and Ramadan for example. Set the task of designing and making a card for their favourite time or event and for a specific person. Discuss the materials that are available for the task. What size their cards will be when finished? Will they need to be folded, scored, and trimmed?

Activity 215: Design and make a group wallhanging or collage

Whatever subject is chosen (a jungle or birthday party) there will be a number of common considerations. What

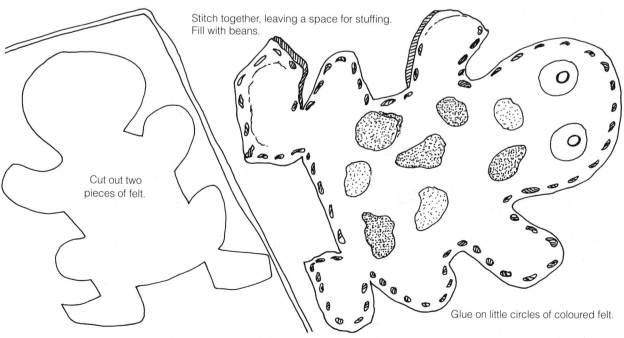

Stitch together, leaving a space for stuffing. Fill with beans.

Cut out two pieces of felt.

Glue on little circles of coloured felt.

Frog design

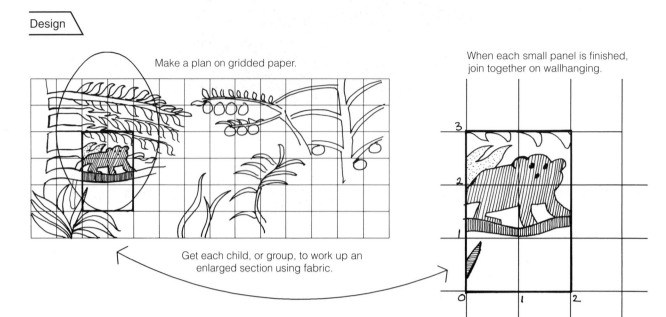

Make a plan on gridded paper.

When each small panel is finished, join together on wallhanging.

Get each child, or group, to work up an enlarged section using fabric.

Scaling up a wallhanging

size will the finished piece be? What sort of plan will be needed? Will each child make one section? How will all the elements be fixed together? How will it be possible to ensure that colour is used consistently throughout the design?

As children approach Key Stage 2 you can introduce ways of using grids for planning and scaling up. Use **Copymasters 17** and **18** to demonstrate how an image can be enlarged accurately to a larger scale. Draw a cube or simple cartoon character on the smaller scale grid and then using the larger one plot the same figure but now twice as big.

If, for example, the finished design is to be about 3 m long by 1 m wide then you should select a scale on one of the gridded sheets and draw a rectangle that is 3 × 1 (it may, of course, be 30 cms × 10 cms). Discuss the elements that your class want to include in the hanging and work with them to plan and sketch an outline drawing of the whole design. If you have 30 children in your class you can get them to divide up this design into 30 equal rectangular sections. Each child's finished piece of work for the design measuring 50 cms × 20 cms. (Initially your children can plan out their part of the design on a piece of grid paper measuring 10 cms × 4 cms). When all the elements are complete they can be brought together according to the original plan and be fixed ready for display.

Activity 216: Design and make a poster on railway safety
If possible arrange for a railway worker to visit your school and talk about the dangers of playing near railway lines. Perhaps he or she can also bring along posters to point out the message. Look at some posters and talk about what is important. For example impact, simplicity, keeping text to a minimum, colour (or silhouettes of contrasting tones). Also consider what will be important for this particular poster, speed? machinery? wheels? signals? What kind of shapes would be good? What about lines? Make a list of key features and get your pupils to sketch them out, using relevant source material. When they are familiar with the things they will use for their poster give them pieces of paper, pencils, scissors, paint, mixing trays, glue and rulers. Do not forget that posters can be made by combining cut-out shapes (including lettering) of coloured paper glued onto a contrasting background. This approach can be more effective than using paint.

Activity 217: Design and make a model rocket ship
You will need a collection of well organised junk materials so that your children can work on a large scale. Give them a limited choice of materials to use, get them to list which items they will use and then design a model rocket ship to be produced only from those materials. Get them to make up their designs using glues and paints to finish their work.

GLOSSARY OF TERMS

Colour scheme
The use of dominant colours in a carefully orchestrated whole to give an overall unified impression.

Dry mounting
Method of mounting work by sandwiching a dry laminate between the work and mount and then heating it to melt the laminate and fixing the work in place.

Mat cutting (mounting)
Cutting window mounts for improved display of work.

Portfolio
Large folder for keeping work in good condition.

Template
Useful pattern device for repeating standard motifs or shapes, like a stencil.

DRAWING

Drawing is the vital element underpinning all other practical Art activities. For many primary teachers it is important to grasp what drawing is. For the purposes of this book, drawing is copying something on to paper or another surface, with a pencil, chalk, pen or brush using elements such as marks, dots, lines and shapes. The 'something' is a subject, either from observation (nature), memory, the imagination or feelings.

Drawing with infants

At the beginning of Key Stage 1 children will be at various levels of achievement in drawing. Some will be scribbling while others may have progressed to well-developed schematic drawings with which they represent and analyse their worlds. The development of these schematic drawings (which use a range of symbols to represent different things) dominate these years. Children should be encouraged to look closely before making observational drawings. Typical of work at Key Stage 1 is the direct use of a variety of materials and a gradual change from play to structured exercises.

For infant children drawing has a swiftly evolving function. Between the ages of four and seven, children start by using symbols to communicate impressions about what they have seen, imagined or remembered. At this stage they should be introduced to drawing descriptively from familiar objects together with their making of story-telling drawings. Children draw naturally in a vibrant and unconscious way, remaking the world for themselves through drawing from nature, imagination, fantasy and memory. As children grow the function of drawing extends to:

- drawing from natural and made objects (use questions to encourage careful observation)
- close observation of animals
- drawing themselves, family and pets
- characters in stories (often made up by the children)
- their feelings
- information and diagrams
- cartoons, sequences of drawings to tell a story
- playing with drawing materials, making many different types of marks, using shapes and using found objects with which to draw.

Drawing is not merely a matter of method, it depends on vision, imagination and understanding. You should provide plenty of opportunities for young children to work spontaneously. Such freedom, does not, however, negate the need for teaching skills. Freedom is governed by skills and control. Even children aged five can benefit from taking a directed look at the world around them. Indeed they can gain a tremendous sense of achievement in producing drawings that are 'better than they

Symbols and drawings

97

expect'. Of course, it is important not to push young children too far and you need to restrict to some extent the materials that they use. Offer a greater variety as children grow.

Until age six or seven children's drawings do not obviously refer to adult or traditional forms of visual representation. Space, marks, scale, movement and time are often successfully mixed in one drawing. This mixture is the quality that gives young children's drawings such vitality. As children grow this happy imagination can be lost as they develop the ability to use more formal ways of visual communication. They try to make their drawings look like the 'real world'. At the same time their literacy skills are becoming more powerful and the crucial, irrepressible need to draw as a way of direct communication loses its importance. Imagination need not die. If you try to build skills whilst

giving the freedom to experiment and the confidence to value their own efforts for their own sake you may form a happy marriage of technical skill and imagination.

This part of the book gives clear instruction in the technique of drawing. It also points to opportunities for the various purposes of drawing that include the personal expressive needs of each individual, the use of drawing as a preliminary to other activities or for explaining the world as seen through the eyes of children. Please ensure that your children are given opportunities for drawing without the constraints of these exercises. The sequence of activities is a progressive framework that will form a sound basis for effective and original work. The elements of this growth include, dots, marks, lines, open and closed shapes, tone, textures, structure and colour.

MATERIALS AND EQUIPMENT

C8, 17, 18, 26
43, 77, 83–5

Brushes, cartridge paper, chalk, charcoal, coloured pencils, crayons (wax), Conté crayons®, erasers, felt tip pens and markers, paint, pastels, pastel paper, pens, pencils, rulers, tracing paper.

Before you start
The exercises in this section are intended to help your children see and understand relationships between parts and the whole. They cover the basic building blocks and you should get your children to use thinking, seeing, observing, touching and handling as ways of feeding their drawings. Introduce the idea that it is good to think about what is going to be drawn before picking up a brush, pencil or felt tip pen. Your children will work with dots, lines, (enclosing lines) shapes. For very young children these exercises encourage a grasp of flat shapes and a facility to make expressive marks and lines. Later on solid shapes or forms composed of length, breadth and thickness can be introduced. Draw attention to 'thinking, seeing and drawing'. Include these words in your display.

The more that children think and observe the better their control will be. Taking such an approach will help drawing develop as a natural activity that grows as experience and skills are extended.

Activity 218: Drawing flat shapes
Get the children to do simple drawings of comparatively flat objects such as leaves. Try to find the centre of the leaf, then use dots or points to map the important features, working from the centre towards the circumference, indicating the important internal and external boundaries. Once the outline is dotted use lines (light ones to start with), to more clearly define the enclosed shapes. Do not try to make the drawing appear solid, resist the temptation to smudge shadows, keep the drawing clean and linear.

When introducing this drawing from nature activity it is a good idea to talk about the way the leaf has grown

from its stem through its veins to the tip. This will help children to empathise and to produce drawings that are in tune with the feeling of natural growth. There are good links here for movement and dance.

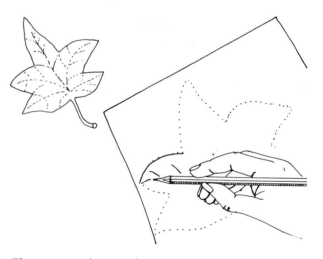

The centre and circumference

Activity 219: Finger, wrist and arm strokes
Holding pencils or other drawing materials can be exactly the same as writing. Making drawings of small details or careful shading can best be achieved by using finger strokes. For more sweeping and bolder lines other types of movement are preferred.

Get the children to use wrist strokes. These allow supple, large scale, fluid lines or curves to be drawn. Exercises that encourage free movement of the wrist are illustrated. Get the children to try loose free lines away and towards their bodies.

Place some large sheets of newsprint on to a table. Young children find it easier to work on a flat horizontal surface than an easel. Use full arm strokes with crayons, pastels, large marker pens or brush and paint.

Finger strokes

Activity 220: Thick, thin, curved and straight lines

Using a piece of paper (approximately A3) make as many types of lines as possible. Vary the size, thickness and direction of the lines, using finger strokes, wrist and arm strokes. Do not allow the sheet to become a mess. Pay some attention to the relationships between the lines and the shape and size of the paper.

Activity 221: Handwriting patterns

An excellent way to encourage fluid yet controlled drawing is to use a bridge between handwriting and pattern work as developed many years ago by Marion Richardson. The 'life' in the lines of handwriting can be developed and used as part of a lively drawing style as children grow. The simple curves used to draw leaves should be no more difficult to produce than the natural graceful lines of children's letters. Pick any letter (J is a good one to start with) and ask your children to start

Encourage fluid strokes.
Fill shapes with colour.

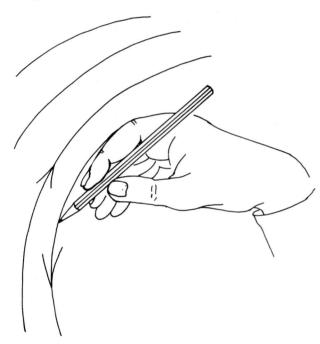

Wrist strokes

Handwriting patterns

Full arm strokes

99

with normal sized capital letters and gradually increase the size until the letters are 10–15 cms high. For the larger letters use charcoal. Your children will discover that they can draw large, sweeping graceful curves with loops and down strokes. Ask them to produce a pattern of linked letters across a sheet of newsprint. This exercise can be extended, with advantage, to include almost every letter of the alphabet. These exercises will help to develop manual dexterity. For older children the exercises can involve the use of pens and brushes as well.

The shapes formed by the pattern of 'open and closed areas', can then be coloured in using pencils. As different shaped letters may lend themselves to certain colours rather than others young children can become selective in their use of colour. As children progress to Key Stage 2 calligraphy can extend their use of graceful and fluid lines.

Activity 222 : Using dots for tonal value

Show the children photographs of newspapers or images on television using a magnifying glass. They will

Dotty drawing

see that the size and number of black dots show how dark or light an object is. You can ask the children to extend their work on drawing leaves (Activity 218) by using dots to build a feeling of structure and to give an indication of light and dark. Limit the media to fine felt tip pens or pen and ink. Every dot should have its own careful shape, try to be careful with every mark that you put on your paper. (If you are undertaking the exercises yourself choose subjects that include round solid objects set with the light from one side).

Activity 223: Lines from natural and made forms

If the weather is good, this will make a good outdoor activity. Alternatively ask the children to collect a range of natural and made objects that contain a variety of lines. Ask the children to find and draw as many examples as possible of lines in natural and made forms. Find and draw examples of straight, twisted, curved, bent, hard and soft lines. Find examples and draw how lines grow and join together to form more complicated forms. Make two or three careful line drawings of leaves or objects in or around the school. Remember to ask the children to measure and map the key features working from the centre to the circumference. Use pencil first, using a soft rubber to correct mistakes. Later use a fine felt tip to finish the drawings. Do not shade the drawings.

Activity 224: More flat shapes

Get your children to search and make a list of natural and made objects that are circular, elliptical, triangular or square. Using outlines only get them to make a drawing that includes all the shapes listed, they can overlap or butt up against each other. The shapes in these designs can be coloured. An extension of this activity can be found by using **Copymasters 83–5**.

Measuring
At Key Stage 1 children are generally too young to measure and select in a standard artist's way. You can

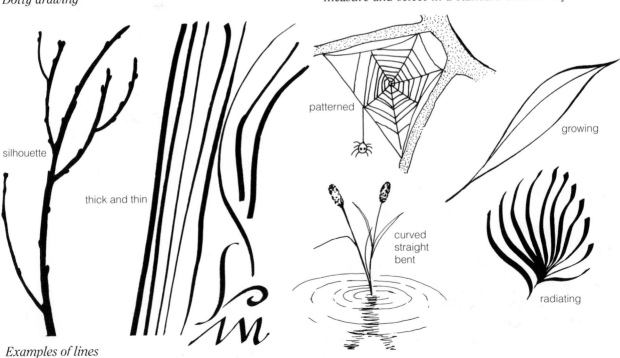

silhouette

thick and thin

patterned

growing

curved
straight
bent

radiating

Examples of lines

Abstract shapes from houses

help, however, to bring a greater facility in composing, selecting and judging relative elements by using simple rectangular viewfinders. Make a rectangular viewfinder from a piece of card. When cut out this can be used to make selections from illustrations and photographs.

Activity 225: Using a window or viewfinder
This is most suitable for children towards the end of Key Stage 1. Get the children to choose a medium size rectangular window for close-up work. For landscape or views out of the classroom window get them to cut out a larger rectangular shape. Explain to the children that in order to use a viewfinder effectively they need to try to keep their head in the same position, relative to the viewfinder. Also, make sure that the proportions of the viewfinder match the proportions of the drawing.

Activity 226: Identikit

Look at examples of police identikit pictures, illustrations of face shapes and individual features such as eyes and noses. With the children working in pairs, concentrate in turn on the shape of their partner's face; their eyes, ears, nose, mouth and hair. Each element is to be drawn on separate pieces of paper which are then cut and assembled with great attention to the right positions for each individual piece, colouring, and of course checking that the scale of the parts match each

other. When the portraits are finished they will make an interesting class display. Get the children to discuss what they have done and how they did it. The main point of the exercise is the enhancement of the analytical drawing skills.

Activity 227: Self portrait
Combining imaginative, recording and drawing from memory in one activity can be achieved by getting your class to make self portraits from touching their own faces. The textures, the lines and shapes require a variety of media including pencils, charcoal, pastels and perhaps felt tip pens. Other self portraits can be set working from spoons or mirrors. Make sure that the spoons are really reflective and you may find that using Mirriboard® is a safe option.

Activity 228: Continuous line drawings
A useful technique in developing childrens' spatial awareness is to set the task of working with a free-

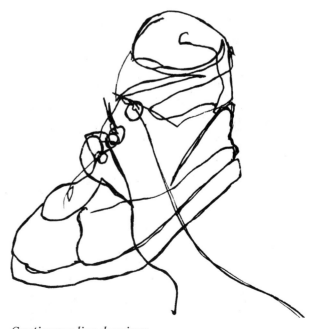

Continuous line drawings

flowing fine-tip felt pen in which they draw a picture of their friend without removing their pen from the paper nor looking at the paper while drawing. Children should concentrate on feeling their way across the paper as they map their friend's features. This contour drawing exercise is different to simple outline drawing in that outlines are merely flat silhouettes whereas contours (like contour maps) have a hint of three dimensions. This exercise should not be hurried. These drawings can be coloured.

Activity 229: Measuring body proportions

Use **Copymasters 8** and **43** to explain the approximate proportions of the human body in stages of maturity and get the children to check this against their own observations. Put large sheets of lining paper on the floor and trace the outlines of children and adults, measure the parts and compare them.

Activity 230: Drawing buildings

Talk about houses, homes and buildings. Discussion will help avoid the production of very standard stereotype images composed of rectangles with windows stuck in the corners. Ask questions and focus attention by looking at the work of Klee and others including Lowry. As children approach Key Stage 2 you can start to discuss ways of drawing solid forms using simple perspective. Nearby buildings or models of houses made from cardboard boxes can be viewed through a camera obscura and sketched onto tracing paper with felt tip pens. These drawings can be measured and comparisons made. You may wish to wait until Key Stage 2 to introduce perspective work, nevertheless buildings of all kinds can be an excellent stimulus for observational and imaginative work.

Activity 231: Scaling/distorting

The copymaster sheets include a variety of different grids. Such simple drawings as in the illustration can be scaled up by young children. Get them to do simple line drawings on a copy of **Copymaster 17** and enlarage it on **Copymaster 18**.

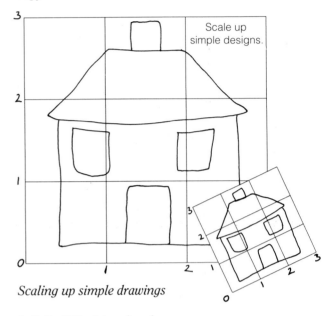

Scaling up simple drawings

Activity 232: A tonal scale

Give the children an HB pencil and a charcoal pencil. Using **Copymaster 102** get them to produce equivalent tonal values to the printed samples. You may need to use an atomiser to fix the charcoal drawings.

Activity 233: Using strong directional light

In the corner of a half-dark room set up a still-life and light it strongly from one side. Use simple forms such as a bowl of fruit and a packet of cornflakes. The light will lift the objects out of the common day into a dreamlike

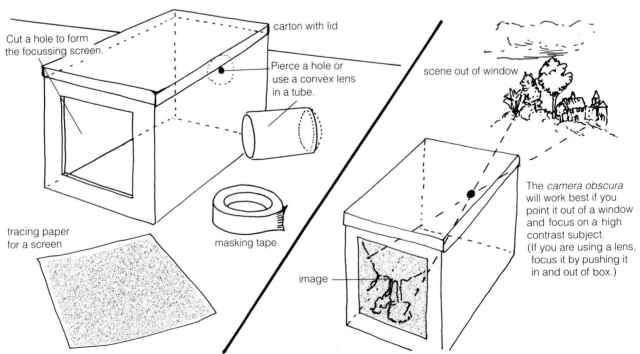

How to make and use a simple camera obscura

Lit from the side familiar objects become dramatic.

Highly lit tonal drawing

world of wonder and delight. Get the children to use pencil and charcoal pencil as they used for their tone scale to produce a drawing of the still-life.

Activity 234: Using shading techniques

Shading, varying the tonal value, can be achieved in a number of different ways. An obvious approach is to cover an area of paper with a continuous tone from pencils. Alternatively, using felt tip pens, pencils or pen and ink hatching or cross-hatching can build up tones by the proximity of individual lines to each other or the openness or filled in quality of a lattice of lines. Your children can also experiment with using pen and wash techniques. See the section on painting for applying a wash (page 115).

Activity 235: Textures

Give your children a range of different materials including different grades of pencil to express 'furriness', smoothness, detail and softness of a variety of toys. Use erasers and combine different materials together.

Activity 236: Different viewpoints

Take your children around the playground get them to look up, down, through and across familiar landmarks. Ask them to make three or four drawings from different viewpoints. Use **Copymaster 26** for this.

Activity 237: Magnifying minibeasts

Collect insects from the school grounds. Give the children magnifying glasses and get them to make detailed studies of the creatures. Encourage your children to make the drawings big. Use a variety of materials to suit the kind of insect. **Copymaster 77** can be used with this activity.

Activity 238: Traditional costumes

Make a display of traditional or multi-cultural costumes. Get your children to examine the fabrics, textures, shapes and colours of the costumes closely. Make detailed drawings using coloured pencils.

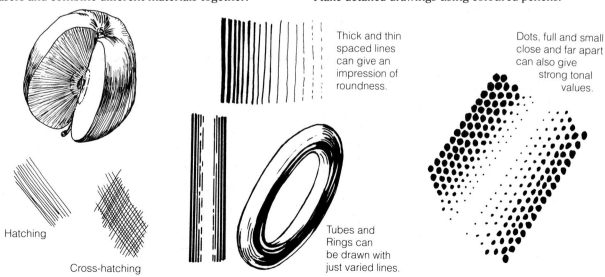

Thick and thin spaced lines can give an impression of roundness.

Dots, full and small close and far apart can also give strong tonal values.

Hatching

Cross-hatching

Tubes and Rings can be drawn with just varied lines.

Shading techniques

GLOSSARY OF TERMS

Bird's eye view
Overhead view of a subject.

Calligraphy
Handwriting art, undertaken with lettering pen or fine brush.

Camera obscura
Optical device that projects an image onto a surface which can then be traced accurately. (Used by many artists.)

Carbon pencils
Fine drawing pencil made from carbon rather than graphite.

Cartoon
A full size preparatory drawing.

Cartridge paper
Inexpensive good quality drawing paper.

Charcoal
Soft black crayon usually made from willow. Drawings must be fixed to resist smudges.

Conté crayons
High quality French pastels.

Contour drawing
Drawing made when artist fixes eyes on subject and draws without looking at the drawing, nor removing pencil from paper.

Crayons
General term for stick drawing material.

Cross hatching
Pattern of drawn lines that form a net, the closer the lines the darker the tone.

Cross section
Drawing of section through object.

Enlarging
Making a picture larger without altering the proportions of the elements in it.

Felt tip pens and markers
Nylon and felt tipped drawing tools.

Horizon line
A real or imaginary line in a picture. It is a basis for relating other elements in the picture together through perspective.

Lay figure
A small articulated figure, useful for approximating human poses.

Life drawing
Drawing the human figure from a model.

Line drawing
Drawing in which forms and shapes are shown entirely by use of lines.

Outline drawing
Drawing of object in which only the outline is shown with an even line. No tone, texture or internal aspects are shown.

Pantograph
A mechanism for copying, reducing or enlarging drawings.

Pastel
A coloured crayon composed of pigment and water-based binder.

Pastel paper
Special textured paper designed to hold pastel firmly to its surface.

Pencils
Used to refer to small pointed brush, now covers large range of coloured, carbon, flat, charcoal and graphite pencils. Pencils are often on a scale from 6H through HB to 6B, H being hard, B being black or soft.

Perspective
A way to show a three-dimensional scene in two dimensions so that the picture accurately represents the scene from a fixed viewpoint.

Render
Accurate way of drawing.

Scale
Relationship between drawn items and the original, i.e. 1:50.

Scraperboard
Type of scratch board.

Shading
Merging of one tone into another.

Sketch
A preliminary drawing sometimes done quickly.

Stump
Tightly rolled paper used to blend or smudge pencil or charcoal to give a smooth finish.

Tone
The lightness or darkness of colour or monotone.

Vanishing point
Imaginary point where parallel lines converge on the horizon.

Worm's eye view
A picture produced from a low level point of view.

MOVING FROM TWO TO THREE DIMENSIONS

C17, 18

Most children experience working in two dimensions and while they will be happy working with clay, working with other materials in three dimensions brings extra demands. These include the need for more time to be allowed, extra storage, and an unfamiliarity with new materials. You may find that building pictures up into reliefs and making collages with cut out silhouettes and dioramas is an easy way to introduce three-dimensional work in solid or sheet materials to young children.

Modelling skills cross the boundary between art and design and technology. Much of the three-dimensional work of infants is cross-curricular and has a strong design and technology element. Working as artists rather than technologists, children will emphasise their own personal responses to materials and express personal ideas and feelings. This section divides three-dimensional work into the processes of construction, modelling and sculpture.

Materials and equipment
Three-dimensional materials are not limited to the traditional sculptural ones of clay, stone, metal and wood. Children should also experience using plastics, wood, paper, card, scrap materials, textiles, malleable materials such as clay and Plasticine®, and construction kits. For information about textiles see pages 124–8.

You need
Various types of card including squared (use **Copymasters 17** and **18** photocopied on to card), paper, glues, scissors, craft knives, cutting board, steel safety rulers, balsa wood, dowelling, small craft saws or junior hacksaws, junk of all kinds, guillotine, clay, (Newclay®, Plasticine®, baseboards for clay work (1 cm chipboard pieces approx 45 cms × 35 cms), pencils, paints, brushes, glazes, slips, rolling pins, rags, clothes and sponges, papier mâché, foils. Protective smocks for children (old shirts).

Safety
Safety is a prime consideration with all cutting tools; this is particularly important for craft knives. Always provide metal safety rules, cutting mats and good quality sharp knives. Demonstrate the correct method of cutting, showing that fingers are kept away from the direction of the cut. Then, with the blade at a slight angle, draw the knife towards the body in the line of the cut. It is better to establish the cut slowly and finish the cut with a series of light strokes without forcing. It is important to supervise young children carefully when they are using potentially dangerous tools.

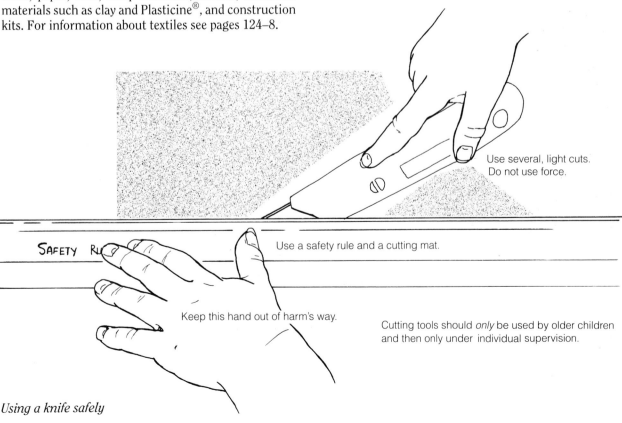

Use several, light cuts. Do not use force.

SAFETY RULE

Use a safety rule and a cutting mat.

Keep this hand out of harm's way.

Cutting tools should *only* be used by older children and then only under individual supervision.

Using a knife safely

CONSTRUCTION

Construction involves joining materials together, whether they be clay slabs, wood or card. Constructing in paper and card is not the same as sculpture or origami. It usually involves cutting, creasing, folding and fixing pieces together with glues, tapes or fasteners. For young children you should keep activities simple and remember that models can be clad in textured papers or paint. **Copymasters 30–37** contain a number of different brick, stone and tile patterns that can be used for decorating model buildings.

As mentioned earlier, an important part of learning to work with sheet material such as card, is investigating the many ways in which it can be folded, shaped and formed to give it increased strength and rigidity. Probably the quickest and simplest way to stiffen a sheet of card is to use strips of card folded at right angles and stuck onto the sheet.

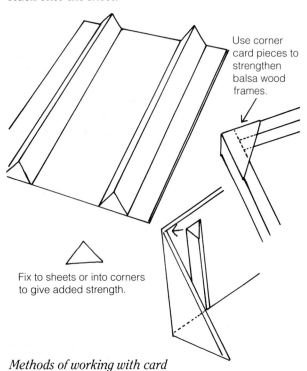

Use corner card pieces to strengthen balsa wood frames.

Fix to sheets or into corners to give added strength.

Methods of working with card

Containers, boxes and solids can all be constructed from card. It is important that exercises should not be made boring by expecting too much technical success. Use **Copymasters 99–100** to produce simple regular geometric solids. Care should be taken in cutting, scoring and gluing. Cut and form sections as shown to strengthen the sides of the solids. Use corner pieces and balsa wood to strengthen corners. Collect examples of different small folded card packs, such as sweet containers. Get your children to carefully open them out to discover the nets. Get them to design simple nets and make up solids. Use Polydron® (flat shapes with edges hinged for ease of construction) to help plan nets. As an extension to this get your children to design and paint the surface of a cube before making it up to be used as a jewellery box for Mother's Day or for Easter eggs.

Activity 239: Robots or cars from boxes
Modelling can be introduced to very young children by using cardboard cartons. Children can transform simple cartons into all kinds of things. For example, take a medium sized carton and fix all panels firmly in place. Cut holes for arms, head and body, so that a child can put the box on rather like the tin man from the 'Wizard of Oz'. Get a couple of really big cartons (used to pack fridges); these can be fixed together, opened up in places and have chairs put inside to make a car. The children can paint wheels, cut open windows and generally enjoy their make-believe car. Space ships, houses, boats can all be made this way.

Activity 240: Pop up or stand up raised pictures
This is a simple form of diorama, or card projection. First take a sheet of card and fold it so that it forms a horizontal base and a back wall. Now the background can be painted and figures and objects arranged on the base as silhouettes supported by tabs. This exercise can introduce some ideas of perspective. You will need to help with this activity.

tabs

Silhouettes supported by tabs

Activity 241: Diorama
Take a piece of stout card (Tri-wall), about 40 cms wide by 30 cms high and cut out a rectangular hole about 30 cms by 20 cms to form the proscenium. Now take a larger piece of card about 75 cms by 30 cms, fold over ends as shown and fix with split pin paper fasteners in a semi-circular backdrop. This interior curved wall can be decorated with scenery and freestanding silhouettes. Now place the framework on two other pieces of card, trace the outline and cut to form a base and roof to the diorama then glue walls to roof and base. You will have to help with this and Activity 242 following.

Making a diorama using split pins

Activity 242: A puppet theatre
This is an extension of the previous two activities and develops the skills of constructing with card. The theatre will be a useful prop for many further activities so the development of skills will have real purpose.

Making the theatres
Get each group to work out where to cut out the proscenium arch and the hole in the base (through which the puppets will be operated). Strengthen the window (the proscenium arch) and the opening in the base with water-soluble brown adhesive tape. Carefully paste decorative paper over the outside of the theatre walls. Line the inside with coloured paper using blues or light grey.

Making scene changes
Make a number of scene backdrops for the escape, the inn, and the stable. These can be hung in place as shown in the illustration. Free-standing scenery can also be used. Design and make a curtain that can be pulled back easily from the sides.

Activity 243: Making a boat
This activity involves marking out, cutting, fixing and finishing. As a starting point, your children can use

Copymaster 55 that contains a simple plan of parts and information about making a simple boat. Based on this the children can make their own designs up. The model is going to be made from flat pieces of card joined together. Cut out the shapes making sure that the tabs are cut out as well. If you photocopy the copymaster on thin card, the children can cut out the outline with scissors. The children should fold the pieces roughly into shape and should discuss how to use the tabs and which is the most logical way of sticking the boat together. Glue the parts together and allow to dry. When the model is dry, it can be decorated. This exercise is prescriptive, nevertheless, it will help children make links between two and three dimensions that can be used in their own work.

Activity 244: Making a crane
Using your collection of junk materials, set your children the task of making a model crane that can lift a small weight in a container. Cornflake, biscuit and margarine containers and string make good cranes.

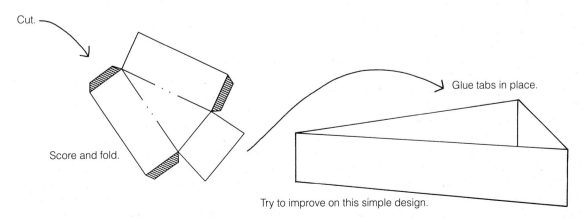

Cut.

Score and fold.

Glue tabs in place.

Try to improve on this simple design.

Fixing the boat parts

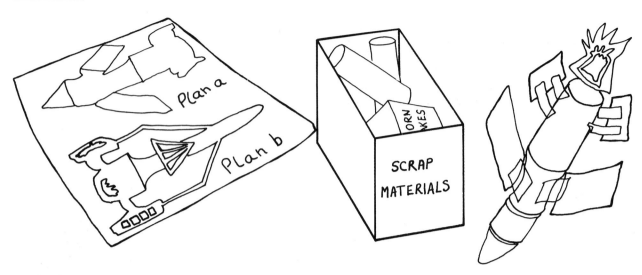

Rocket design

Activity 245: Making a rocket ship

Get the children to design a rocket to be made out of available junk materials such as toilet rolls, strips of paper and glue. It is important that the children know what is available before making their design. The point of the activity is to introduce planning and the model should be made after the drawing. The items chosen to make the model should be exactly those in the drawing. Children will enjoy working to their plans. The models can be painted and displayed as mobiles.

Activity 246: Monster with moving parts

A good starting point for a project like this is to read the story, *Not now, Bernard*. If children have previously made faces with moving parts, they will need little discussion or help with this activity and can apply their knowledge of the use of butterfly clips. The monsters should have moving legs, arms and head. Eyelids should be folded and glued along the top to open and close, and the mouth can be glued along the ends to allow a tongue to slide up and down.

Activity 247: Making a cooker

Using junk materials, glue, paint and scissors, set the task of making a cooker with an oven below. Two boxes, one supporting silver foil cups for the hob and the other cut with a door and fitted with a handle made up of layers of card, will provide one solution to the problem of making a cooker. Illustrations and magazines with cookers in them are essential for this activity.

Activity 248: Fixing wheels and axles

Wheels can be attached in a variety of ways to cardboard vehicles and mechanisms. Accurately mark the position where the axle is to pass through the side of the vehicle and punch holes with a hole puncher. If the card is thin, use an additional washer made from card to strengthen the place where the axle passes through. **Copymaster 66** contains a net for a simple lorry that can be used to demonstrate the fixing of wheels.

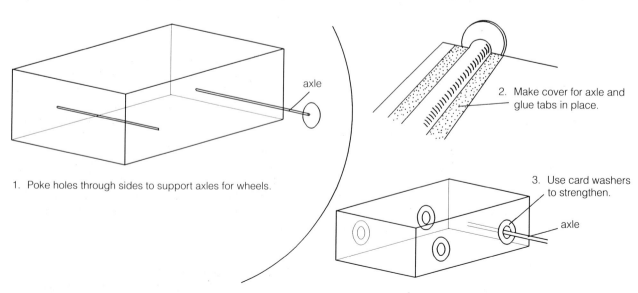

1. Poke holes through sides to support axles for wheels.

2. Make cover for axle and glue tabs in place.

3. Use card washers to strengthen.

Fixing wheels

Activity 249: Pop ups
Children may need to make pop ups for greeting cards or presents. There are a number of ways of making pop ups in which horizontal and vertical surfaces can form backgrounds, where horizontal surfaces can stand parallel to the card and v-folds which are very often used for greeting cards. See the illustration below.

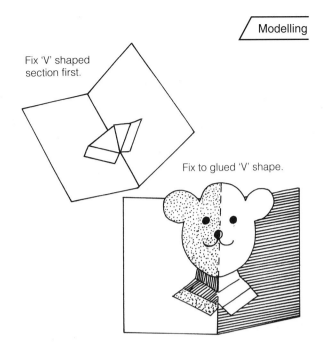

Fix 'V' shaped section first.

Fix to glued 'V' shape.

Activity 250: Making simple geometric shapes
Copymasters 99 and **100** contain nets of simple geometric solids. These are produced on a background grid that will be useful for measuring and other mathematical activities. Children can make up numbers of the solids which can then be used as building blocks for all kinds of constructions.

MODELLING ▶

Modelling involves making forms by manipulating materials. Children can convey feelings, observations and ideas through using solid and sheet materials such as junk, paper, card and balsa wood and soft materials such as clay, plasticine, and papier mâché. Modelling can include the skills of designing, cutting, folding, fixing, colouring, sawing, pinching and rolling. Modelling offers a bridge between working with flat shapes and solid forms. Modelling with clay develops children's physical perception in an immediate way that requires few tools. Squeezing, pinching, rolling and coiling are typical ways to make forms.

Children best learn how to do things through direct experience. Many young children find that working with clay (and other malleable materials) is the most natural and accessible way of expressing ideas and feelings. Clay is a wonderful material: children (and adults) love the messiness of clay and the easy way that all kinds of shapes can be made. Learning to model clay will be enhanced if you ask children to squeeze, pinch, roll, bend, dig into, fold and join the clay in relevant activities. Children should be encouraged to undertake observational and expressive or storytelling modelling. Children should discuss and handle natural and man-made objects before modelling them. Ask questions such as: How big is it? What is it for? and, How is it made? Look closely at details of insects, buildings, fruit, shells, bottles and pieces of machinery. Clay can be used to describe an event or a memory such as a birthday party or a role play which children can base their models of characters on, or a cartoon can be made in a series of tiles. Modelling can also be used in a factual way to support other areas of the curriculum. Children can, for example, model sections through volcanoes or features from history like castles.

General points
Clay can be used by very young children to build animals and all kinds of forms without any special tools.

As children progress they will need tools to cut slits, to scoop out and to texture the surface of clay. Properly used, clay is no more messy than paint or papier mâché. It is best to provide an absorbent surface. Avoid polythene or a vinyl covered table. Hessian, card, wooden boards or thick hardboard are the best. Make sure that if you are going to fire models that you hollow them out to minimise the risk of the piece shattering. Guidance on storing, colouring, drying and firing clay is given in the section on Ceramics.

Activity 251: Modelling animals
Give each child a handful of clay with which to experiment. For very young children the greatest aid you can offer is to provide rich stimulus materials. Books are fine but better by far are mounted specimens from your school museum service. Being able to sketch and model directly from real birds or animals will transform this activity.

Activity 252: Making basic shapes
You may wish to guide the play of slightly older infants and extend the activity of making animals. Suggest that they look for the basic shape of their animal. This may include cylinders, cubes and cones which can be made by rolling or wedging (banging on the table). They can then add small pieces of clay to build up the shape and add texture. A simple pebble shape can be changed by scratching the surface or impressing the surface with various objects or by painting the dry animal shape with water-based paints (but only if you are not going to fire the piece).

Activity 253: Fixing basic shapes together
You may suggest further that each piece is considered and made separately: the body, head, legs and tail. Fix

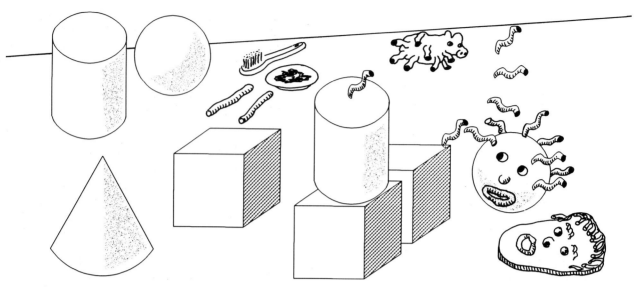

Using basic shapes

these together using slip (mixture of clay and water applied with finger or toothbrush) and pressed firmly together.

Other methods for modelling such as slabwork, pinchwork, coilwork and carving cheese-hard clay can be found in the Ceramics section.

SCULPTURE ▶

Sculpture, like modelling, includes the processes of casting, moulding, modelling, assembling, as well as carving into solid blocks. It often involves decorating the surfaces of sculpted forms with textures, glazes and stains. It may include carving into such materials as wax, wood, plaster and soap. It is a process that needs special attention and sound planning.

Papier mâché is a useful modelling and sculpting material. It is cheap and shows how waste materials can be transformed into strong and light products. The recipe below can be used in most activities that call for papier mâché.

Activity 254: Making papier mâché

Ingredients
Papier mâché (enough for 1/2 gallon, reduce for smaller quantities):

> One complete newspaper
> 4 tablespoons of whiting
> 4 tablespoons of Gloy®, or white paper paste (do not use cellulose paste that includes antifungal agents and do not use PVA)
> 2 tablespoons of either raw or boiled linseed oil
> 4 tablespoons of white flour
> 4 drops of wintergreen or oil of cloves (acts as a preservative)

Method
1. Tear newspaper sheets into small pieces, approximately 2 cms square. Place the pieces into a bucket and cover with water, soak overnight.
2. Boil the mash for approximately 20 minutes having added 4 pints of water. Mash the mixture to a pulp.
3. Place this pulp into a strainer to remove surplus water.
4. The pulp should now be a soft wet consistency.
5. Add to the pulp the whiting, glue and linseed oil. Stir the mixture thoroughly then add the flour and oil of cloves. When the mix is thoroughly stirred it is ready to use.

The quantities specified can be varied considerably. More glue makes a stronger finished product; more whiting makes a whiter denser mâché. If the mixture is too watery just add more flour until it is a pliable stiffish consistency.

The glue and the paste bind the mixture, the whiting acts as a filler and colouring agent while adding to the density of the mix. Linseed oil is an 'extender' and adds to the pliability and strengthens the finished products. Oil of wintergreen or cloves acts as a preservative, preventing the mixture from going off.

Activity 255: Making a papier mâché mask
An old cardboard box can be used with papier mâché to produce four different masks. First of all, draw mask shapes over the corners of the cardboard box. The masks need to be long enough to cover the children's faces. Cut out the basic shapes and then the eyes, nose and mouth. Make sure that the holes are big enough to see and speak through. Apply a coat of PVA to the basic mask shape. Let it dry and then your children can build up the features of the mask with papier mâché in whichever way they like. When dry, the mask can be painted and finished with string, feathers or other scrap materials. Fix the mask with elastic, so that it is comfortable when worn.

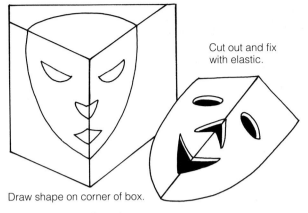

Cut out and fix with elastic.

Draw shape on corner of box.

Making masks from box corners

Activity 256: Mixing plaster

To prepare the plaster, take a plastic bowl and fill it about a third full with water. Make sure your hands are dry and then gently sprinkle the plaster into the water. When the plaster forms a mound so that the top sticks out of the water, you are ready to start mixing. Put your hand below the surface of the water and gently stir the plaster. You will feel that all of the powder plaster is absorbed without lumps and it is the right consistency to use. Pour the plaster into the moulds for the blocks, casts or tiles that you have previously prepared. Adding a little washing up liquid to the water, will tend to slow down the action of the plaster going hard. Your children can learn a lot by observing the heat that is given off as the plaster turns from liquid to solid.

Activity 257: Simple plaster casting

Use a mould, as described above, to contain the object to be cast and the plaster. Use a small piece of clay to make a relief model of a face or an animal and place on the base of the mould. Make sure that it is below the level of the top edge of the mould. Mix and pour plaster over the clay model until it reaches the top edge of the mould. Let the plaster 'go off'. When the plaster is solid, remove the mould and turn the plaster upside down. Remove the clay from the plaster. When all the clay has been removed, wash out the plaster. To make a cast, let the plaster dry out thoroughly, paint the surface well with

two or three coats of washing up liquid. Mix up a small quantity of plaster and pour into the plaster mould. When dry, the plaster cast should come out easily, providing there are no undercuts.

Activity 258: Repoussé work

This relief work is normally produced by working with a hammer and punches of differing shapes on the back of a sheet of metal fixed over a soft or yielding material. If the relief required is very slight it may be obtained by simply laying the metal sheet onto a piece of soft pine. For work with young children repoussé may be introduced by using thin metal foils over a shaped former and simply pressing the foil into the indentations. When complete carefully remove the foil and mount onto a card support.

Activity 259: Making mobiles

Many different elements may be hung in mobiles. These include cut out shapes from cardboard, motifs made from multi-coloured Mirriboard®, light or transparent appliqués made from cellophane or acetate stretched across frames of twisted cane and found objects. To make frames simply take thin cane cut a length of 60 cms and bend it to form a circle. Overlap the ends and strap them together with cotton and PVA glue. Such frames can be placed onto sheets of acetate or tissue paper, traced, and the backing shape cut out and glued to the frame. Once the backing has been cut additional pieces of paper can be cut and stuck in place. For older children the canes can be used as a support for embroidered designs for mobiles.

Once the designs on the elements have been finished you will need to hang all the elements so that they balance and move freely. The main hanging support can be made from cane, dowelling or wire. Whatever you use, the successful hanging of the mobile will depend on a trial and error approach. Use invisible threads to support the individual elements. Hanging the whole mobile is worked out by balancing the different weights of each element against the distances from the fulcrum points on the supporting bars or canes. The diagram below gives a simplified view of a standard arrangement. If your children wish to suspend heavier items then, of course, the strength of supports and threads will have to be suitable.

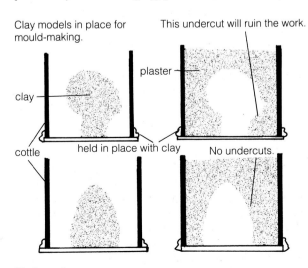

Clay models in place for mould-making.

This undercut will ruin the work.

plaster

clay

cottle

held in place with clay

No undercuts.

Undercuts

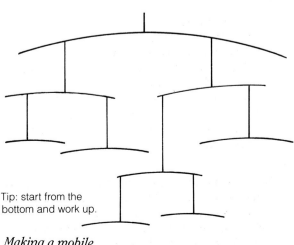

Tip: start from the bottom and work up.

Making a mobile

GLOSSARY OF TERMS ▶

Acetate
Transparent coloured plastic, useful for projecting coloured lights and for mobiles.

Artcor
Laminated foam board, light, strong with card surface ideal for quick clean model making and for mobile elements.

Armature
Skeletal support for sculptures made from plaster, clay or papier mâché.

Balsa wood
Useful and light traditional material, needs to be glued or pinned.

Bas relief
Type of relief work.

Callipers
Wooden or metal device with movable jaws for measuring across such three-dimensional shapes as the width of someone's head.

Card
There are various types including pulpboard, folding boxboard (used in cartons for sweets and chocolates), manila, strawboard and corrugated.

Casting
To produce (or reproduce) an object by using a mould and casting material such as plaster of Paris.

Corriflute
An expensive corrugated plastic with rather limited use.

Corrugated card
There are various thicknesses, the Tri-wall type being particularly strong. Cartons can be cut into panels and used for many purposes.

Diorama
A representation of a scene in three dimensions often on a small scale. Clever use of perspective and painting can give realistic impressions when viewed from the right position.

Folding boxboard
Surfaced thin card used for containers such as chocolate boxes, toothpaste packets. A very useful product. Easily cut and scored with scissors.

Glues
For general use PVA is excellent either diluted or neat. Be wary of hot glue guns and solvent based adhesives.

Manila (or pasteboard)
Easily cut and folded coloured thin card, often in four sheet thickness, easily cut with scissors.

Maquette
Sketch version of sculpture (in clay) often on a smaller scale than the finished piece.

Modelling tools
Tools for shaping clay or plaster, made from boxwood, open wire ended. Some are pointed, serrated or rounded.

Papier mâché
Excellent modelling or moulding material made from torn paper and binder (for recipe see page 110).

Parting compound
Material, such as soft soap or wahing up liquid, used to ensure that cast separates from mould.

Patina
The finish on bronze sculptures that results from natural aging or weathering, the removal of patina is mistaken and can destroy much of the character of fine pieces.

Plaster of Paris
White powder when mixed with water is used for casting. When plaster 'goes off' it becomes hot and hardens, the speed at which plaster goes off can be changed by adding liquid detergent or PVA.

Pulpboard
Often used for mounting purposes, it is six sheets thick and often needs to be cut with craft knife or guillotine.

Relief
Shallow modelling or sculpture, a head for example on coins is an extreme form of relief work.

Replica
An exact copy as opposed to a mere reproduction, often made by the original artist.

Repoussé
Method of decorating thin sheets of metal by hammering the back of the piece, infants can use thin metal foils such as embossing foil from NES Arnold.

Scrim
Open fabric used with plaster to build strong light weight moulds or casts.

Strawboard
Stout board used for folios and bookcovers. Needs to be cut with craft knife. Does not fold but panels are useful strengtheners.

PAINTING

PAINTING AND INFANTS

Painting and drawing are so closely related that they often develop simultaneously. For very young children painting's only distinguishing features are that it concerns colour and texture more than any other art activity. Infants enjoy the tactile qualities of paint and love bright colours. Although infant paintings are often seen as bold and powerful expressions, given the right materials and teaching, the range of expression can include subtle, precise and demanding work. Dexterity with tools and materials increases as infants mix colours and take greater control over the marks and images they make. Many paints are hard to handle and children can easily be frustrated by messiness and the difficulty of using some tools. You will need to demonstrate how to use paint pots and brushes effectively. Schematic designs will tend to dominate children's early drawings but will develop as the vehicle of colour extends their expressive vocabulary. Painting should not be limited to work on paper or to a small scale, textiles and pottery can be painted and group murals can give children an exciting experience of changes to scale. As children approach Key Stage 2 try to increase their opportunities to move from one medium to another and link preparatory drawings more positively to finished paintings. Such activities will enhance their knowledge of artistic processes and build progression into your scheme of work.

Painting activities also need to provide opportunities to develop the imagination. For example, ask the children to make a painting of a friend and discuss it as it progresses and change it in the light of the discussions; make an imaginary portrait of themselves when grown up; make a large painting based on a favourite story or piece of music; make a group collage based on the theme of jungle.

Materials and equipment
Children need to work with good quality materials and tools. The tendency of painting to be a messy and frustrating activity can often be overcome by providing the right materials. Even simple instruction about how to take paint up onto a brush can make life much easier for infant artists. Manual skills will develop more easily and quickly by choosing the right materials and equipment for the chosen task. The following items will be needed: card and papers, drinking straws, lino printing rollers, marbling colours, mixing trays, overalls or large shirts for smocks, water-based paints and dyes including acrylic and powder, finger paints, tempera blocks and cold water dyes such as Brusho; paintbrushes (a variety of sizes and types, some flat tipped, some pointed), paper clips, pencils and crayons, scrap materials and sponges for pads.

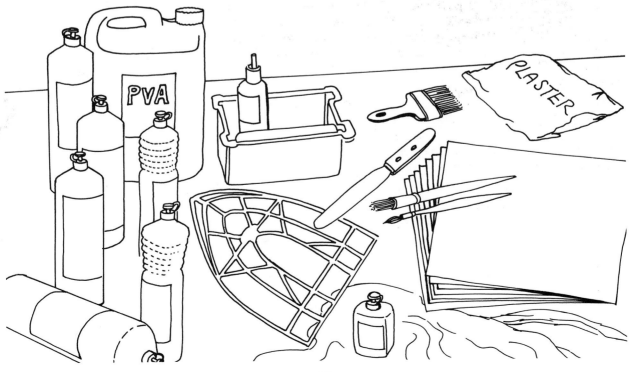

Before you start
Ensure that the children are well protected by overalls. Besides managing the physical aspects of painting well you need to remember that children should have the opportunity to build progressive skills in painting. From playing with paint infants should develop control over tools and materials as they make imaginative and observational paintings. As they mature, it may be appropriate to plan paintings.

Activity 260: Playing with paint
Paint can be smooth, thick, thin, watery, dry, textured, brilliant, muddy, happy and sad. Children should be given the opportunity to experience these different qualities of paint. They should also be given the chance to use a variety of materials and find out how to make different kinds of marks and mix a range of colours through games and observation.

Finger paints offer a link between painting, drawing and print-making. Use a clean plastic tray and give your children a limited range of bright colours. Painting can be done directly on paper or pictures can be made by drawing fingers through the paint that has been applied to a plastic tray or piece of perspex. Finger paints can dry out quickly so children should be aware that they need to work reasonably quickly. Direct paintings on paper can be based on subjects close to home, such as 'My family', 'Going for a drive', or a subject from a favourite story. Mood pictures also can be very successful. If children are working with finger paints on a plastic surface, a print of the picture can be produced by placing a clean sheet of paper over the still wet picture and smoothing it onto the paint.

Activity 261: Colour matching
Mixing colours together creates new colours. Discuss with your children how new colours can be identified, sorted and described. Focus attention on the importance of primary colours: blue, yellow and red in mixing colours. Introduce dry powder colour and acrylic paints to produce secondary colours (orange, green and purple). Use colour mixing games, matching, making favourite colours and finding out how many colours can be made from one by adding water and white and black. Demonstrate how colours can be changed by mixing. Mix red and green together to produce brown, add a little white to produce a beige colour. Also show how to pick up enough paint on a brush and remove the excess on the lip of the container. Show how adding water can make paint easier to handle.

You can choose any object or accessible subject for colour matching exercises. Make a collection and produce an exhibition with questions about colour, books, and pigments. Autumnal leaves are a very good way of adding sensitivity to young children's perception of colour. This is simply because the natural process of change in the leaves produces a wonderful range of primary and secondary colours. Make sure that the collection of leaves is generous and contains really good examples of variations of colour. First get the children to draw the leaves as described in the drawing section of this book and then, with good quality brushes, carefully map out the colours as they appear on the leaves.

Activity 262: Dry and wet, paper and paint
Provide pieces of two or three types of paper, such as sugar, cartridge and newsprint, also make available powder paint, PVA paint and Brusho®. Cut the pieces of paper into two, then get your children to soak one piece of each type of paper in turn with a wet sponge and ask them to drop powder paint, drip PVA and float Brusho® onto the surfaces of the papers. Now ask them to see what happens when the same is done on dry paper and what happens if you wash over dry powder paint on a piece of dry paper. Discuss with your children whether certain techniques they have used might be good for painting skies, seascapes or faces. Can they apply colours in different ways, using scrap materials for example? Mount and display good examples of wet and dry work.

Activity 263: Combing paint
This is really an extension of work with finger paints. Spread out some finger paint into a plastic tray. If children use more than one colour, put one colour in one area and another in a different corner so that pure and mixed colours can coexist. Take a piece of card

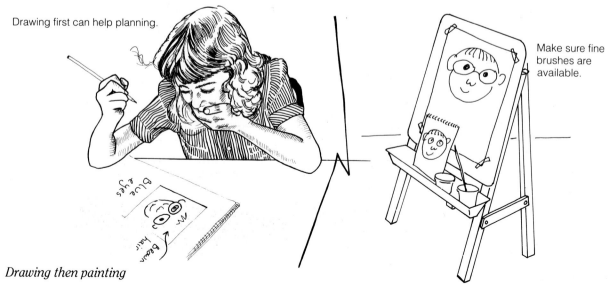

Drawing first can help planning.

Make sure fine brushes are available.

Drawing then painting

smaller than the tray and cut it to produce notches of different thicknesses. Draw this comb through the finger paint to produce a pattern and take a print by placing a piece of clean paper on the surface.

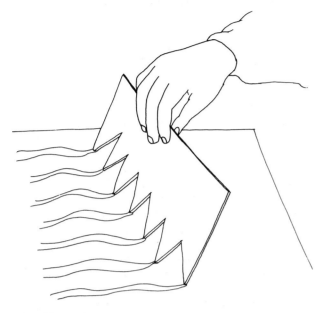

Combing paint

Activity 264: Brushes, sponges and rollers

Different kinds of tools and materials can produce different kinds of marks. You need to make available a variety of tools with which to apply paint. These may include sponges, brushes of different sizes, found objects, card and, of course, fingers and hands. Make an organised collection of scrap materials (soft, hard, textured, smooth), various brushes, soft and hard rollers, and fabrics. Give the children scrap paper and some good paper to work on after they have experimented. They will also need sponge pads and plastic trays into which the colour can be worked. Ask your children to produce as many kinds of marks as they can, applying paint to make up images and pictures. At first it is important that your children try out their experiments on scrap paper, otherwise they will waste a lot of materials. Pressing scraps into a pad of paint or dye and being applied to paper may result in pictures that have been made from marks using only soft or hard materials. Children may use rollers by charging them with colour and rolling across paper as a background for further painting, or they may pick up an image from an already painted object and transfer it to the paper on the surface of the roller.

Activity 265: Using a brush

Try to ensure that you are able to provide more than one medium sized brush. Children really need an opportunity to work on both a large and a small scale. A medium size bristle brush is too big for fine work and too small for mural work. Try to avoid the particularly nasty extremely cheap synthetic brushes. Good quality synthetic brushes last longer and are much better for developing manual skills. Sizes 3, 5, 8 and small decorating brushes will give your children a good scope. Using smaller brushes, ask your children to paint a series of flowing continuous lines. To do this, the paint will need to be of the right consistency, so they will need to experiment. Set them a task of painting a black line, over the surface of a piece of paper. When complete, ask them to colour the open shapes in a way that will be attractive to them. Ask them to make examples of straight, curved, swirling, bent and zig-zag lines. Working on a larger scale children will need to experiment to find the right consistency of paint for the brushes they are using.

Activity 266: Applying a wash

It will often be necessary for a thin wash of colour to be applied over the whole of a piece of paper as a

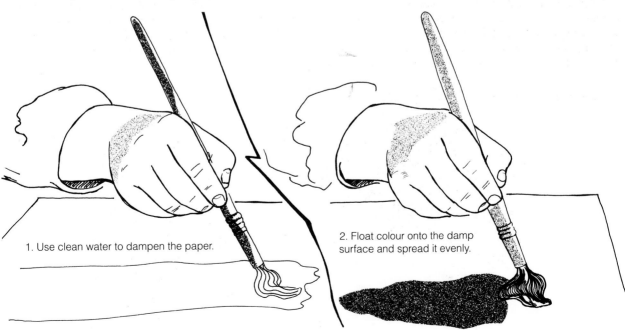

1. Use clean water to dampen the paper.

2. Float colour onto the damp surface and spread it evenly.

Applying a wash

115

background. With a clean large brush (or piece of wet sponge) apply clean water in consecutive bands across a sheet of clean, good quality paper. While the paper is still wet, apply the background from top to bottom, the paint will run together and produce a soft blended impression. Pictures can be painted directly using this wash technique and will look very different to paintings made on dry paper.

Activity 267: Adding textures
Different kinds of textures can be added to PVA paint by mixing in quantities of sand, semolina, polycell, sawdust and liquid detergent. PVA paints are most suitable as they already include a glue base that can fix any added materials. Thickened paint can be applied with brushes and palette knives and is very useful as a medium for fixing collage materials, such as buttons, sequins or papers and fabrics.

Activity 268: Wax resist
This painting technique can be a useful introduction to batik work as well as being a valuable cross-curricular science link. Wax crayons will not mix with water: they resist it. Give your children pieces of sugar paper and a selection of wax crayons. Set a subject that is relevant to your topic and ask your children to make a drawing using the crayons applied thickly. When complete, choose suitably coloured inks as a background to the picture. Paint across the whole picture. The ink will colour the unwaxed areas and saturate the background.

Activity 269: Planning painting
Children are happy when drawing or painting directly but there is, unfortunately, a tendency to view painting as 'colouring-in'. Such an approach ruins many perfectly good drawings and causes confusion and frustration as the manual skills of painting are often not up to the job of completing drawings with colour. Painting is not the second stage of drawing, it has as much to do with sculpture as it has with drawing. It can be useful, nevertheless, to plan paintings by drawing.

Ideas need to be discussed and tried out before painting is started. As children grow, get them to use a sketch book to make notes and drawings for future use. The National Curriculum suggests that, for infants, sketches of scenes made on the spot from observation can be used as the basis for a large painting upon return to class. Other activities that can be undertaken before making a painting include testing colours, brushes and papers, drawing from selected source materials, making small studies and outlining important areas of a painting with a light colour (light blue). The picture can be adjusted as it progresses.

Activity 270: Collage based on drawing
Get your children to rip up a selection of coloured papers and illustrations from magazines into small pieces. The pieces should be about 1 or 2 square centimetres of any shape. Make sure that the subject for the collage is relevant to your main topic or theme. Using a piece of tinted paper as a background ask your

Sketch on visits.

Back in class, use sketches for paintings, wax resists or other activities.

Using a sketch-book

116

children to make an outline drawing of the subject and then with PVA affix small pieces of paper to make up their collage. Naturally, your children should consider the colours to use carefully before fixing them permanently.

Activity 271: Using pastels or watercolour pencils
Try out water-soluble pencils before tackling a finished piece of work. Apply strokes of pencils close together and blend them with a wet brush. Provide your children with a limited palette of pencils or pastels. You can set a variety of still life subjects. Include leaves, shells, minerals, bottles, found objects and mechanisms. Set the task of making as accurate representational pictures as possible by carefully blending and merging the colours.

GLOSSARY OF TERMS

Acrylic colours
Most useful liquid colours that include a fine adhesive. This enables the paints to be used in thin transparent overlaid washes, impasto techniques (when used with thickeners), and collage.

Advancing and retreating colours
Generally reds advance and blues retreat into a picture.

Background
The parts in a picture which appear to be furthest away from the viewer.

Binder
Material used to hold pigments in suspension, such as PVA, oils or wax.

Bird's eye view
A view from above a subject that includes the whole of the subject.

Blending
Merging together two or more colours, tints or tones.

Broken colour
A colour produced by breaking pure colours together, such as when blue and orange are mixed.

Collage
Pictures made by fixing fabrics, papers and all kinds of found objects to a background support.

Colour circle
A simplified way of representing the ways colours mix and are complementary to each other.

Complementary colours
Pure colours that when mixed produce a neutral grey (black in theory); such as blue and orange; red and green; yellow and purple.

Cool colours
Those that seem to suggest a feeling of coolness, often thought to be the blue and green range of colours.

Dominant colour
The main colour in a painting or colour scheme.

Encaustic
Ancient painting system that uses hot wax as a binder for pigments.

Finger painting
This method is often associated only with infants. The method, however, of making direct marks with fingers in paint is very similar to methods used by professional artists and should be used progressively throughout Key Stage 1 and Key Stage 2.

Foreground
The part of a picture that appears to be closest to the viewer.

Impasto
Method of building up a thick textured surface to paintings.

Landscape
A picture whose subject is landscape or scenery.

Mosaic
Small pieces of coloured tiles (tesserae) arranged so as to form pictures. The images were originally set in plaster and were often made up from small pieces of coloured glass. Cut sticky paper is a simple way to introduce infants to this craft.

Mural
Paintings done either directly onto a wall or on a frame in a wall. Modern murals are often used to decorate the ends of houses, tube stations or panels around building sites.

Paint
A material made by suspending pigments in a binding medium.

Pointillist
Technical name given to painters such as Seurat who used small points of pure colour, juxtaposed to produce other colours by optical mixing (the colours appear to mix when viewed from a distance).

Restricted palette
For some exercises it is sensible to restrict the palette of infants to the primary colours and black and white. Doing so will encourage them to experiment with mixing colour.

Still life
A subject that often includes fruit, bowls, fabrics, shells and other found objects arranged on a table.

Wash
Paper is first wetted thoroughly and the washes of watercolours are brushed over the surface in such a way that there are no hard edges, everything is smooth and soft. Often useful as a background to landscapes.

PRINT-MAKING

WHAT IS PRINT-MAKING?

Printmaking in some ways serves the same functions as drawing and painting. In printmaking, however, a mark or a picture is transferred from one surface or material to another. This is very exciting in itself but there are also technical considerations that make it important. These include the fact that overprinted colours and textures give a variety of results. Marks and pictures can be repeated so that patterns are formed and the activities of stencilling, cutting and pressing produce images that have different qualities to those of painting and drawing and this adds to the richness of children's' visual language. The ability to produce repeated images gives printmaking an important position in art and design, and design and technology activities. Printmaking has aesthetic and mass communication aspects. Basically we have two types of process involved in printing at Key Stage 1, that is pressing or relief printing and resist printing, which includes stencilling.

Printmaking and infants
Pure play using finger paints to produce monoprints will often develop into more structured activities that make printing a logical extension of children's drawing and painting. It is important to make a variety of materials available and to encourage using combinations of marks, colours and textures to develop infants' image making beyond typical schematic pictures.

The activities given below include relief printing techniques and some resist techniques. Often the same methods can be used to print onto paper, fabrics and other materials. Besides teaching the techniques, a number of printing activities can be tackled. These include using printed marks to illustrate a story, using a collection of printed materials to make a collage and using different materials to make different marks.

Before you start
Ensure that your children and working surfaces are well protected as some of the colours used can stain permanently. Tools should be in good condition and when cutting with craft knives please demonstrate and often reinforce the correct way to cut. Use a safety rule and cutting mat.

Activity 272: Rubbings from natural and made objects
Get your children to collect a good variety of manageable natural and made materials. Suitable items will include well grained pieces of wood, embossed wall-paper, stones, coins, string bags, paper doilies, leaves, shells and bricks.

Crayons are particularly useful for taking rubbings, simply place a sheet of paper over the surface to be rubbed and while holding everything steady, apply the side of a crayon evenly across the image area. Children can build up a collection of rubbings which can be categorised and used in displays. This activity can be extended to produce rubbed images from card. This is most easily done, working from simple designs of animals or scenes that are then built up by gluing cut sections of card, string or other scrap materials to a base board.

You need
Chunky wax crayons, lining paper or newsprint, materials from which to take rubbings, **Copymaster 39**.

Rubbings

Activity 273: Using found objects to make printed marks

The same kind of objects used in Activity 272, can be used to produce printed images. The simplest approach is to pour some liquid paint onto a sponge pad contained in an old icecream box. Objects are pressed onto the paint-covered pad and then pressed onto a sheet of sugar paper.

Printing onto fabric can be done easily using dried leaves and dyes. Place the leaves on a sheet of newsprint and one at a time carefully apply dye to the leaves. Place the leaf face down onto the fabric and cover it with a piece of paper which is then rubbed gently to print the leaf onto the fabric. Remove the paper and the leaf carefully and repeat the operation with different colours and using a clean piece of paper for each printing.

You need
Paints or inks, pads of sponge or fabric, articles from which to print, natural fabrics such as cotton, backing papers, paper.

Activity 274: Creating simple patterns

Potatoes, carrots and cabbages can all be used to produce simple patterns on paper or fabric. Half a potato can be shaped so that a simple design can be repeated over a large surface. The design is pressed into the pad of paint or dye and applied to the paper or fabric. If you are using fabric, then it is a good idea to tape the surface onto the table, so that a regular and even impression is made. Before printing on fabric, it is good practice to try out the pattern on scraps of paper first. It is also best not to put too much dye or ink on the pad at once.

You need
Paints or inks, pads of sponge or fabric, articles from which to print, natural fabrics such as cotton, vegetables, backing papers, paper.

Simple patterns

Activity 275: Making a simple block print

Give your children squares of polystyrene. Get them to draw images into the surface with a modelling tool or biro. Ink up the prepared polystyrene surface with water based ink or paint and take a print by laying a piece of paper onto the paint loaded surface. Rub carefully to transfer the image. Modify the block if the first impression is not satisfactory.

You need
Polystyrene tiles with smooth surfaces, water-based inks, rollers, biros or modelling tools, paper.

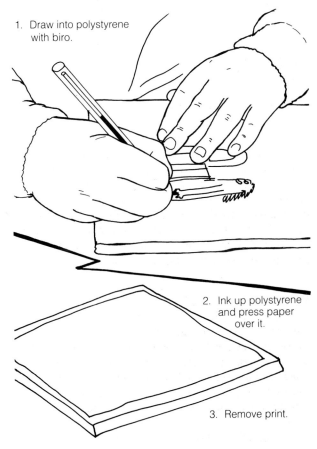

1. Draw into polystyrene with biro.

2. Ink up polystyrene and press paper over it.

3. Remove print.

Block printing

Activity 276: Monotype printing

Details of this technique can be found on page 37.

Activity 277: Marbling

Using special oil-based inks your children can pattern paper with images of swirling water. Marbled papers can be used for many other craft activities including covering books, as backgrounds to collages or for finishing the interiors of model houses.

Prepare your work area and materials well. Half fill a large photographic dish with clean water. Cut paper so that it is a little smaller than the size of the dish. Carefully float a little colour onto the surface of the water. You can use more than one colour at a time. Stir the surface of the water gently so that the colour is dispersed over the whole surface, taking care not to cause the colour to settle in blobs on the bottom of the tray. Drop a sheet of good quality paper on to the

119

surface, remove and lay out face up on a piece of newsprint to dry. You can repeat this process on the same piece of paper with different colours. You can also use special combs to change the types of patterns made.

You need
Dishes, marbling colours, paper, a stick for stirring, newsprint.

Activity 278: Printing with clay

This is introduced as a method that is similar to potato printing. A small ball of clay is thumped onto a table and objects pressed into the flat surface which is tapped once more onto the table to ensure its evenness. It can now be used for printing: press the clay against a pad of ink or paint and take a print. Repeat patterns in a single colour of a simple shape may be extended in the following way:

a) a random or abstract arrangement printed in two or more colours,

b) pull a piece of clay away from the main lump, thump this abstract tear onto the table and print this unusual shape regularly,

c) make a shape that will tessellate, impress marks into the surface and print regular tessellated patterns from the carefully formed block of clay. Try using objects such as tools and hands.

Make sure that the children work in a clean way and wipe the blocks clean after each colour. Favourite clay printing blocks can be allowed to harden and be reused over a long period of time.

You need
Clay, clay boards, texture making surfaces or tools, paints, paper.

Activity 279: Simple stencilling

This is the simplest form of resist printing. Young children can easily be introduced to the method in the following way. Give each child a square of paper. Fold it in half, draw a symmetrical pattern or motif on the folded paper. In fact they will draw half of the motif centred on the line of fold as shown in the diagram.

Take a pair of scissors and cut out the shaded area. Open out the paper and wax the edges that form the stencil. Using a piece of sponge, or stippling brush and paint, take an impression by forcing paint through onto a clean piece of paper.

You need
Paper squares, paper to print or stencil onto, paint, sponge or stippling or stencilling brushes.

Activity 280: Screen printing

Use a strong wooden frame as shown in the diagram. Use brown water based tape to secure the internal edges of the stretched fabric (organdie or voile). Make sure you seal both surfaces of the fabric by sticking brown tape around the printing area on the underside of the screen too. You will then need to coat the brown tape with button polish to make it tough and waterproof. Give it two good coats. You now have a tough screen, suitable to print high quality images.

Make up paper stencils large enough to cover the open area of the screen. Place the stencil on a clean piece of newsprint. Place the screen on top so that the paper stencil is nicely positioned to cover the whole open area of the screen. Pour a little paint or ink along one edge of the screen, taking care not to let it go into the area where the stencil openings are. Now using a squeegee held at the angle shown in the diagram draw the ink across the screen. This action accomplishes two things. First it sticks the stencil to the underside of the screen, second it makes your first print as ink is forced through the open areas of the paper stencil. As children grow into Key Stage 2 different types of screen stencils can be used. For example water-soluble PVA painted directly onto the screen and allowed to dry, is then ready for a few impression to be taken. The PVA can be washed out and the screen dried for reuse.

Do not waste money on cheap frames as they do not last and will be expensive in the long run. A couple of solid frames from Sericol will last you for a long time. Also buy good (soft quality) squeegees from Sericol. Do not waste money on cheap ones. Young children can also hold these chunky squeegees with surprising ease.

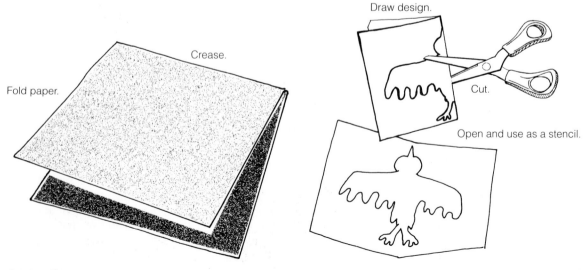

Simple stencils

Screen printing with a stencil

Place the stencil as shown.
Lay the screen flat in place and pour some ink along the inside edges.
The first pull with the squeegee will stick the stencil in place and print at the same time.

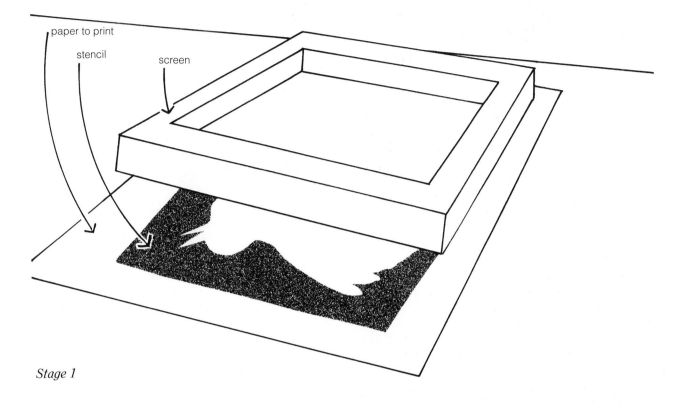

paper to print

stencil

screen

Stage 1

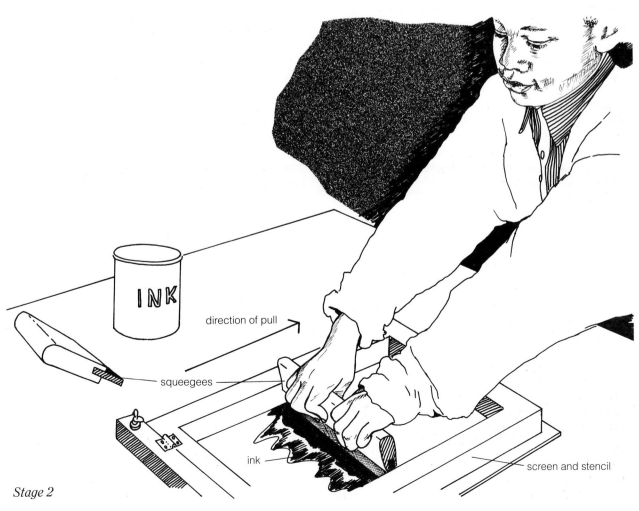

INK

direction of pull

squeegees

ink

screen and stencil

Stage 2

121

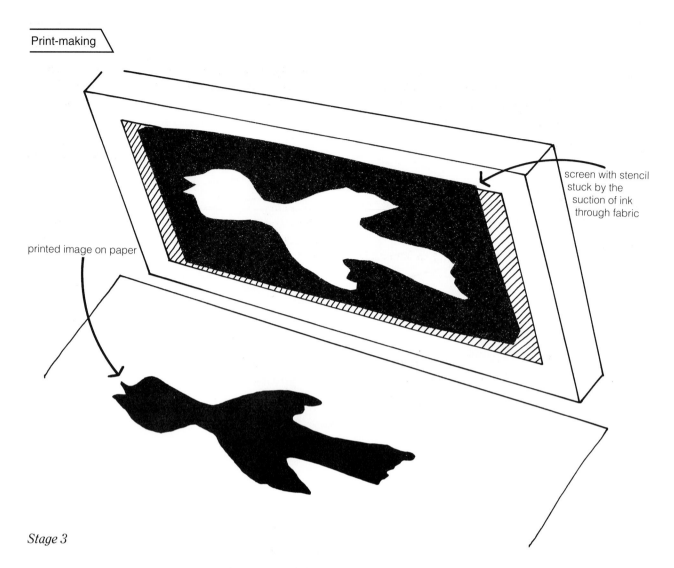

printed image on paper

screen with stencil
stuck by the
suction of ink
through fabric

Stage 3

There are some particularly bad screen inks available from some suppliers. As screen printing can be done on fabrics and paper I suggest that you buy one ink type which will work well on both surfaces. Buy a few one litre tubs of Texiscreen inks from Sericol. These are self curing, water-soluble inks which are safe to use. You will get excellent results if you wish to produce T-shirts, or paper. The cost of these inks is lower than those sold in small quantities, and they are far better and easier to use.

GLOSSARY OF TERMS ▶

Card prints
Prints taken from cut out shapes of card. Individual elements can be printed separately to make up a composition such as a face (see page 8).

Decal
Prints onto transfer material which can then be fixed onto fabrics, especially T-shirts.

Linocut
Block printing method suitable for Key Stage 2 and onwards.

Marbling
Resist method of producing monotype images from the surface of water.

Monotype
'One-off' prints from fingerpaints or other kinds of paint. Designs are made by using the media on a smooth surface such as perspex or formica and picking up the image on a piece of paper by smoothing over it when placed on top of the wet surface.

Pad and block printing
Using a block (potato, impressed clay, lino or polystyrene block) inked up with a loaded pad of paint or dye. Paper placed over the inked-up block is burnished with the back of a spoon and picks up an impression.

Paper-stencil screen process method
Described on pages 18, 53, 61.

Press printing
Inked-up blocks pressed against paper or fabric.

Relief prints – assemblages
A backing board is used to affix found objects or lines of PVA glue or string. The finished assemblage is then inked up and a print is taken in the normal way.

Resist
Method of printing when the passage of ink onto the receiving surface is halted. The most common method of resist printing for infants is simple stencil work, where ink only passes through the open areas of the stencil.

Rollers
Soft (sponge) and hard rubber rollers are used to roll out ink onto plates or to ink up blocks directly. Soft rollers can be used for stencil work.

Rubbings
Basic method for introducing printing to young children. Paper placed over the surface from which an impression is required is rubbed firmly with chunky wax crayons.

Serigraphy, silk screen or screen process printing
All refer to the process outlined in its simplest form on page 120.

Stencilling
Holes and shapes cut into paper or manila are used to produce simple or complex prints on a variety of surfaces.

TEXTILES

TEXTILES, WEAVING AND JEWELLERY WITH INFANTS ▶

The crafts listed below combine sound educational ideas with a generous helping of therapeutic and soothing activities. You may prefer to leave some activities, such as using a spinning wheel or batik work until Key Stage 2, but with good supervision all can be tackled by infants.

General points
This section includes activities that concern textiles, weaving and jewellery. It is organised in the following way:

- activities to do with making, dyeing, preparing and using threads
- activities to do with making, dyeing, printing and using fabrics
- a range of activities to do with jewellery and accessories

Textiles
Threads are made by twisting and spinning raw materials such as wool, cotton or synthetic materials. Once threads are made, they are interlaced together to make textiles. This method of producing textiles has been used since ancient times. Textiles can be introduced to young children through topic work on clothes. Here in this skills section we look at individual processes in more detail. It is almost impossible to give firm guidelines as far as the suitability of activities for particular ages of children – you will be able to judge whether or not your children have progressed far enough to tackle the activities outlined below. Simple well-known activities such as French knitting can be also included. Just give each child a French knitting bobbin and yarn and follow the manufacturers instructions.

THREADS

C10, 42

Activity 281 : Appliqué with fabrics and threads
Collect together as many different materials, threads, strings and wools as possible. Give each child a piece of fabric or card upon which to assemble their pictures. For making an appliqué use a piece of fabric as a background and, for a thread and string collage, use a piece of card. For young children, the subject for their work needs to be simple, such as a windy or snowy day, 'my favourite footballer', or a pet. To make an appliqué, your children will need to cut out a variety of fabrics to form the main elements and then glue or sew them in

place on the back board. To make a thread collage, get the children to look at the available threads first and choose the right ones for their design. Get them to draw out their design first and then stick pieces of thread, string or wool in place with PVA glue.

Activity 282: Dyeing using natural substances
A selection of cochineal, henna, indigo, madder and yew chips can all be used to produce natural dyes. Most natural dyes require mordants to fix the colours. Check

1. Get children to draw a T-shirt.

2. Use scraps of fabric and glue into place.

Appliqué T-shirt

with your supplier for specific information about the right mordants.

Natural fabrics and raw wool are suitable for dyeing with natural dyes. If you are using wool you will first need to scour (clean) it. To do this first open out the fleece in hot water (50 degrees). Leave it in the bowl until the water is cold. Prepare another bowl of soapy water at hand temperature. Place the fleece in the soapy water and squeeze it to flush out the dirt and natural grease (lanolin). You will need to repeat this and then rinse in tepid water. If you are going to dye yarn prepare it in the form of tied skeins.

If you use lichen first then you will not need to use a mordant as it is naturally colourfast. Collect lichen in damp weather. Layer lichen, fabric, lichen in a large bowl. Cover with soft water and heat gently for two or three hours. Remove, rinse and dry.

The most common mordants are tin, alum, iron and chrome. Test these carefully with some of the range of natural dye sources given above. Natural dyestuffs have to be boiled with mordants so you will have to do this yourself for safety reasons. When prepared your children can test and record results.

You need
Large and small containers, dyebaths (a big stainless steel bowl to hold hot liquids), saucepans, smooth sticks for stirring, muslin bags for holding dyestuffs, sieve, scales, hot ring and soft water (if possible).

Activity 283: Embroidery
Copymasters 10 and **42** are for use with embroidery activities. There are over 50 different embroidery stitches, but infants need to learn just one, cross stitch, to make really lovely things. Cross stitch is easily done on canvas by counting the threads; pattern and back-ground are all worked in the same stitch. You can do cross stitch in two ways. One is by making one diagonal of each stitch all the way along, and complete it coming back by putting in the second stitch. The other way, more satisfactory, is to complete each cross as one goes along. In either case, each cross must be identical, the first stitch always in the same direction and the second in the opposite. Your children can make up their own simple designs using **Copymaster 42** and coloured felt tip pens. Simply mark crosses as part of the design and transfer to canvas or Binca®. Alternatively use **Copymaster 10**.

You need
Real canvas or Binca®, needles, embroidery cottons, **Copymasters 10** and **42**, scissors, felt tip pens, pencils.

Activity 284: Spinning
Try to arrange to borrow a simple spinning wheel such as the Louet type and a number of finger spindles. Before spinning with either the wheel or spindles you will need to prepare the fleece. If you have difficulty getting hold of fleece contact the Wool Board. Use clean fleece. First take a little fleece and place on one of the pair of carders, comb the fleece with the other to align the fibres. After carding for a few minutes you should be able to produce a rollag. Having a rollag is essential to spinning. Use a piece of ready spun wool to attach a strand of wool from the end of the rollag to the spinning wheel or spindle. After this you start spinning. Try to tease a little of the rollag gently onto the spindle in a spun form. This can take some getting used to but is a lot of fun.

You need
Finger spindles, spinning wheel, clean fleece, carders, knitting wool.

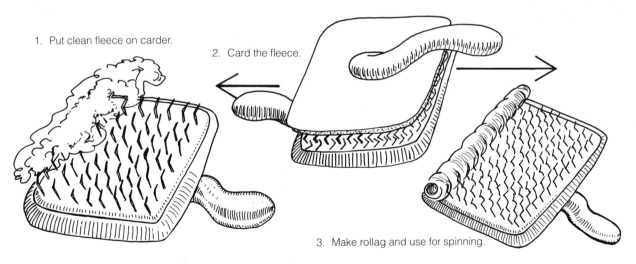

1. Put clean fleece on carder.

2. Card the fleece.

3. Make rollag and use for spinning.

Making a rollag

FABRICS

C50, 51–4
57–9

Felt is a material that is very suitable for work with infants. It is soft, easily handled and comes in many beautiful colours. Not only simple garments, soft toys and things such as book-marks can be made with felt, it is often useful for making appliqué. The simplest way to make appliqué is to form a base from a coarse material while the pictorial elements are shapes cut from felt and stitched or stuck to the base fabric. Your children can spend many happy hours making small, useful articles as birthday or Christmas gifts. **Copymaster 50** contains a pattern of a small bag that can be made up from felt.

Activity 285: Making a book-mark

Cut a piece of felt 18 cms long by 5 cms wide, pointing it at one end. Finish the edge with a double row of small running stitches, interlaced with a contrasting colour. Use embroidery cotton for this. Cut out a design in two or more colours of felt and tack them down into position. Secure these with a small running stitch close to the edge, using a coloured thread. Leave some of the threads used for running round the edge loose at the pointed end. Knot these to form a tassel, or make a separate tassel and attach it to the pointed end.

Activity 286: Making gloves or mittens

This activity can be modified to make a glove puppet. First get your children to draw around both right and left hands on newsprint to form simple patterns, use dotted lines for this. Before cutting out the patterns draw a 1 cm border around the hand profiles as shown in the diagram. Cut out the patterns as shown. Now place the patterns on two pieces of felt, mark around with chalk. Cut out. Take the paper patterns and cut them along the dotted lines. Place these on to the cut felt shapes so that there is an even border. Mark these outlines to establish the position for sewing. Secure these pieces with tack stitches. Turn the mitten inside out and finish the edges with blanket stitch. Make the other mitten.

You need
Felt, tracing paper, scissors, chalk, pencils, no. 6 needles and thread.

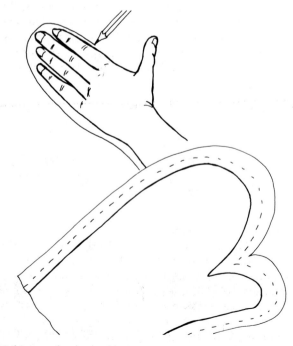

Making and using patterns

Activity 287: Making soft toys or dolls

On pieces of A4 paper get your children to do a simple outline drawing of an animal or baby. Or use the simple animal and sea creature shapes on **Copymasters 51–4** and **57–9**. You need to ensure that the article can be stuffed easily when made up (an octopus will have to be stuffed from the head). Trace the drawing or transfer the outline from the copymaster. Draw an extra border around the drawing of about 1 cm. Transfer the extended drawing onto two pieces of contrasting coloured felt. Follow the procedures given above for making mittens. Tack around the perimeter of the design, leaving an edge untacked so that the stuffing can be done. Turn the article inside out, stuff and finish by using blanket stitch all around the edges. Eyes, noses and mouths should be fixed or sewn before stuffing.

You need
Felt, tracing paper, paper, pencils, chalk, no. 6 needles and thread, stuffing material, buttons and sequins.

Activity 288: Batik

Wax resist work is introduced at any age by drawing with wax crayons and applying water-based paints or ink over the whole surface of the work. New elements can be introduced in a progressive way, and eventually, in small well supervised groups, top infants can start to do batik.

Get your children to make a design on a piece of paper and, when they are happy with it, transfer a rough outline onto a piece of fabric. Use a piece of cotton about 30 cms square or silk (if you use silk the work can be combined with silk painting). Now using either brushes or tjantings (batik pens), paint or draw molten wax onto clean cotton or silk fabric. When the first part has been done crumple up the fabric to crack the wax drawing. The dye will be resisted where the wax is applied but the rest will be dyed. Place the fabric in a bath of cold-water dye (Dylon) with salt as a fixative. Remove, rinse, dry and then iron between sheets of newsprint (not newspaper!) to remove the wax. Repeat with different colours until the desired effect is achieved. Try to remove all the wax at the end of the process otherwise the fabrics will feel heavy and horrid, not the beautiful, delicate and softly decorated pieces of cloth that they can be.

Jackson Contra-Banned of Huddersfield sell an excellent set of batik samples from Bali that clearly show sequences of the processes of waxing and dyeing involved in batik work. You may find that a set for display and reference will be a useful addition to your resource collection.

You need
Tjantings, brushes, wax and suitable heater (double boiler) or a specially made batik wax pot (NES Arnold), cotton or silk, pencils, paper, newsprint, dyebath (plastic bowl), cold-water dyes and an iron.

Activity 289: Tie dye

This is another resist method. Take a length of cotton and tie it at selected points, tightly and in some case more loosely. Soak the fabric with water then immerse in a bath of chosen and prepared cold-water dye. Leave for a while (an hour or so), remove and rinse until the water runs clear. Open, retie and repeat the process until the results are pleasing. Finally dry and iron.

You need
Cold-water dyes, dyebath, cotton, string and an iron.

WEAVING

C40, 41

Woven fabric is made when a vertical set of threads, called the warp (each individual thread has its own warp end), is interlaced by a sequence of horizontal threads called the weft. Your children can understand this structure easily by fraying the edge of a scrap of fabric and looking at it through a magnifying glass. Get the children to pull out a single thread to see how it is permanently waved from the over and under threads that crossed it.

Weaving is an excellent activity involving interesting problems of pattern and colour. It helps develop manipulative skills and dexterity without causing eye-strain. A progressive course can be planned for infants and juniors supplemented with dyeing activities. **Copy-masters 40** and **41**, are drawings of woven patterns that can be coloured over and under. Young children may find that using these helps them to plan their own simple designs.

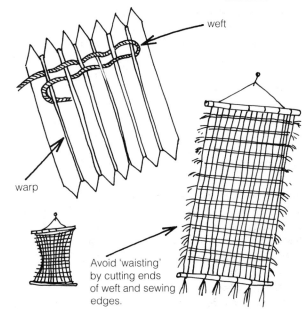
weft
warp
Avoid 'waisting' by cutting ends of weft and sewing edges.

Activity 290: Strip weaving
See Activity 79 in the topic on Clothing.

Activity 291: Cardboard looms
See Activity 81 in the topic on Clothing.

JEWELLERY AND ACCESSORIES

Elsewhere in this book you will find details of how to make badges (p 9), pasta jewellery (p 26), edible jewellery (p 46) and bangles (p 25). Details are given below of how to introduce beadwork and making tassels.

Activity 292: Beadwork
Large wooden beads, suitable for infants can be purchased in a variety of colours. These can be used to make a variety of bangles, anklets, and necklaces by threading them onto a cord. Also there are large packs of small plastic beads available for traditional work or for making up designs which are then ironed with a hot iron (on top of a piece of baking foil). The heating which fuses the beads together, must be undertaken by an adult.

As a separate activity your children can make their own clay beads. Give each child a small lump of clay and get them to roll it out into a sausage about 2 cms diameter. Cut this into small sections about 3 cms long. Pierce the pieces with a piece of thin dowelling. The pieces can be rounded and further finished when the clay has dried a little. Dry, fire and glaze and use to make all kinds of beadwork.

You need
Clay, clay boards, clay knives and tools, glazes, brushes, cord.

Activity 293: Threading and knotting
Endless patterns and combinations of colours can be created by threading beads. Strong carpet thread made from linen is excellent for large beads. Needles will be unnecessary with stiff cord. You may need to use knots to separate the beads and to finish off the article. Use a simple overhand knot as in the diagram for separating and a granny knot to finish. Tie the ends to fasteners (findings).

You need
Cord, findings.

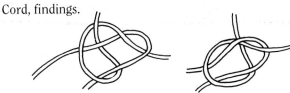

Activity 294: Tassels
A tassel can provide a good finish to many kinds of fabric and jewellery work. A simple way to do this is to knot a cord a few centimetres from the end, fringe it, and cut the tips evenly. This gives a tassel effect, though it is not a real tassel. Another way is to take a group of strands of wool or cotton, made in the usual way by winding around a book. Pass them through the closed ends of a cord and tie and finish as shown in the diagram.

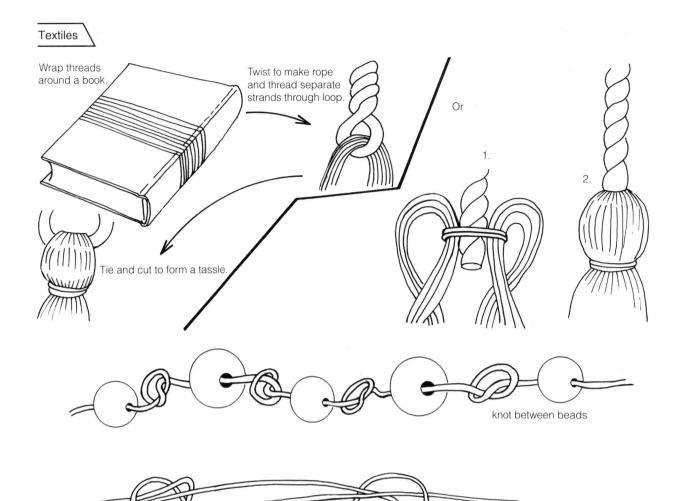

Wrap threads around a book.

Twist to make rope and thread separate strands through loop.

Or

1.

2.

Tie and cut to form a tassle.

knot between beads

adjustable slip ties

Making tassels and beaded cords

GLOSSARY OF TERMS

Appliqué
Decorative art in which pieces of material are fastened to a surface to form a design. Cloth is often sewn or glued in place.

Basketwork
It involves weaving strong fibres to produce baskets, or materials are first coiled together and then stitched coil by coil to form containers. Many people agree that this kind of fabric work is the earliest of all.

Beadwork
It involves threading different kinds of beads on a cord. They are also used in other craftworks such as macrame, knitting, crochet, embroidery and metal jewellery.

Dyes
Materials used to colour fabrics.

Embroidery
Pictures and patterns made usually on canvas or linen by combining a variety of stitches and coloured threads.

Findings
Small fittings for jewellery, connectors and clasps.

Knitting
Interlocking loops of yarn that then form a fabric, often produced on knitting needles.

Macramé
Heavy, coarse lacework that can be used in abstract designs and a form of sculpture.

Resist
The use of a resisting material such as wax to form patterns and images on fabrics when dyed.

Rollag
Clean fleece that has been carded so that all the fibres are roughly parallel and ready to be fed onto the spinning bobbin.

Sewing
Fastening of fabrics by using thread stitches. Simple stitches such as the blanket stitch are suitable for infants.

Spinning
Method of producing yarn by twisting raw material (often wool) into a fine thread.

Tassels
Decorative finish to cords and ropes.